DUALITIES IN SHAKESPEARE

DUALITIES IN
SHAKESPEARE

Marion Bodwell Smith

University of Toronto Press

Preface

THE QUALITY OF MIND, the intellectual attitude which links Shakespeare with his age and accounts in large part for both his universality and his individuality is a lively awareness of contradictions accompanied by a particularly keen sensitivity to interdependent relationships. It is this double vision to which I have applied the inclusive label "duality." This double view of life manifests itself in a variety of ways both to divide and to integrate; it is basic to Shakespeare's comprehensiveness of purpose and technique, and especially to his dramatic and poetic use of language and his symbolic use of myth and ritual.

In the following pages I have tried to indicate some of the evidence which has led me to these conclusions and to demonstrate some of their critical applications. The task has involved a re-examination, in the context of the concept of duality, of the text[1] of the plays and poems, conducted as far as possible without critical preconceptions but with the application of whatever critical approaches seemed relevant for a particular work. The introductory chapter—a necessarily limited and superficial survey of those aspects of Renaissance thought which have particular relevance for Shakespeare—is intended to provide a setting in time and place for the consideration of Shakespeare's dualities. Chapter II traces the development of these attitudes from the early to the late works. Since the manifestations of duality in theme and form are not equally significant in every play, some have been treated at moderate length, others more briefly, and still others merely mentioned as providing parallel or supporting evidence. The later chapters deal with the fusion of artistic and intellectual dualities in particular works, emphasizing, in each instance, one aspect of technique. Such an

[1] All textual references are to the Tudor edition of *William Shakespeare the Complete Works*, edited by Peter Alexander (London and Glasgow: Collins, 1953).

approach makes it possible to conduct an investigation in depth into a
particular aspect of a particular work, but does not make it possible,
however regrettably, to give full consideration to any one work as an
organic whole.

In addition to the specific obligations acknowledged in the notes, I
am conscious of my general indebtedness to the scholars, critics, and
teachers who have afforded me stimulation and insights over years of
reading, and I am happy to acknowledge, here, my obligations to that
goodly fellowship. It is a pleasure, also, to express my gratitude for
assistance of many kinds: to the University of British Columbia, which
granted me a year's study-leave, and to Professor A. L. Wheeler of
the Department of English of the University of Manitoba, whose for-
bearance made it possible for me to complete the writing of this study
early in 1964, I am indebted for that first requisite of scholarship—time.
For financial assistance my thanks go to the Canada Council for the
award of a Senior Research Fellowship for 1962–63, to the Leon and
Thea Koerner Foundation for a grant towards the costs of travel, and to
the President's Research Fund of the University of Manitoba for grants
to cover the costs of final typing and for a further grant for
assistance in proof-reading and the compilation of the index. The
Humanities Research Council, using funds provided by the Canada
Council, and the publications fund of the University of Toronto Press
have assisted publication. I should like to extend particular thanks also
to Mr. John Wain, without whose cheerful encouragement and practical assistance in arranging for housing in England both the book and
its author would be the poorer. I am grateful to Professor Geoffrey
Durrant of the Department of English of the University of Manitoba,
who, along with Professor Wheeler, has been kind enough to read the
manuscript and give me the benefit of critical comment. My thanks
are also due to Mr. Geoffrey Ursell for his help in proof-reading and
indexing, to two excellent typists, and to the staffs of the Shakespeare
Institute at Stratford-upon-Avon, the Bodleian Library, the British
Museum Reading Room, and the libraries of the University of Reading,
the University of British Columbia, and the University of Manitoba.
Finally, I should like to thank my son and daughter, my students, and
my colleagues, for uncomplainingly allowing themselves to be used as
sounding boards for ideas in process of definition.

I am grateful to W. J. Gage and Co. for permission to reproduce
here some of the materials of chapter ix, "Mockery and Cherished
Purpose in The Tempest," published under that title in Thought, 1960.

University of Manitoba, Winnipeg   M.B.S.

Contents

DUALITIES IN SHAKESPEARE

I

The Humanist Synthesis

> Methinks I see these things with parted eye
> When every thing seems double.
> (*A Midsummer Night's Dream*, IV, i, 186–7)

THE DOUBLE VISION OF LIFE is not confined to lunatics, poets, and lovers who awake on a May morning in a wood near Athens; it is the hallmark of the questioning, the creative spirit, which is not satisfied with simple answers to complex problems or with the application to human experience of watertight categories and rigid value-judgments. It is a state of mind which cannot entertain a concept without a simultaneous and lively awareness of its opposite, which is "capable of being in uncertainties, mysteries, doubts, without any irritable reaching after" not merely "fact and reason"[1] but consistency and certainty. It is one of the manifestations of that "duality" which is both a condition of human existence and an attitude towards it, which is present equally in the interdependence of birth and death and the most trivial pun, which keeps reality in view without losing sight of the vision.

Contradictions and paradoxes are characteristic of the thought and culture of the Renaissance, but it was given to Shakespeare more than to most writers of his time to use his insight into the duality of things as an effective instrument of his art. When Shakespeare holds the mirror up to Nature it is more often than not a double rather than a single image which is reflected there, though its doubleness is more often than not indicative of an underlying unity. It is an image which shows "the soul of goodness in things evil" as seen by a mind which has the understanding, as well as the patience, to "distill it out," but a

[1]Keats on Shakespeare's "negative capability." Letter to George and Thomas Keats, December 21, 1817.

mind which sees, too, the frequency with which goodness is made use
of for evil purposes. As a creative artist, parallels, duplications, contrasts, puns, paradoxes, innuendos, and ironies of theme, situation,
character, style, and language are his stock in trade, the "noted weed"
of his "invention." Often his tone and attitude are ambivalent and
evoke contradictory responses from his audience. He both exploits and
mocks conventions, social and literary, sometimes in the same play; he
even, on occasion, burlesques his own work. He paints both manners
and men, is individual and universal, the microcosm of his age and
himself alone.

The purpose of this study is to examine some of the ways in which
Shakespeare's plays and poems reflect the pervasive dualities of the
Renaissance as modified by his personal vision of life, and the ways in
which these dualities find expression in language which for richness of
connotation, subtlety of meaning, and range of relevance is the glory
of English literature. My concern, therefore, is not with the Renaissance as a whole but with its dualities. I shall not attempt to account
for, or delimit the duration of, the explosion of intellectual activity
which, during the fifteenth and sixteenth centuries, made itself felt in
every area of life, or to trace its powder-train back to the thirteenth or
earlier centuries. The Renaissance will be accepted at its own estimate
of itself, as a period of "large discourse, looking before and after,"
which rejected the heritage of the recent past in favour of an older one
not as a retreat but as an advance, and for which discovery and redis-
covery went hand in hand. But the dualities of the Renaissance are not
confined to the Janus-view associated with any period of far-reaching
and rapid change, or to its concern with the positive and negative
implications of time, tradition, and inquiry. Renaissance eclecticism is
not an uncritical assembling of contradictions but an attempt to reconcile them, and at its height, if not in its decline, it accepts dualities
consciously and gladly as the necessary ingredients of completeness,
directing its attention outward towards the infinite and inward towards
the individual in a confident search for the elements of transcendent
good in the diverse realities of human experience.

Confidence in its quest for truth is the keynote, particularly, of
Renaissance humanism, which did not hesitate to bring all received
concepts, all orthodoxies to the bar of human reason. Its temper is
nothing if not critical, but its criticism, however searching, is not so
much destructive as constructive in intention. It professes to oppose all
authority which confines and to embrace all sanctions which liberate
the human spirit. Therefore it is equally characteristic of the new
learning to question authority and to seek for and cite it as model,

guide, and support. But any authority, even that of the ancients, might be circumvented, or refuted, or ignored if it threatened to put obstacles in the way of creativity and enlightenment. In every area of creative activity, especially, practice outran precept, and most theorists were also practitioners. But even such stout upholders of classical precedent as Ben Jonson warned their disciples that all rules are not set by the square of Greece or Rome, and advocated imitation of classical models as a first step towards creative emulation.

The humanist ideal is integration, and its particular enemy separatism. Therefore the humanists attacked, for the greater glory of God and the greater well-being of man, not the Church as such, but those doctrines of the Church which, in their view, tended to keep man apart from God and those of its practices which kept the Church apart from man. For them the Church was the macrocosm which unified the varieties of spiritual experience, the body which gave significance to the function of each of its members. Humanist thought makes Christianity its spiritual frame of reference but does not regard the teachings of the Christian Church as the sole source of spiritual enlightenment. Rather it attempts to trace in the varieties of human belief the components of that ultimate good which is the divine image. Pico della Mirandola, for example, hoped to accomplish the reconciliation of all philosophies with Christianity, each contributing its "quintessence of truth." And the "wise and godly ordinances" of More's Utopians were based not upon a single revelation of social justice, but upon the learning of the ancients, information about new developments obtained from visitors to their country, and the lessons of experience.

The integrity at which humanism aims is based not upon homogeneity of substance but upon the harmonious fusion of differences, "there being nothing wherein nature so much triumpheth," as Sir Walter Raleigh writes in the Preface to his *History of the World*, "as in dissimilitude": "From when it cometh, that there is found so great a diversity of opinions; so strange contrariety of inclinations; so many natural and unnatural; wise, foolish; manly and childish affections and passions in mortal man."

To the humanist, difference is not an obstacle to truth but a means to it, and he neither ignores contradictions nor is too deeply disturbed by them. The eyes of the humanist see separately, but when each is functioning properly and both are focussed upon the same object each contributes to a single image. It is only among the blind that the one-eyed man is king. Thus, the humanists do not regard Philosophy and Religion as divided and distinguished worlds but as parallel aspects of the same activity—man's search to know the good, which is infinite.

The focus of both studies—"the object and end of the mind, the origin and end of the soul"—is, according to Ficino, the infinity of universal truth and goodness. If the goodness of God is infinite his creation must be so also, and so strong is this conviction that Giordano Bruno will go to the stake rather than renounce his belief in the infinity of the physical universe. Since infinite goodness includes all forms of the good, knowledge of its truth may be derived from many sources—from natural magic (for example, scientific experiment) and from the Platonic dialogues, as well as from the Scriptures and the teachings of the Church.

Christian Platonism did not, of course, spring into being with the Renaissance. The Gospel of St. John is evidence that many of Plato's teachings had been assimilated into Christian doctrine very early in the Church's history, and as incorporated into the Augustinian tradition these teachings dominated early medieval thought. Nor were the Platonic ingredients wholly submerged by the Christian Aristotelianism of St. Thomas Aquinas and his followers any more than it, in turn, was overwhelmed by Renaissance Neoplatonism. What was new in the Platonism of the Renaissance, besides its wider and more accurate textual basis, was its insistence on the equal status and identity of purpose of philosophy and theology. Humanist philosophy is religious and humanist religion philosophical.

But Renaissance Neoplatonism is compounded of many elements, though it is grounded on classical Platonism as expounded by the Alexandrian Greek, Plotinus, who contributed to the Platonic teachings certain mystical and stoical ingredients. To these, Pico della Mirandola, the translator of Plato's Dialogues, added certain still more exotic concepts derived from his studies of the Jewish Cabbala. "Renaissance Platonism," says W. C. Curry, who disapproves of it heartily as a kind of intellectual *pot-au-feu*, "was a heady concoction, calculated to obstruct clear thought and inflame the imagination. One cannot expect writers of this period to be consistent. They were uncritical eclectics, at once Christian, pagan, or otherwise, choosing from this and that tradition such elements as filled their needs or pleased their fancy."[2] No humanist philosopher would have been able to understand by what sort of logic such judiciously pragmatic selection as theirs could be called "uncritical." They would have been equally at a loss to understand how the word "dilettantism," the enjoyment of a variety of intellectual and cultural pursuits, could have acquired its present pejorative connotation.

The elements of Neoplatonism which most often seemed to fill the

---

[2]*Shakespeare's Philosophical Patterns* (Baton Rouge: Louisiana State University Press, 1937), p. 150.

needs or please the fancy of the writers of this period were those concerned with reconciling the contradictions of human experience, which attempted to find an answer to the human dilemma by seeing in these very contradictions (as Gerard Manley Hopkins was to do in the nineteenth century[3]) a manifestation of the divine purpose. One such conceptual reconciliation of differences which seemed to fill their needs was that of Plato's celestial harmony, in which opposition was conceived of as the basis of order, and conflict as a creative force:

God hath appointed . . . that in diversity there should be order. . . . Seeing that without this the Same should have . . . no motion or generation. . . . as harmony doeth consist of many sounds and intervals . . . which, when they be mixed and tempered together, make Song and melodie. . . . Thus having conceived and comprised *the Same* and *the Other* by the similitudes and dissimilitudes of numbers, making accord of difference, thereof the life of the universal world became wise and prudent, the harmony consonant. . . . Empedocles named concord and discord together, Heraclitus the opposite tension and harmony of the world, as of a bow or harpe, wherein both ends bend one against an other: Parmenides, light and darknesse.

For as Heraclitus was wont to say: Hidden harmony is better than apparent, for that therein God who tempered it, hath bestowed secretly and concealed, differences and diversities.[4]

A second such concept was that of the World Soul, which emanated as Light throughout the universe until it finally dissipated itself in matter, which it shaped and informed.[5] Through contemplation of these emanations of the divine spirit as embodied in the things of this world, man might move upward in soul towards the spiritual perfection of ultimate truth through the comprehension of the reflection in them of the patterns laid up in heaven, those Platonic Ideas which, for the later Neoplatonists, were synonymous with the thoughts of God. The doctrine is most familiarly known in its application to Platonic Love, of which the statement most often echoed by Renaissance writers is that of Cardinal Bembo in Book IV of Castiglione's *The Courtier*:

. . . in our soul there be three manner ways to know; namely, by sense, reason, and understanding: of sense, there ariseth appetite or longing, which is common to us with brute beasts; of reason ariseth election or choice, which is proper to man; of understanding, by the which man may be partner with angels, ariseth will. Even as therefore the sense knoweth not but sensible matters and that which may be felt, so the appetite or coveting only desireth the same; and even as the understanding is bent but to behold

[3]See his poetry in general, but especially "Pied Beauty" and "God's Grandeur."
[4]"The Creation of the Soul," in Plutarch's *Morals*, tr. Philemon Holland (1603), pp. 1043 ff.
[5]See Spenser's "An Hymne to Beauty," especially,
　　　For of the soule the bodie forme doth take.
　　　For soule is forme and doth the bodie make. (ll. 132–3)

things that may be understood, so is that will only fed with spiritual goods.

Man of nature endowed with reason, placed (as it were) in the middle between these two extremities, may through his choice inclining to sense, or reaching to understanding, come nigh to the coveting sometime of the one sometime of the other part. . . .

The lover . . . that considereth only the beauty in the body loseth this treasure and happiness as soon as the woman beloved with her departure leaveth the eyes without their brightness, and consequently the soul, as a widow, without her joy. . . . To avoid, therefore, the torment of this absence, and to enjoy beauty without passion, the Courtier, by the help of reason, must full and wholly call back again the coveting of the body to beauty alone, and . . . behold it in itself simple and pure, and frame it within in his imagination sundered from all matter, and so make it friendly and loving to his soul, and there enjoy it. . . .

. . . among these commodities the lover shall find another yet far greater, in case he will take this love for a stair . . . to climb up to another part higher than it. . . . meddling all beauties together, he shall make an universal concept and bring the multitude of them to the unity of one alone. . . . And thus shall he behold no more the particular beauty of one woman, but an universal that decketh out all bodies. Whereupon, being made dim with this greater light, he shall not pass upon the lesser, and burning in a more excellent flame, he shall little esteem it that he set great store by at the first. . . .

When our Courtier . . . be come to this point . . . he may come into his wit, to behold the beauty that is seen with the eyes of the mind. . . . Therefore the soul . . . , purged with the studies of true philosophy, occupied in spiritual, and exercised in matters of understanding . . . openeth the eyes that all men have, and few occupy, and seeth in herself a shining beam of that light which is the true image of the angelic beauty partened with her, whereof she also partneth with the body a feeble shadow. . . . And therefore . . . she ariseth to the noblest part of her (which is the understanding) and there, no more shadowed with the dark night of earthly matters, seeth the heavenly beauty.

But yet doth she not for all that enjoy it altogether perfectly, because she beholdeth it only in her particular understanding, which cannot conceive the passing great universal beauty; whereupon . . . love . . . giveth unto the soul a greater happiness. For like as through the particular beauty of one body he guideth her to the universal beauty of all bodies, even so in the last degree of perfection, through particular understanding he guideth her to the universal understanding. Thus the soul . . . seeth the main sea of the pure heavenly beauty and receiveth it into her, and enjoyeth that sovereign happiness that cannot be comprehended of the senses.[6]

The return to Plato was a natural consequence of humanist opposition to certain aspects of Aristotelianism as expounded by the Scholastics, but it did not involve a total rejection of Aristotle. It would have been impossible, even inconceivable, for any Renaissance thinker to

[6]As translated by Sir Thomas Hoby, 1561. Quoted from *Prose of the English Renaissance*, ed. Hebel, Hudson, Johnson and Green (New York: Appleton-Century-Crofts, 1952).

discard the Aristotelian conceptual frame of reference in which he had been educated and within which all studies were pursued. There was nothing to put in its place. Therefore the humanist philosopher formulates his definitions according to the Aristotelian categories and accepts the principle of dialectic as a fundamental law of nature governing the composition of matter and the movements of the heavenly bodies, however loudly he may cry out against the schoolmen's abuses of dialectic reasoning. In all things, the humanist's way is the *via media*. The opposite extreme to scholasticism is to be found in Luther's wholly negative attitude, which rejects uncompromisingly Aristotle and all his works, especially the *Ethics*, which he regarded as contrary to God's will and the Christian virtues. The humanists found Aristotle's enlightened pragmatism almost as congenial to their way of thinking as Plato's idealism. Their chief objection to scholasticism was to its neglect of larger issues in concentrating on the minutiae of logical "questions" and the logical hair-splitting which resulted from the application of dialectic reasoning to such trivia. Their ideal of "wholeness" was in part a reaction against the doctrines of the Averroists which separated logic and metaphysics, and those of the Occamists which postulated a universe of absolute and separate entities held together by an abstract notion of "order," a concept which reduced sense experiences to the status of mental phenomena.

The purposeful eclecticism of humanist thought is demonstrated both in what it accepts and what it rejects. All is grist to the mill which reconciles or assimilates contradictions, which does not undermine the ideals of completeness and of relevance to human experience. Amplitude is more highly regarded than consistency. Thus humanism could embrace as diverse ways of looking at truth and as guides to the good life the denial of moral absolutes implied in Aquinas's doctrine of "ends," the absolutes of Neoplatonic transcendentalism, and the pragmatic relativism of the Aristotelian mean. The good life, as the Renaissance humanist conceived of it, did not involve denial of the world and the flesh as alien to the divine, although they were acknowledged to be inferior and transitory, but rather embraced them as aspects of experience which, sharing in the divine nature of all created things, could contribute to the knowledge of the good. In turn, the varieties of knowledge of the good must be applied to the enlargement and enrichment of human experience. Education should therefore be the training of all the human faculties to perform (and in so far as possible to enjoy) "all the offices both public and private of peace and war," as Milton expressed it in his Tractate *Of Education*.

Another indication of the importance of wholeness in humanist thinking is the high estate which it accords to literature as an integrating study. The poet is peerless, as Sidney insists in his *Defense of Poesy*, because he combines the functions of philosopher and historian in providing both precept and example, and in so doing adds the grace of pleasure to the profit of instruction. Since the proper end of all earthly activity is the achievement of the good life, poetry is the queen of sciences, since it serves best to teach the "architectonic," or ultimate end of all study, "which stands, as I think, in knowledge of a man's self, in the ethic and politic consideration, with the end of well-doing, and not of well knowing only . . . the end of all learning being virtuous action." But Sidney makes a still higher claim for poetry, directly challenging Plato's condemnation of it in *The Republic* as an imitation of an imitation of the ideal reality. It is more than a teacher, for in going beyond nature it is the most fully creative of human activities and therefore the one in which man most closely emulates his divine Creator:

Only the poet . . . lifted up with the vigour of his own invention, doth grow, in effect, into another nature, in making things either better than nature bringeth forth or quite anew—forms such as never were in nature . . . he goeth hand in hand with nature, not enclosed within the narrow warrant of her gifts but freely ranging within the zodiac of his own wit. Nature never set forth the earth in so rich a tapestry as divers poets have done; . . . her world is brazen, the poets only deliver a golden.

One of the most attractive aspects of Renaissance humanism is this optimistic eclecticism, this conviction that it is possible to have the flesh, the world, and heaven too. It maintains, of course, a scale of values, but to recognize one aspect of experience as contrary or as inferior to another is not to condemn it out of hand. Man must be accepted as fallible, but he is also regarded as capable of desiring, comprehending, and perhaps even attaining perfection. The sovereign light of knowledge could show him the road to perfection and take him some way on it. Even the utopian state was conceivable, though, as More admitted, it might be "wished for rather than hoped for." To recognize man's weaknesses and glory in his strengths, to point out the imperfections of this world and show how they might be remedied by seeking after the best of all worlds, a harmony in which abstract and concrete, ideal and actual, active and contemplative, fleshly and spiritual values would all play their parts: such was the mission of humanism. But confidence in its success in comprehending, let alone attaining to the ultimate perfection of goodness, truth, and beauty became progressively more difficult to sustain, for the movement bore within it the seeds of its own destruction. Too many obstacles troubled men's senses "with conceit of foil." The doctrine of perfectibility clashed head-on with original sin and man's consequent mortality. The liberty of inquiry which pushed back the frontiers of knowledge made it increasingly difficult for the individual to take all knowledge to be his province. Liberated individualism often set its own good above the good of the whole. As divisions multiplied, the frame of order came to be seen less as Bembo's circle of beauty with good as its centre than as a bridge between differences. The circle integrates differences; the bridge seeks to reconcile them. But in all the conflicts of the later Renaissance, the high destiny of poetry is not lost sight of, and ideas similar to Sidney's are found everywhere in the very considerable body of literary criticism published in late Elizabethan and Jacobean England. Poetry, like love, was regarded as a reflection of the ordering, creative forces of the universe; it combined the functions of teacher, law-giver, and entertainer, and however he might occasionally seem "to write with no moral purpose," no writer of the time could have been unaware that it was his business to instruct and to delight.

Nevertheless the separatist trends became more clearly marked in all areas of activity, and as the conflicting views moved farther from the centre of compromise and nearer to the poles of opposition, even the humanists found it increasingly difficult to avoid being forced to choose between alternative views of the truth. The unity of learning was threatened not only by the practical difficulty of mastering its entirety but also by the opposed convictions that to seek to go beyond the accepted limits of human knowledge was to re-enact the sin of Eden, and that only by establishing a clear line of demarcation between matters of faith and matters of reason could the reason be truly free. In religion, the forces of Reformation and Counter-Reformation insisted more and more rigidly upon uniformity of belief and conformity of practice, and on both sides divergences once tolerated were anathematized as heresies. As with learning, reason and faith drifted or were forced into opposite camps, reason frequently allying itself with skepticism and faith with bigotry. However strong a man's personal belief might be, he had lost the assurance of belonging to a communion which embraced all of Christendom. The eternal verities had become not merely matters for rational speculation but for common and passionate controversy—often of political expediency. Was man to be saved by works or by faith? If by faith, by which faith? Was all mankind to be saved, as some reformers claimed, or was salvation predestined by special grace to some and denied to others regardless

of faith or works? The state of a devout, intelligent, and deeply concerned mind in this turbulent situation is presented in John Donne's
Holy Sonnet XVIII:

> Show me deare Christ, thy Spouse, so bright and clear
> What! is it She, which on the other shore
> Goes richly painted? or which rob'd and tore
> Laments and mournes in Germany and here?
> Sleepes she a thousand, then peepes up one yeare?
> Is she selfe truth and errs? now new, now outwore?
> Doth she, and did she, and shall she evermore
> On one, on seaven, or on no hill appeare?

Politics took on the passionate intensity of the religious dissension
with which it was so closely bound up that the line of demarcation
between heretics and traitors wellnigh disappeared. It became more
and more difficult to avoid rendering to Caesar that which was God's,
whether Caesar were a monarch by divine right, or the high priest and
governor of the City of God at Geneva, or the viceroy of his most
Catholic majesty of Spain, or an Italian *condottiere*; whether the
sanctions of power were based on Saint Paul's Epistle to the Romans
or on Machiavelli's *The Prince*. Yet the identification of the ruler with
divine authority or with the righteousness of might did not make for
unity but gave reinforcement to divisions both religious and political,
and in both areas sects and schisms representing every shade of
opinion, from the more-or-less constitutional absolutism at which the
Stuarts aimed to the near anarchism of the Levellers, grew and
proliferated.

Added to all this was the disruption caused by the "new philosophy"
which, if it was not alone in calling "all in doubt," is symptomatic of
the whole process of separation and its effect upon the minds of men.
The substitution of a Copernican for a Ptolemaic universe broke the
cosmic circle which was the emblem of divine perfection, and while
the Copernican system was not generally accepted until well on in the
seventeenth century, its postulates were widely discussed in the sixteenth,[7] and its threat to the received concept of order had made itself
felt long before Galileo published his findings in 1610. The new
pattern of the universe destroyed the authority of the macrocosm not
only as the image of the microcosms of state and individual but as the

---

[7]Thomas and Leonard Digges's edition of *Prognostication Everlasting* (1576,
reprinted in 1578, 1583, 1585, 1592, 1596, and 1605) considers (with approval)
the heliocentric theories of Copernicus and translates the relevant passages of his
De revolutionibus orbium coelestium, Book I. The Copernican system was certainly

visible evidence of the workings of the divine purpose. It untuned the sky as it undermined "degree," for gone with the spheres was the music of the spheres, Plato's celestial harmony which reconciled discordant elements and showed how all things worked together for good. Now that the Earth was no longer the centre of the universe, how could Man be regarded as the measure of all things? He no longer, in Pico's phrase, could be said to "comprehend the world"; indeed not only his soul but his senses had failed to "comprehend" its "wondrous architecture." The proud boast of Marlowe's Tamburlaine had been based upon an illusion; the climb "after knowledge infinite" had reached an infinity which seemed, to most men, to reduce man to insignificance and leave little room in its vastness for God. It was a frightening and incomprehensible abstraction which provided no comforting pattern of existence. That grand design must be sought elsewhere, and more and more it came to be sought not in the shattered macrocosm but in the microcosm, in man as the measure of himself. The measuring of "every wandering planet's course" and the reaction against it go hand in hand, and the force of both outward and inward searching is reflected in literature well before the end of the sixteenth century.

One happy result of this turning inward of speculation was to give strength, significance, and status to various forms of personal and popular literature, most of all to the drama, that "fair, lively, painted picture" as Ascham had termed it, "of the life of every degree of man." Montaigne boldly announced that the object of his *Essais* was to record his observation of "moi-même," and in his *Apology for Raimond Sebond* he denied that a pattern of moral absolutes or of natural law could be deduced from any such conceptual framework as the Great Chain of Being, for example. What can man know of the nature of God

---

known to John Norden, who alludes to it in Stanza xiii of his *Vicissitudo Rerum* [1600] in such a way as to suggest that he expects his readers to be familiar with it:

Some eke affirm the earthly sphere to err:
First set the Centre of the concave Spheres
Now start aside (supposed not to stir).
If so, the Power that Earth and Heaven Steers
By it forshows the purpose that he bears,
That all creatures that he made so fast,
Shall by degrees alter, wear and wast.

The stanza is an effective illustration of the reflection of mental conflict in ambiguity of language. "Made so fast" may mean "made so quickly," or "made to stand firm and secure." "Shall by degrees alter" suggests not only the gradualness of inevitable change but the altered concept of the universe, in which the earth rotates through the degrees of a circle. "Wast" is a variant of "waste" and sometimes (as in "the dead wast and middle of the night," *Hamlet* I, ii, 198) of "vast."

or the nature of beasts? What certitude can he have, indeed, of anything which lies outside his own experience?

Similar conclusions are reached in Sir John Davies' *Nosce Teipsum*:

> . . . how may we to others' things attain,
> When none of us his own soul understands?
> For which the devil mocks our curious brain,
> When Know thyself, his oracle commands. . . .
> All things without, which round about we see,
> We seek to know, and how therewith to do;
> But that whereby we reason, live, and be,
> Within ourselves we strangers are thereto.
> We seek to know the moving of each sphere,
> And the strange cause of th'ebbs and floods of Nile;
> But of that clock within our breasts we bear,
> The subtle motions we forget the while.
> ("Of human knowledge," 82–96)

But the search for self-knowledge resulted in reassurance only for those who could accept man's duality:

> I know my soul hath power to know all things,
> Yet is she blind and ignorant in all;
> I know I am one of nature's little kings,
> Yet to the least and vilest things am thrall.
> I know my life's a pain and but a span,
> I know my sense is mocked with everything;
> And to conclude, I know myself a man,
> Which is a proud and yet a wretched thing.
> (173–81)

Yet this very duality is evidence that goodness cannot wholly be overcome by evil, and therefore:

> . . . whoso makes a mirror of his mind
> And doth with patience view himself therein,
> His soul's eternity shall clearly find,
> Though th'other beauties be defaced with sin.
> ("That the soul is immortal," 29–32)

In spite of the divisive tendencies of the later Renaissance the humanist search for a synthesis died hard, and nowhere harder perhaps than in England, where, because its course was interrupted by the religious and political upheavals of the middle years of the century, the latter stages of Renaissance development were compressed and their characteristics intensified. The second phase, occupying roughly the two final decades of Elizabeth I's reign, is marked by an intense concern for the ideal of completeness and an equally keen awareness of the forces which threatened it. An obsession with contradictions rather than an acceptance of them is characteristic of the later humanists, however confidently they may proclaim that in the universal frame of reference these contradictions lose their significance, however fervently they may hope that in spite of the seeming triumph of Mutability this world of change and decay is indeed "stay'd upon the pillours of Eternity."

For most Elizabethans, as for Sir John Davies and Hamlet, man was both the paragon of animals and the quintessence of dust, a creature who, compounded of contradictions, often found himself ill-at-ease in his "isthmus of a middle state." For Pico della Mirandola, man's dual nature had constituted a challenge and an opportunity. It was for the intellect and will of the individual to determine whether he would be "reborn into the higher or divine state or decline into the lower or brute creation." Later writers were to be more concerned with the frustrations than with the challenge of the situation. Hamlet is again their spokesman, and his "How all occasions . . ." soliloquy (IV, iv, 32–66) is perhaps the most familiar statement of the dilemma. Whatever his reason and will might consciously choose, man continued to be pulled in opposite directions; his vision was not always effectively focussed on the ultimate good; too often it persisted in presenting a double image.

Even for Sidney, though as poet a man might go beyond nature towards the divine, as lover, as *Astrophel and Stella* makes clear, he found the ascent of the Platonic staircase from sensual to spiritual and thence to heavenly love neither easy nor satisfying:

> It is most true that eyes were meant to serve
>   The inward light, and that the heavenly part
>   Ought to be king. . . .
> True that true beauty virtue is indeed,
>   Whereof this beauty can be but a shade,
>   Which elements with mortal mixture breed.
> True that on earth we are but pilgrims made,
>   And should in soul up to our country move;
>   True, and yet true that I must Stella love.   (v)

"Passion and reason self-division cause," as his friend Fulke-Greville lamented, commenting on the

> wearisome condition of humanity,
> Born under one law, to another bound;
> Vainly begot, and yet forbidden vanity,
> Created sick, commanded to be sound.
>   ("Chorus Sacerdotum," *Mustapha*)

In the end, Sidney seems to have abandoned the struggle to reconcile the claims of mind, soul, and body, abjuring the "love which reachest but to dust" and turning from the poetry in which he both celebrated and questioned the doctrines of courtly and Platonic love to the active life of public service.

Spenser, on the other hand, failing to find satisfaction in the sphere of public action allotted to him, found his poetic reconciliation of the oppositions of flesh and spirit in Christian marriage as the right, true end of Platonic love, a sacrament which, in mirroring the union of Christ and his Church, unites the earthly and the heavenly to the greater joy of man and the greater glory of God. He found a further reconciliation in achieving a fusion of heroic poetry and spiritual allegory which treats of internal and external virtue, spiritual contemplation, and public action. And here, too, the symbolic marriage of the earthly and the heavenly finds its place.

Donne, in both his sacred and his profane poems, attempts to obliterate the division between flesh and spirit by writing of one in terms of the other. All three, and most other Elizabethan writers, assume with Plato that love is both a means to and a manifestation of order, but they are keenly aware of the problems of reconciling the physical and the spiritual manifestations of love. Whatever lip-service they may pay to the "staircase" symbol, they tend to regard these manifestations as opposed rather than complementary aspects of man's nature.

It was not the poetry of love alone, however, which produced masterpieces motivated by the desire to sustain the ideal of wholeness in a divided world. Hooker's *Laws of Ecclesiastical Polity* is a literary monument to this ideal, as the Anglican Compromise which it celebrated was an attempt, if for practical rather than philosophical ends, to put that ideal into practice. Both inclusiveness and compromise as means to the good have their personifications in *The Faerie Queene*, Arthur being the embodiment of all the virtues and Guyon, the hero of Book II, of Temperance. Paradoxical characters—wise fools, lovable rogues, uneasy Machiavellians, and honest whores—abound in fiction and drama. The interest in psychologically abnormal or one-sided characters is also an index to the temper (or lack of "temper") of the times. Such works as Burton's *Anatomy of Melancholy* are evidence of a general desire to understand the nature of mental disorder in order to correct it, and the Jonsonian Comedy of Humours upholds the ideal of the balanced man by ridiculing its opposite. It is almost impossible to discuss the themes of Elizabethan and Jacobean literature without associating them in pairs that involve overt or latent oppositions—time and eternity, appearance and reality, growth and decay, love and friendship, love and honour, law and liberty, art and nature, the governor and the governed.

To a great extent it is the search for some principle of coherence in the face of the rising tide of division which accounts for the juxtaposition of opposites, the association of diverse elements of experience not in theme and characterization alone but in every aspect of literary activity. It accounts for contrasts in tone and mingling of genres, for the prevalence of dialogue and of formal debate, of oxymoron and stichomythia, for the fully explored analogy between physical and emotional concepts, and for the metaphysical conceit. Dr. Johnson appears to have regarded this yoking of heterogeneous ideas together as evidence of intellectual perversity. Its purpose, rather, appears to have been to demonstrate the unity of human experience by showing that even between areas seemingly quite disparate an intellectual nexus could be found.[8] It was an outward and visible sign of an inward resistance to the dissociation of intellect and sensibility.

The earlier sixteenth century had found its reassurance of unity in the emblem of the microcosm, in the Platonic harmony which fused diversity into unity, in the Aristotelian concept of the composition of matter from four opposed elements, founding its order on the balance of oppositions, and on the interdependence of the links of the Great Chain of Being. When these traditional cosmic emblems had begun to lose their intellectual if not their imaginative validity the attempt was made, in the metaphysical conceit for example, to apply similar patterns of reconciliation to the associations of the individual mind. Often, of course, the literature of the turn of the century uses the traditional concepts in a new way, extending their areas of application to new kinds of physical, mental, or emotional experience rather than discarding them. Writers still wanted to have the best of both worlds, to use the resources of the new philosophy and at the same time to resolve the doubts of the old for which it was responsible.

[8]In Chapter XIV of *Biographia Literaria*, Coleridge comments on the importance of this integrating function of the poetic imagination, which ". . . diffuses a tone and spirit of unity, that blends, and (as it were) fuses, each into each, by that synthetic and magical power, to which we have exclusively appropriated the name of Imagination. . . . This power . . . reveals itself in the balance or reconciliation of opposite or discordant qualities: of sameness with difference; of the general with the concrete. . . ." T. S. Eliot ("The Metaphysical Poets," *Selected Essays* [London: Faber and Faber, 1951], p. 287) speaks of ". . . [the] poet's mind . . . constantly amalgamating disparate experience; the ordinary man's experience is chaotic, irregular, fragmentary . . . in the mind of the poet these experiences are always forming new wholes." The periods of human history which have proved most fertile in poetry seem to have been those in which the general consciousness of "the oppositions," in Jung's terminology, has been particularly acute.

Such were the dominating ideas of Shakespeare's intellectual heritage, such the conflicts of attitude and opinion which dominated men's minds at the time when he was beginning to consolidate his position as poet and playwright, such the evaluations of man, doing and suffering, which he accepted, questioned, and reshaped according to his personal dramatic vision.

Two Distincts, Division None:
The Nature of
Shakespeare's Dualities

> Property was thus appalled,
> That the self was not the same;
> Single nature's double name
> Neither two nor one was called.
> (*The Phoenix and the Turtle*)

SHAKESPEARE'S TREATMENTS of the theme of duality range from the simple to the abstruse, from the "passions of some difference" which vex the soul of a particular man to the multiple oppositions inherent in the unity of cosmic nature. In establishing the elements of dramatic conflict and in achieving poetic tension the principle operates in a variety of ways both simple and complex, straightforward and subtle. Sometimes the unity of things is stressed, sometimes the differences, and if most often, as in *The Phoenix and the Turtle*, the unifying force is the alchemy of love, at other times love's elements, if not fully reconciled, operate to divide. The ethical assumptions of the plays, whether explicit or implicit, are the assumptions of the humanist synthesis. Tolerance, temperance, and charity—the golden mean and the golden rule—are the manifestations of a harmonious ordering of differences in the personal and social spheres, as duty and responsibility are the elements of political order. All these concepts imply distinctions, but not divisions, between the self and the other. The forces of disorder, on the other hand—pride, self-aggrandizement, greed, envy, jealousy, artifice, double-dealing, hypocrisy, self-deception, and self-righteous-ness—do involve such divisions.

The pattern of all nature, at once single and dual, is reflected in the individual, and in Shakespeare's dramatic world the character who does not recognize this pattern as operating in his own nature, who disregards or denies one element of his dual heritage, is doomed to ridicule or disaster. For Shakespeare, the happy man is he who in learning to know and accept his own dualities has learned to know and accept the world. In the plays, separation from the world is usually the result of disorder in the external world or a symptom of it in the internal one, and the restoration of order—internal, external, or both—is often symbolized by a return to the world.

The simplest form of duality is the numerical, and it has been argued[1] that many of the structural conventions of Elizabethan drama, such as double plots, the introduction and suppression of minor characters in pairs, followed by the introduction of new pairs, and the like, evolved because of the necessity of doubling rôles in the small travelling theatrical companies of the mid-sixteenth century. However these conventions may have originated, whether from the practice of doubling parts or from the desire to present in morality plays "the life of every degree of man" by having the action proceed on two social levels—the upper serious, the lower comic—as Empson suggests,[2] Shakespeare exploited to the full the dramatic opportunities presented by the numerical dualities of contemporary drama.

The term "dialogue" indicates one reason for the introduction of characters in pairs, and the two sides of a dramatic conflict each with its protagonist suggest another reason, but the variety and subtlety of Shakespeare's use of pairs of all kinds seems to have been motivated by something more than these elementary considerations. His paired characters sometimes duplicate or parallel, sometimes contrast with, sometimes complement each other, and the two sides of an external conflict, each of which has its champion, may be waging a private war within the nature of one or both of these. That he was the father of twins may have made Shakespeare especially interested in that particu-lar phenomenon of biological doubling which exemplifies "single nature's double name," for in two plays he exploits its comic possibili-ties. The second of these will be reserved for discussion in a later chapter, but the first repays examination as indicative of certain of Shakespeare's basic dualities.

---

[1] David M. Bevington, *From Mankind to Marlowe: Growth of Structure in the Popular Drama of Tudor England* (Cambridge: Harvard University Press, 1962).
[2] *Some Versions of Pastoral* (London: Chatto and Windus, 1935), p. 11.

The Comedy of Errors, generally regarded as an early play, is a farce, hilariously effective when produced with pace and verve. Yet its rhetorical style and careful observance of the unities of time and place are as "academic" as its source, the *Menaechmi* of Plautus. As everyone knows, Shakespeare multiplied the confusion of identity by doubling Plautus' original pair of twins, adding twin servants of the principals, born on the same day as their masters. What is less often noticed is that the successive episodes of mistaken identity follow an almost mathematical pattern of permutations and combinations between the inner group of four, consisting of the twins, and an outer group of six, consisting of Balthazar, Angelo the goldsmith, the First Merchant, Adriana, Luciana, and the Courtesan, until, in the final scenes, the complications so proliferate as to include the minor characters of the main plot and those concerned primarily with the frame story. It is all as carefully worked out as the line-endings of a sestina, as is a somewhat less complicated pattern in *Love's Labour's Lost*. Also, the same kind of episode is repeated on two levels: Antipholus of Syracuse is claimed by Adriana, Dromio of Syracuse by Luce; the master becomes involved in a financial tangle, and immediately thereafter the man finds himself in a similar mix-up.

In style, *The Comedy of Errors* is a microcosm of early Shakespeare: the frequent rhymes, the end-stopped lines, the quibbles, the rhetorical dialectic of question and answer in a single speech, the oxymoron and stichomythia, the echoes of Kyd and Marlowe,[3] all are there. It is also a compendium of devices and situations Shakespeare used in other plays, early and late. The twins, the circumstances of the shipwreck, the kindly merchant, the comic exorcist, and the visitor who is convinced that the town is bewitched, appear in *Twelfth Night*, the turbulent wife lessoned in *The Taming of the Shrew*, the irrevocable law not enforced in *A Midsummer Night's Dream*, the parallel comic episodes on two social levels in the "ring business" of *The Merchant of Venice* and the Jaquenetta-Costard-Armado triangle in *Love's Labour's Lost*, the quest for the lost child in *Pericles*, and the lost child and wife restored in *Pericles, Cymbeline,* and *The Winter's Tale*. The doubling of pairs occurs in *Love's Labour's Lost*, which has four pairs of lovers instead of the customary two and shapes its central action on the patterns of a dance. The same device is used in *As You Like It* to illustrate four varieties of love. It is not surprising, therefore, that we can find also in *The Comedy of Errors* many characteristic Shakespearean dualities other than the numerical.

[3]For example, Adriana's complaints of her husband's neglect are very much in the style of the similar complaints of Isabella in *Edward II*.

Since his plot gives almost unlimited opportunity for the confusions, ironies of situation, and *double-entendres* which can be derived from mistaken identity, Shakespeare emphasizes here the comic aspects of appearance at variance with reality. It is a theme which he explores and re-explores in his Sonnets, Histories, Comedies, and Tragedies, as long as he can hold a pen. In *The Comedy of Errors* the two Antipholi resemble each other in personality as well as in appearance, but only outwardly are they identical. Both, in the tradition of Latin comedy, are choleric towards their servants, but in other respects Antipholus of Syracuse is the milder and less rash, the more courteous and considerate of the two. Where Antipholus of Ephesus meets obstacles head-on and is with difficulty persuaded by his friends to make the best of a bad situation, Antipholus of Syracuse is more inclined to go with the tide rather than fight against it.

To his two sets of twins Shakespeare adds a pair of sisters, and between them the differences are more marked. Indeed their two personalities are almost opposites, as is frequently the case with Shakespeare's siblings—honest Don Pedro and villainous Don John in *Much Ado About Nothing*, Edgar and Edmund, Isabella and Claudio, Antonio and Prospero, Katherine and Bianca, vacillating Clarence and single-purposed Richard, honourable Prince Hal and dishonourable Prince John, Cordelia and her sisters, Hamlet's father and Claudius, Oliver and Orlando in *As You Like It*, are some of them. "Good wombs have borne bad sons." But why? The paradoxical workings of nature by which the same elements of inheritance can be so variously compounded as to produce opposite characteristics in brothers and sisters are, for Shakespeare, one of the persistently fascinating anomalies of existence, and often a well-spring of tragedy.

But since this is a comedy, the characters of Adriana and Luciana complement rather than conflict with each other. Luciana's mildness balances Adriana's shrewishness, her submissiveness Adriana's jealous resentment of her husband's authority and liberty. Both, were they not mitigated by other qualities, might be seriously destructive, as such extreme characteristics are in other plays. But again as is appropriate to comedy, the attitudes of the sisters move closer together rather than farther apart, and the rapprochement is made easier by the fact that neither Adriana's curstness nor Luciana's mildness is as extreme as it professes to be. Adriana admits that she thinks her husband better than she says, and Luciana, for all that she preaches the whole duty of wives, does not hesitate to take the supposed Antipholus of Ephesus to task for his neglect of her sister. In the end she has come so far that she rebukes Adriana for her submissiveness: "Why bear you these rebukes, and answer not?" and Adriana, who has been taught self-knowledge by Aemilia's cross-examination, replies, "She did betray me to my own reproof." The conflict between husband and wife ends in the triumph of order: Adriana has learned that "to obey is best" and has admitted her error. But it is not alone Luciana's scolding of the wrong Antipholus which suggests that Adriana is not solely at fault. That her husband is also culpable is indicated by the subtle and characteristically Shakespearean device of a buried biblical allusion in his complaint to the Duke:

> Justice, sweet Prince, against that woman there!
> She whom thou gav'st to me to be my wife,
> That hath abused and dishonoured me
> Even in the strength and height of injury.
>
> (V, i, 197–200)

In Shakespeare's plays the cry for "Justice!" is seldom heard without the accompaniment of some sort of irony.

Other characteristic dualities are the interweaving of the stories of two generations and the mingling of tones and genres. In setting his farce in a frame of romance Shakespeare departs from the New Comedy norm in which the conflict is between generations.[4] His fathers are often enough, like Egeus in *A Midsummer Night's Dream*, "full of vexation" against their children, and that vexation is usually unjustified, but he seldom bases the main action of a comedy on their opposition to the wishes of the young people. For Shakespeare the conflict of parents and children is the material of tragedy, and he reserves it as serious plot-motivation for tragic or tragi-comic action.

The declaration of Antipholus of Syracuse's love for Luciana adds a lyric note to the predominantly farcical main plot, and the romance frame is not entirely without touches of satire, or at least tongue-in-cheek burlesque. If the Duke's pompous exposition of the law which condemns Aegeon is not sufficient warning not to take too seriously the threat which surrounds the central comedy, what follows it makes the signposting unmistakable. Can Aegeon's reply,

> Yet this my comfort: when your words are done,
> My woes end likewise with the evening sun.
>
> (I, i, 27–8)

[4] See Northrop Frye's analysis of comic patterns in "The Argument of Comedy," *English Institute Essays, 1948*, ed. D. Robertson, Jr. (New York, 1949), developed at greater length in *An Anatomy of Criticism* (Princeton University Press, 1957). Professor Frye comments that "Shakespeare's main interest is in getting away from the father-son conflict of ironic comedy towards a vision of a serene community" (*Anatomy*, p. 286).

be taken otherwise than as indicating that the Duke's platitudes are among the woes? The gently ironic tone of the scene is underlined when, immediately afterwards, Aegeon takes no less than 105 lines (in three "fits") to speak his "griefs unspeakable." In reply, the Duke demonstrates that in Ephesus as elsewhere the public scale of values sets legality above justice and official dignity above individual life by stating that though "his soul would sue as advocate" for Aegeon he cannot recall the sentence passed against him, "but to our honour's great disparagement." He does, however, allow him the great boon of according him a whole day in which to collect (in a city in which he is an utter stranger) the sum needed to ransom him. In his "natural" search for his lost son Aegeon has innocently violated an "unnatural" commercial blockade. The penalty is the forfeit of his life or a fine of a thousand marks. The satire is not stressed, but here we have another of Shakespeare's favourite themes of opposition, the disparity between law and justice, between the fertility of life and the sterility of "barren metal." And what sort of "honour" is it that is founded on injustice?

The Duke is an ambiguous character, a well-meaning but not too effective representative of public order. He knows that there is no fault in the man, but considerations of legality and public policy tie his hands, as they did those of Pilate. It is not only Shakespeare's "helpless governors," however, who demonstrate the inefficacy of platitudes, the futility of applying the parmaceti of general truth to the inward bruise of particular grief.

> I pray thee, cease thy counsel,
> Which falls into mine ears as profitless
> As water in a sieve. Give not me counsel;
> Nor let no comforter delight mine ear
> But such a one whose wrongs do suit with mine,

Leonato begs Antonio (*Much Ado about Nothing*, V, i, 3–7), and his protest is echoed in Brabantio's:

> But words are words: I never yet did hear
> That the bruis'd heart was pierced through the ear.
> (*Othello*, I, iii, 218–19)

"Why tell you me of moderation?" cries Cressida on hearing she must leave Troy, and Troilus. To know that sorrow is "common" does not console the one to whom it is "particular." In terms of the play's assumptions, however, Luciana is not only right but well-intentioned in her brief exposition of the orthodox view of domestic harmony:

Why, headstrong liberty is lash'd[5] with woe.
There's nothing situate under heaven's eye
But hath his bound, in earth, in sea, in sky.
The beasts, the fishes, and the winged fowls,
Are their males' subjects, and at their controls.
Man, more divine, the master of all these,
Lord of the wide world and wild wat'ry seas,
Indu'd with intellectual sense and souls,
Of more pre-eminence than fish and fowls,
Are masters to their females, and their lords.

                                        (II, i, 15–24)

This is Ulysses' famous "degree" speech in little, but Adriana has no appetite for boiled Hooker.[6] She makes the standard reply:

They can be meek that have no other cause.
A wretched soul, bruis'd with adversity,
We bid be quiet when we hear it cry;
But were we burd'ned with like weight of pain,
As much, or more, we should ourselves complain.
So thou, that hast no unkind mate to grieve thee,
With urging helpless patience would relieve me;
But if thou live to see like right bereft,
This fool-begg'd patience in thee will be left.

                                        (II, i, 33–41)

Recent scholarship has devoted a great deal of attention to Elizabethan doctrines of natural and political order as reflected in Shakespeare's plays and in particular to the concept of degree as exemplified in the Great Chain of Being.[7] Indeed so much attention has been given to them that we are in danger of forgetting that Shakespeare's attitude to conventions of all kinds, and especially to

[5]This is an early example of a typically Shakespearean latent ambiguity of the sort in which all senses of a word—in this instance, "driven," "chastised," and "bound"—are appropriate in the context. For other examples, see Empson's discussion of Type Three, in *The Seven Types of Ambiguity* (New York: Meridian Books, 1955), pp. 117–50.

[6]Perhaps the most famous sentence in *The Laws of Ecclesiastical Polity* (Book I, Section III, 2) begins, "Now if Nature should intermit her course . . . ," goes on to list the results of disfunction in the various "degrees" of physical Nature, and ends, ". . . what would become of man himself whom these things now do all serve?" "See we not plainly," Hooker concludes, "that obedience of creatures unto the law of Nature is the stay of the whole world?"

[7]A few of the many works of criticism in this area are: Lily B. Campbell, *Shakespeare's Histories: Mirrors of Elizabethan Policy* (San Marino, Cal.: Huntington Library, 1937); Alfred Hart, *Shakespeare and the Homilies* (Melbourne University Press, 1934); Robert Speaight, *Shakespeare and Politics* (Royal Society Lecture, 1946); E. M. W. Tillyard, *The Elizabethan World Picture* (London: Chatto and Windus, 1943); and *Shakespeare's History Plays* (London: Chatto and Windus, 1944).

conventional statements of orthodox ethical principles, is consistently inconsistent. Ethical, political, or literary, he uses the conventions of his age to point a moral or adorn a tale when it suits him to do so; he questions, or modifies, or rejects them when it does not. In the later plays any orthodox statement sententiously expressed is suspect; indeed such statements become themselves conventional indications that the speaker is either insincere or at a loss for words, if he is not speaking "officialese."[8] Even when a predominantly sympathetic character like Ulysses utters a formal dissertation on the principle of "degree," this is no assurance of Shakespeare's unreserved acceptance of the principle, especially since the wily Greek is using the argument for the express purpose of undermining the operation of the principle in the particular context in which he is speaking.

This is not to say that Shakespeare was not deeply concerned with the problems of order. Such problems are inseparable from any serious consideration of human experience and from the reconciliation of the conflicts of human existence towards which all serious drama is directed. As Arthur Sewell expresses it: "The dramatist gives dramatic form to that dialectic through which all of us, in our own way, seek to fashion—but can never perfect—our address to the world."[9]

For Shakespeare the form of that address to the world is not single but multiple, and the degree-symbolism only one of its guises. Most of the critical insistence on his championing of the Tudor orthodoxy with regard to political order is based upon plays with a political or historical theme, to which the chain-of-being emblem is appropriate and in which its premises are most frequently stated. It provides an over-all thesis for the two tetralogies which span the course of English history from the reign of Richard of Bordeaux to that of Richard of Gloucester. In addition, by taking Henry of Bolingbroke's usurpation as a violation of the natural order which called down misfortune on his family and his country Shakespeare was following the classical precedent of the curse of the Atreidi and demonstrating the fulfilment of the biblical warning that the sins of the fathers would be visited upon the children to the third and fourth generation, thus gaining for his series of chronicle plays the prestige of scholarly precedent combined with moral justification and the popularity of the "Tudor myth." But the political dialectic of rights and duties in the framework of

---

[8]The classic instances are perhaps Claudius's throne speech (*Hamlet*, I, ii) and Macbeth's outburst of rhetoric describing the finding of Duncan, "His silver skin lac'd with his golden blood" (II, ii, 114–24).

[9]*Character and Society in Shakespeare* (Oxford: Clarendon Press, 1951), p. 8.

degree is not the only theme dealt with in the Histories, though, as might be expected in a dramatic series dealing almost exclusively with a period of civil strife, the theme of order predominates.

Nevertheless, most of the questionings of "order" made explicit in the tragedies are implicit in the Histories, and in the later plays the questions are often more dramatically significant than the ready-made answers. Most of the questions raised in the Histories are concerned with the dual relationship of governor to governed, but there are others which involve the establishment of a line of demarcation between opposites in a world of conflicting values, of civil war external and internal—a favourite Shakespearean correspondence. Where is the line of truth and virtue to be drawn between honour and fame, for example? between political duty and moral duty? between royal privilege and private justice? between mirth and folly? between being and seeming? between the shadow and substance of kingship? between piety and weakness? shrewdness and deceit? means and ends? good and bad wars? friendship and favouritism? between defence of one's own rights and the usurpation of others? The answers to these questions, where they are given, are seldom unequivocal; they give us a sense of what has gone wrong rather than of what would have been right. If, as Tillyard suggests, the hero of the History Plays as a whole is England, and the cycle is a tragi-comedy, it should be possible to evaluate actions on the basis of their effect on this central character. The evils which cause civil war are made clear enough— favouritism, irresponsibility, ingratitude, vanity, suspicion, scorn, and weakness on the part of the ruler; ambition, hypocrisy, treachery, jealousy, negligence, vindictiveness, disobedience, murder, adultery, witchcraft, and usurpation on the part of the subject. Most of the world's ills are due to one or another of these causes. It is clear also that it would have been better for England if the royal power had not been shared by mutually jealous uncles during the minorities of Richard II and Henry VI, and given over to a wicked uncle of the youthful Edward V. "Woe to the land that's govern'd by a child!" But would it have been better for England to have remained mis-governed and bankrupt under the legitimate Richard II rather than capably managed at the usurping hands of Henry IV? Which was pre-ferable as commander and ruler, the weak-willed and shallow-brained but saintly Henry VI or his efficient if fiend-like queen? In the Histories what is politically good is frequently morally evil, and what is morally acceptable and politically expedient—the rejection of Falstaff for example—we find repugnant if not intolerable. What is spiritually decadent, like Falstaff's view of honour, is factually accurate, and what is monstrous, like the actions of Richard III, is nevertheless amusing. Elizabeth I was well aware that the Histories are not reliable as Tudor propaganda. For her the stated "moral" of *Richard II* was less significant than the force of example in the presentation of his character and its results. Considering the frequency with which she was accused of favouritism it is small wonder that this was not her favourite play. The eight History Plays are an examination of the problems of kingship in the context of British history, but they present a report, not dogma.

In the tragedies "Nature" takes the place held by "Degree" in the Histories as the dominant concept of order,[10] but there are two concepts of Nature, and the disorder of the new challenges the order of the old. Yet the unnaturalness of evil is not a new theme; it appears in the *Henry VI* trilogy and dominates *Richard III*. For Richard is not merely the end product of the original violation of "degree" in the usurpation of Henry IV and deposition of Richard II, the incarnation of ultimate disorder by whose excesses the corrupt realm will be purged of its evil and so made ready to receive the blessings of the Tudor peace under Henry VII. He stands outside human nature:

> I have no brother, I am like no brother;
> And this word 'love', which greybeards call divine,
> Be resident in men like one another,
> And not in me! I am myself alone.
>
> (*III Henry VI*, V, vi, 80–3)

Four of Shakespeare's tragic heroes are thus divided from humanity— Richard before birth (*III Henry VI*, III, iii, 153), Timon by circum-

---

[10]Some recent studies which discuss external Nature as the exemplar of moral order, Christian or otherwise, in Shakespeare's plays are: John F. Danby, *Shakespeare's Doctrine of Nature: A Study of King Lear* (London: Faber and Faber, 1951); Willard Farnham, *The Medieval Heritage of Elizabethan Tragedy* (Berkeley: University of California Press, 1936), and *Shakespeare's Tragic Frontier* (Berkeley: University of California Press, 1948); Northrop Frye, *An Anatomy of Criticism* (see note 4); R. B. Heilman, *This Great Stage* (University of Louisiana Press, 1948); G. Wilson Knight, *The Wheel of Fire* (Oxford University Press, 1930; London: Methuen, 1949); M. D. H. Parker, *The Slave of Life* (London: Chatto and Windus, 1955); R. N. Siegel, *Shakespearean Tragedy and the Elizabethan Compromise* (New York University Press, 1957); Irving Ribner, *Jacobean Tragedy: The Quest for Moral Order* (London: Methuen, 1962), and *Patterns in Shakespearean Tragedy* (London: Methuen, 1960); Robert Speaight, *Nature in Shakespearean Tragedy* (London: Hollis and Carter, 1955); Theodore Spencer, *Shakespeare and the Nature of Man*, the Lowell Lectures (New York: Macmillan 1942; Macmillan Paperbacks, 1961); H. S. Wilson, *On the Design of Shakespearean Tragedy* (University of Toronto Press, 1957).

stance, Macbeth by choice, and Coriolanus by upbringing. Of the four, only Richard III could be termed "naturally unnatural." His unnaturalness is visible; it is indicated by the circumstances of his birth and by the mis-shapen body which his deformed soul informs. The orthodox concept of natural order has no relevance for Richard of Gloucester, who is the forerunner of Edmund in representing the self-regarding Nature of Montaigne as opposed to the providential Nature of Sebond, the polity of Machiavelli as opposed to that of Hooker. His unnaturalness also exemplifies the Aristotelian disorder of excess and defect which plays so prominent a part in Shakespeare's tragic vision.[11] The qualities he has to excess are virtues, as he himself recognizes in the opening speech of *Richard III*, only in the disordered world of war, and especially of civil war. Shrewdness, boldness, mercilessness, the ability to deceive, may be the qualities of the successfully ambitious man, but it is only the big wars that make ambition virtue. The qualities appropriate to peace and good order—honesty, natural affection, respect for authority, and capacity for love—he totally lacks. He is completely self-regarding, and his double-dealing is single-purposed. Because he is not typical, because he does stand outside "that great bond" of humanity, we feel we may safely laugh at his trickery; yet because "no one ever loved" him we must pity him.

The examination of received concepts of order becomes more searching in the tragedies, the questioning more insistent. And the questions are not merely implied; they are spoken: "Is there no pity sitting in the clouds / That sees into the bottom of my grief?" "Did not great Julius bleed for Justice' sake?" "What is a man / If his chief good and market of his time / Be but to sleep and feed?" "Why should our endeavour be so loved and the performance so loathed?" "Who can control his fate?" "Is there any cause in nature that makes these hard hearts?" "How is't with me when every noise appalls me?" "Is Antony or we in fault for this?" "Think'st thou it honorable for a noble man / Still to remember wrongs?" "Who would be so mocked with glory?" And the answers, when there are answers, are more likely to be ironical or ambiguous than conclusive.

Therefore, even if the statements or implications of the plays are admitted as evidence of the author's attitudes, that evidence presents an uncertain image of order. The theme is developed under several concepts, not one, and the various dramatic amplifications of any

[11]See Spencer, *Shakespeare and the Nature of Man*, and Lily B. Campbell, *Shakespeare's Tragic Heroes, Slaves of Passion* (Cambridge University Press, 1930; New York: Barnes and Noble, 1960).

single concept do not lead to consistent conclusions. Sometimes the contradictory elements of a particular aspect of the human dilemma are resolved by modifying and qualifying them to a point of harmonious reconciliation; sometimes order is achieved through sacrifice of the good, or by the purgation of evil[12]—the driving out of the irreconcilable element, or by the cyclical processes of regeneration[13] and restoration, or by a combination of such methods.

Conventional notions of order are questioned less seriously and less often in the early plays than in the later ones. For example, *The Taming of the Shrew*, like *The Comedy of Errors*, upholds the principle of degree in the domestic microcosm:

> Marry, peace it bodes, and love, and quiet life,
> An awful rule, and right supremacy;
> And, to be short, what not that's sweet and happy?
>   (V, ii, 108–10)

Yet Desdemona's wifely submissiveness brings her to no such happy end. Why? Her love for Othello, which others term "unnatural," is the ideal love which does not alter "when it alteration finds." When Lady Macbeth and Cleopatra step out of their appointed station as women to play the roles of men the result is chaos; when Portia does the same thing in *The Merchant of Venice*, order is restored. At a crucial moment Cordelia tells less than the truth and Desdemona lies, yet each is invested with the spirit of grace which, as is said of Cordelia, "redeems Nature from the general curse that twain have brought her to." We are made to identify ourselves with the forces of disorder in *Twelfth Night* and *I Henry IV* and with the protagonists of evil in *Richard III* and *Macbeth*, and "measure for measure" on the lips of Warwick as he removes York's head from the gates of the city to make room for Clifford's (*III Henry VI*, II, vi, 55) means something very different from its significance in the play of that name.

Nor is the treatment of the conflict of reason and passion always the orthodox one. *Love's Labour's Lost* ridicules both love which is not serious and seriousness without love, and ends not with marriage but with putting the lovers on a year's probation to find the point of balance between them for themselves. Lear, Leontes, and Antony may be, in different ways, the slaves of passion, but reliance on reason (or what they think to be reason) and mistrust of emotion contribute to the downfall of Brutus, Hamlet, and Othello. Helena, who pursued

[12]See Frye, *Anatomy of Criticism*, on the archetypes of the dying god and the *pharmakos* or scapegoat in literature, particularly in the drama.

[13]*Ibid., passim,* and sections on "romance," especially pp. 136 ff. and 186 ff.; also Ribner, *Patterns*, Ch. 6.

her reluctant husband to the limits of feminine modesty if not beyond them, and Viola, who "never told her love," are both presented as worthy representatives of their sex. Bertram resists the domination of his noble mother and is universally condemned for his folly; Coriolanus yields to the wishes of his noble mother and finds the consequences "most mortal to him." Black may be the devil's hue, but the soul which informs a black skin may be as stygian as Aaron's, as "fair" as Othello's, or as neutral as the Prince of Morocco's. "Unnatural" characters may, like the same Aaron, nevertheless be capable of natural affection, while "natural" ones, like Egeus in *A Midsummer Night's Dream*, may display little or no tenderness for their offspring. "Natural" sons may or may not be naturally evil: Don John in *Much Ado*, Edmund in *King Lear*, and Faulconbridge in *King John* are all bastards and all profess adherence to the Renaissance equivalent of the "I'm all right, Jack" ethic, yet two are scoundrels and one an engaging hero. Prospero's enforced withdrawal from the world restores him to it a wiser and a greater man; Timon's voluntary if outraged withdrawal from his world destroys him. Falstaff is wrong but irresistible; Thersites, like the Roundheads of *1066 and All That*, is "right but repulsive." Theseus and Henry V woo almost as unnaturally as Richard III, and win their loves doing them injuries, but the prognosis for their unions is as favourable as it was fatal for poor Queen Anne. Heroes come to grief through possessing, like Hamlet and Antony, irreconcilably divided dispositions, and through being, like Coriolanus, "all one thing." The labels applied to a situation or a character are as reliable as the person who speaks them and no more, though sometimes less. In the words of a recent critic: "Words like honour, nobility, justice, harlot, and traitor are often, perhaps more often than not, to be suspected. . . . frequently justice, as the speaker terms it, is to Shakespeare tyranny or worse . . . honour, in its conventional sense . . . deliberately shown . . . as preventing conciliation and conducing to superfluous death."[14] From such diversities and contradictions the only pattern of order that can be derived is that of Friar Laurence:

> . . . nought so vile that on the earth doth live
> But to the earth some special good doth give;
> Nor aught so good but, strain'd from that fair use,
> Revolts from true birth, stumbling on abuse:
> Virtue itself turns vice, being misapplied,
> And vice sometime's by action dignified.
> (*Romeo and Juliet*, II, iii, 17–22)

[14]John Vyvyan, *The Shakespearean Ethic* (London: Chatto and Windus, 1959), p. 12.

Considerations of order inevitably involve dualities, but Shakespeare's presentation of those dualities is illustrative of his own double vision of life.

A. C. Bradley realized that if any principle of moral order can be deduced from Shakespeare's tragedies it is that of ambivalence: ". . . we are left at last with an idea showing two sides or aspects which we can neither separate nor reconcile."[15] Though recent criticism has thrown out Bradley's insights along with his speculations, there are indications of a reaction against those who regard the plays as fixed in the frame of reference of one or another medieval concept of order.[16] Alfred Harbage suggests that Shakespeare's moral enigmas are nothing more than a kind of intellectual "sallet" intended to titillate the audience and appeal to its propensity for moral philosophizing.[17] John Vyvyan, on the other hand, assumes that Shakespeare's questioning of received concepts is sincere if unsettling: "He was not satisfied with conventional answers; yet he needed answers, for his own peace, in terms of life. And his plays are part of his quest for them."[18] Something like Bradley's view of the matter is developed by Geoffrey Bush:

There is a tendency of the mind to seek out meaning; the Elizabethan doctrine of order belongs to this effort towards conclusive statement. . . . And while the idea of order has not survived, *Hamlet* and *King Lear* have survived: they belong to a different enterprise of the mind, concerned with matters more personal, more obscure, and more exacting of our fears and affections. They are experiments in thought that did not end in failure; and what is striking about them is that their outcome is so incomplete and inconclusive.

Nothing is said in *Hamlet* and *King Lear* that has the certainty of knowledge offered by Shakespeare's two most distinguished contemporaries in the theatre. Chapman and Webster take sides, and we know where they stand.[19]

It might be added that Chapman sometimes does not know quite where he stands (though he never admits it) and that Jonson takes a broader view of life but is perhaps more consistent in presenting it, though *The Alchemist* and *Volpone* show ambivalence. But we never know where Shakespeare stands. We only know that he will be found standing sometimes on one side, sometimes on the other, and some-

[15]*Shakespearean Tragedy* (St. Martin's Library; London: Macmillan, 1957), p. 28.

[16]See, for example, A. P. Rossiter, *Angel with Horns, and other Shakespeare Lectures*, ed. Graham Storey (London: Longmans; New York: Theatre Arts Books, 1961), especially Ch. 3: "Ambivalence: The Dialectic of the Histories."

[17]*As They Liked It* (New York: Macmillan, 1947; Harper Torchbooks, 1961).

[18]*The Shakespearean Ethic*, p. 9.

[19]*Shakespeare and the Natural Condition* (Harvard University Press, 1956), pp. 6 ff.

times in the middle, that wherever he is standing he will be keeping both sides in view and will never give the impression, as Beaumont and Fletcher sometimes do, that since there is no sure and single answer to the riddles of life one might as well stop looking and resign oneself to hand-me-down answers or to none.

Though he was not satisfied with conventional answers, Shakespeare made dramatic and poetic capital not only of such answers but also of his dissatisfaction with them, and it is possible to trace some sort of pattern of development in his methods of doing both. In the earlier plays he tries out one principle of resolution after another, just as he experiments with one genre or style after another. At this stage, for the most part, he seems content to take conventional assumptions at face value, or at least to assume, for the purposes of a particular play, that the philosophical and dramatic principles which underlie them are valid. The concepts of order may differ from play to play but are not seriously challenged by characterization, action, or denouement. Good and evil are clearly distinguished, and duality is expressed less in theme than in the mingling of genres and contrasting of styles—as in the lyric passages in the midst of the Senecan horrors of *Titus Andronicus* and the realistic comedy of Launce and his dog amid the idealization of love and friendship in *Two Gentlemen of Verona*. Proteus and the cowardly knight Sir Eglamour are somewhat disturbing because their incongruities are not assimilated into the general tone of the play. The audience finds it easier to laugh at greater cowards and forgive blacker villains in later plays because they have been conditioned to dualities of attitude, often by the careful planting of buried connotative suggestion. In these experimental plays a secondary conventional theme may be used to support the primary one. Thus, the "blood asketh blood" chain reactions of *Titus Andronicus* and the early Histories are associated with violations of the natural order of degree and of the bond of kinship, and the dialectic pattern of action-reaction is interwoven with the star-crossed destinies of Romeo and Juliet.

As he gained confidence in his dramatic skill and (it would seem) began to lose confidence in an absolute scheme of values, he began to dramatize his doubts, sometimes by direct questioning of conventions, as in Falstaff's formal catechism on "honour" and the council-meeting in Troy which demonstrates that so-called honour can be opposed to both reason and justice, sometimes less directly by showing that conventional attitudes can be productive not of reconciliation but dissension. In other plays two characters may be the exponents of conflicting values, not merely in the simple, morality-play fashion as personifications of good and evil but as each possessing a share of both truth and error. In still others, three such characters may be employed, one serving as the mean between two extremes, or as the observer-touchstone who indicates the distribution of truth and error on both sides. These are favourite devices of the middle plays, though the observer-moderator is found as early as Marcus Andronicus, the brother of Titus, and as late as Enobarbus in *Antony and Cleopatra*. Sometimes, however, the observer is mistaken in his analysis, and may even represent the forces of destruction, like Polonius and Parolles, or like Thersites, be an accurate but malevolent commentator. More typical is Prince Hal, the exemplar of the golden mean between the vanity of Hotspur's view of honour and the depravity of Falstaff's. In conditions of extreme disorder the man who is able to see both sides of an issue may be rendered incapable of action, as the Duke of York is in *Richard II*, the most ambivalent of the Histories.

Something very like this happens in *Hamlet*. There are other plays in which the central character is also the observer—*Measure for Measure*, *Macbeth*, and *The Tempest*, for example. But Duke Vincentio and Prospero are firmly in control of the action, in which they are not so much actors as directors—or rather actor-managers. Once he has made his fatal choice, and he makes it early, Macbeth's ambivalence, far from inhibiting him, spurs him to further action in the hope of ridding himself of it. Among the observer-heroes given to self-analysis, Hamlet suffers in a uniquely ambivalent way from maintaining an attitude of intellectual detachment toward a situation in which he is intensely involved emotionally and which he can neither control nor accept. Emotionally, his ambivalence seems to be directed only towards women; with men he knows well enough where he stands. He loves his father, but believes and does not believe the ghost; he hates Claudius, yet would not be passion's slave. He is an intellectually ambivalent perfectionist consumed by a yearning for absolutes, for the unattainable completeness of righteousness in a corrupt world whose corruptness he knows he shares, and in which he has not too little motive and cue for passion but too much. He refuses to kill Claudius at prayer, for that would not be a logically complete and perfect vengeance, but neither would it suffice to assuage his hatred of the man. Yet his reason at the same time rejects the "wild justice" of revenge because it is not "complete justice." Hamlet's active and contemplative sides are both strongly developed but they never work in conjunction. He acts when he does not think, and when he thinks cannot act. Even after the example of Fortinbras' honourable folly (and Hamlet recognizes it as folly) has shamed him into resolving to think bloody thoughts or none, he still seeks the assurance that perfect vengeance will also be perfect justice: "is it not complete justice to quit him with this arm?" And when he has achieved this complete satisfaction at the cost of his own life he is still concerned that his righteousness shall be acknowledged after his death:

> O God! Horatio, what a wounded name,
> Things standing thus unknown, shall live behind me!
> If thou didst ever hold me in thy heart,
> Absent thee from felicity awhile,
> And in this harsh world draw thy breath in pain,
> To tell my story.
>
> (V, ii, 336–40)

The theme of disillusionment and its destructive effect upon those who cannot accept imperfections in themselves or those they love is a dominating one in most of the plays of the middle period, and the revulsion of disillusionment is perhaps seen in the frequency with which, in these plays, normal values are turned upside-down and normal expectations thwarted. Not only do comedy and tragedy mingle in tragi-comedy; conventionally comic situations are taken seriously and conventionally serious ones made to provide the material of comedy. What wisdom cannot discover, fools bring to light, and folly is often the voice of wisdom in a world where vice and virtue, flesh and spirit, restriction and licence, idealization and cynicism, go to extremes.

The jealous husband is the commonest of targets of satiric comedy, but Shakespeare turns him into a tragic hero and insists upon his nobility of nature—or is there a touch of irony in that, too? Certainly Othello's jealousy is noble only in his own eyes. That is part of his self-deception. The nature passion could not shake commits the classic *crime passionel*. Angelo's inhibited lust is aroused not by wantonness but by chastity; women behave like men, or are disguised as men so effectively that women fall in love with them. Public heroes become public enemies. The comic possibilities of inverted values are most fully developed in *Twelfth Night*, the tragic in *Othello* and *Macbeth*. In the former tragedy the external evil which produces internal chaos precedes the fatal act; in the latter the internal evil prompts the action which produces the external chaos. It is in *Othello*, therefore, that we can see the operation of the elements of moral inversion more distinctly. Bradley termed this the most painful of the tragedies because not only is every step of the assault outlined for the audience in advance, but the forces of evil are presented in such a way as to appear irresistible.[20] Certainly, evil prevails over good to an extent

[20]*Shakespearean Tragedy*, p. 143.

that leaves little room for reconciliation, general or particular. This is not a tragedy in which good comes out of evil, but the reverse. Bluff, honest Iago, that caricature of the blunt, honest soldier which so roused the ire of Rymer at the end of the century, assures us at the beginning of his plot that "out of her own goodness" he will make "the net that shall enmesh them all," and he is almost completely successful. Desdemona dies not only murdered by her husband but believing that he loathes her for a sin she cannot even bear to name, much less commit. Othello plays the just judge to the last, executing vengeance on himself and going to his damnation without even the (to the audience at least) redeeming grace of self-knowledge. At the end of the play we are left with a stage full of corpses (and another in the wings), a living villain whose death would have shown "but a trifle here," and a wounded Cassio, the one among Iago's major victims we could most easily have spared. In *Othello* black is white with a vengeance.

All these plays in which inversion is a dominant theme rely for much of their dramatic effectiveness upon irony, tragic or comic, circumstantial or verbal. The comedies often have equivocal titles which we do not know whether or not to take at their face value. *Much Ado about Nothing*, for example, can be regarded with some justice as a play in which there is little enough ado about something, regardless of John Dover Wilson's contention that the least Claudio can do is "to agree to marry the cousin of the supposedly dead girl so that Leonato may not lose his match."[21] *As You Like It* can be taken as meaning "call it whatever you like" or "here is your ideal world—more or less," or "there's something here for all tastes." Similarly, the subtitle of *Twelfth Night*, or *What You Will* may mean "pick your own title," but when we recall what Shakespeare does with that word "will" in the Sonnets and that will has pretty much its own way in the play, we wonder, as we do about the sincerity of the title of that very awkward play, *All's Well That Ends Well*.

The element of parody, already developed in the attack on pedantry and other forms of affectation in *Love's Labour's Lost*, is prominent in the middle plays and in the form of burlesque reinforces the other inversions. The mechanicals of *A Midsummer Night's Dream* burlesque not only the actors of Shakespeare's own or a rival company but the theme of *Romeo and Juliet* and the style of its source.[22] The presence

---

[21]*Shakespeare's Happy Comedies* (London: Faber and Faber, 1962), p. 126.

[22]Brooke's poem was written in "eight and six," printed as couplets of "fourteeners," the metre favoured by Bottom for the prologue to the play of Pyramus and Thisbe, which is in alternatingly rhymed pentameter couplets varied with passionate speeches in mingled dimeter and trimeter couplets. The language of

of elements of burlesque in *Romeo and Juliet* itself I hope to demonstrate in a later chapter.

Burlesque is an element of the comic ambivalence which makes *As You Like It* outstanding among the "mirthful" comedies of the middle period. In it, Shakespeare uses the utopian assumptions of pastoral in the traditional ways, to create a romantic idyll and to expose the artificiality and self-seeking duplicity of court life as contrasted with the innocent, golden-age simplicity of the shepherd's life. But at the same time, he turns this tapestry the other side about and demonstrates that its warp and woof are made of motley, that courtly manners (good and bad) can be found in the wilderness of Arden, along with charitable outlaws, grasping landlords, foolish lovers, scornful ladies, corruptible hedge-priests, and satirical malcontents. Custom may make the life there more sweet than that of painted pomp, but adversity, for all that it wears a rich jewel in its head, is still an ugly toad, and the Duke, given an opportunity to recover his rights, is willing to risk man's ingratitude at court rather than endure the blasts of the winter wind in Arcadia. This ability to take things seriously and laugh at them at the same time, the author imparts to certain of the play's characters, notably Touchstone and Rosalind, who regard themselves with the same clearsighted double vision which they direct towards the world. Jaques possesses a commoner form of this attribute, the astigmatic view of things which enables him to rail at his own vices as he sees them projected on the screen of "the infected body of the world." In connection with this comic ambivalence there is a good deal of parody —of courtly love in the wooing of Phebe by Silvius and of romantic love in the mock-wooing which Rosalind-Ganymede imposes upon Orlando as a supposedly infallible cure for the ailment from which she is the last to desire his recovery. Jaques parodies the *Contemptus Mundi* homily in his speech on "The Seven Ages of Man," and Touchstone's rules for avoiding duels burlesque a handbook of the code of honour.[23]

Romeus and Juliet, however, is closely paralleled in Quince's play. For example, the lines which precede Juliet's drinking of the potion:

> As she had frantic been, in haste the glass she caught,
> And up she drunk the mixture quite, withouten further thought.
> Then on her breast she crossed her arms long and small,
> And so, her senses failing her, into a trance did fall.

[23]Parallels of phrasing indicate that a likely candidate may be *The Booke of Honour and Armes, wherein is discovered the causes of Quarrell, and the nature of injuries, with their repulses. Also the meanes of satisfaction and pacification; with divers other things necessarie to be knowne of all Gentlemen and others professing Armes and Honor* (London: Richard Jhones, dwelling at the Signe of the Rose and Crowne neere Holburne Conduit, 1590). STC 22163.

More puzzling are the instances of parody in *Troilus and Cressida*. O. J. Campbell accounts for the seeming confusion of styles and attitudes in the play by pointing out its affinities with the "comicall satyre" of Marston and Jonson and arguing that it should be regarded as a satire directed against courtly love and the feudal concept of honour.[24] Many of his points are well taken, but the play is surely something more than a satiric exposé of outmoded social values set in the framework of heroic tragedy. Like *As You Like It*, this would appear to be a play of ambivalent intention, which makes straight-forward dramatic use of some elements of a code of values and "debunks" others. To do this with both epic and romantic values in the traditionally opposed areas of love and war is a feat of literary acrobatics less easy of accomplishment in the tragic than in the comic frame of reference. It demands from the audience not only quickness and delicacy of perception but the emotional reactions of a chameleon's colouring, and one can well believe that it was "never clapper-clawed with the palms of the vulgar." Surely we are expected to admire the wisdom of Ulysses, the loyalty, integrity, and courage of Hector, and the devotion of Troilus, but to condemn the unworthy objects which they serve. The self-seeking and self-indulgent vices are painfully evident in *Troilus and Cressida*, but so is "virtue misapplied."

> . . . purest faith unhappily forsworn
> And gilded honor shamefully misplac'd
>
> (SONNET 66)

are the tragic themes of the play. Its satire is directed against the follies which make such virtue tragic, or which make "the service greater than the god."

Ambivalence of intention is apparent, also, in the contrasting styles of *Troilus and Cressida*; they range from the straightforward but compressed tautness of the middle period, which reaches its culmination in the elliptical utterances of *King Lear*, to the most elaborate and stilted of rhetoric. "Valor's show and valor's worth divide" (I, iii, 46) in the speeches of the various epic heroes, and it is not only Achilles and Patroclus who, as Ulysses protests, burlesque "the topless deputation" of great Agamemnon's heroic style in the "fusty stuff" of slanderous imitation:

> like a strutting player whose conceit
> Lies in his hamstring, and doth think it rich
> To hear the wooden dialogue and sound

[24]*Comicall Satyre and Shakespeare's Troilus and Cressida* (San Marino: Huntington Library, 1938).

'Twixt his stretch'd footing and the scaffoldage—
Such to-be-pitied and o'er-wrested seeming
He acts thy greatness in; and when he speaks,
'Tis like a chime a-mending, with terms unsquar'd,
Which, from the tongue of roaring Typhon dropp'd,
Would seem hyperboles.

(I, iii, 153–61)

If Agamemnon's and Ajax's speeches are all wind-machine, there is no "wooden dialogue" in the speeches of Ulysses and Hector.

From *The Merchant of Venice* to *Coriolanus* the dramatic emphasis is upon the contradictions and divisions rather than upon the unity inherent in "single Nature's double name." "So may the outward shows be least themselves. The world is still deceiv'd . . ."—and still deceives itself. The hero is divided against himself in *Julius Caesar*, in *Hamlet*, and in *Antony and Cleopatra*. He is divided from the principle of goodness in *Macbeth*, from love in *Othello* and *Troilus and Cressida*, and from his country in *Timon of Athens* and *Coriolanus*.

> . . . love cools, friendship falls off, brothers divide; in cities, mutinies; in countries, discord; in palaces, treason; and the bond crack'd 'twixt son and father.　　　(*King Lear*, I, ii, 104–7)

Yet in the midst of this chaos the forces of unity are at work, though sometimes in strange ways and with perverse results. In the inverted world of *Othello*, for example, evil is triumphant in the person of Iago, as nearly an absolutely evil character as Shakespeare created.[25] Yet the unity which underlies the duality of good and evil is made clear when they meet and (briefly) merge in the temptation scene.[26] Up to that point hero and villain have been clearly distinguished in language as in attitude. Othello's speech has been "noble," full of the brightness of air and fire; that of Iago has been bestial, its imagery that

[25]*Richard III* may in some ways be more monstrously wicked than Iago, but his evil is less appalling because it is monstrous and we do not, therefore, identify it with the ordinary nature of common man. Iago is not marked as unnatural from birth, as Richard is, nor are his dupes corrupt in the sense that the majority of Richard's are. Iago is presented as an ordinary human being in whose nature the diabolical elements have taken over, and he has almost a monopoly of evil in the play. In *Richard III*, no matter how suspicious they may be, the other characters find it hard to believe that Richard is as bad as he is, but in *Othello* no one doubts that Iago is completely "honest."

[26]This temporary merging of the natures of Iago and Othello has been commented upon by J. I. M. Stewart in *Character and Motive in Shakespeare* (London: Longmans, 1949), pp. 108–9, and by John Lawlor in *The Tragic Sense in Shakespeare* (London: Chatto and Windus, 1960), pp. 93 ff. See also M. M. Morosov, "The Individualization of Shakespeare's Characters through Imagery," *Shakespeare Survey*, 2 (1947), pp. 860–8.

of earth and its lower forms of creation. That "chaos is come again" in Othello's nature when he is "once in doubt" of Desdemona's faith is signalized by the invasion of his speech by the toads, goats, and monkeys of Iago's verbal world. It is now Iago who, professing that his interests and Othello's are identical, swears by the elements of air and fire "that clip us round about" and by the "ever-burning lights above."

The mercy which is the reflection of heaven's grace is called upon to no avail in *The Merchant of Venice,* but reinforced by all-forgiving love it operates to reconcile the disorders of *Measure for Measure.* It is in *King Lear,* however, where chaos predominates on all planes external and internal, public and private, that the positive and negative views of reconciliation meet, and it is here that the characteristic resolution of the final plays is first formulated. In the negative view, the injustices, catastrophes, and disillusionments of life are seen as serving the purposes of Nature. They make the cycle of birth and death acceptable, in that the evil of existence reconciles us to relinquishing it:

> World, world, O world!
> But that thy strange mutations make us hate thee
> Life would not yield to age.
>
> (IV, i, 10–12)

Kent's comment on Lear's death:

> He hates him
> That would upon the rack of this tough world
> Stretch him out longer.
>
> (V, iii, 313–15)

is the final expression of pessimism, but it is not the final impression which most of us carry away from the play, whether or not we believe that Lear has gone to join Cordelia in another world. The issue in the world of the play is not that of Lear's life or death; it is "the question of Cordelia and her father," and the "fitter place" it "requires" is not the hereafter of eternity but the hereafter of the later plays, where it is fully developed. In this play it achieves its resolution in the recognition scene, in which Lear demonstrates that he knows, at last, both Cordelia and himself. His speech is a proud man's triumph in humility:

> I am a very foolish fond old man,
> Fourscore and upward, not an hour more nor less;
> And, to deal plainly,
> I fear I am not in my perfect mind.
> Methinks I should know you, and know this man;
> Yet I am doubtful; for I am mainly ignorant
> What place this is; and all the skill I have
> Remembers not these garments; nor I know not

> Where I did lodge last night. Do not laugh at me;
> For, as I am a man,[27] I think this lady
> To be my child Cordelia.
>
> (IV, vii, 60–70)

All the play is in these lines. Lear has learned to "see better" by learning to look with a double vision upon himself and the world rather than with the single vision of self-regard. He has passed from unreason in sanity through reason in madness to achieve, in his imperfect mind, a clear understanding of an imperfect world in which the issue is not who is sinned against and who sinning, but in which either all stand in need of grace or "none does offend, not one." He has learned that the significance of life does not lie in place and office, or garments, or gold, or in the lance of justice, but in love and forgiveness. So long as he has these, unaccommodated man can take upon him "the mystery of things" and yet laugh and sing "in a walled prison."

This tragi-comic pattern of estrangement and reconciliation is also that of the final comedies, but Shakespeare had not yet exhausted the tragic possibilities of the theme of division: the separated man, divided from his fellows, remains his tragic focus in *Macbeth, Timon of Athens,* and *Coriolanus.* In the two Roman plays of this period the division is political; in *Antony and Cleopatra* the hero's nature mirrors that division; love both accentuates the cleavage and, in the end, acts as an integrating force. Coriolanus, on the other hand, is the most extreme of partisans; he is not a divided man but an incomplete one who possesses the heroic virtues and nothing else. He cannot accept a world which is at variance with the heroic ideal. In his inability to transfer his qualities of greatness from "casque to cushion" he is like Richard III, unlike him as he is in every other attribute save one—self-regard and its consequence, contempt for all who are not in some way identified with himself. For Richard there is no one so identified; he is himself alone, an outsider from the beginning. Coriolanus' contempt is not the result of his exclusion from his world but the cause of it. He begins as the victor whose triumph all factions unite, however briefly, to honour. This unity cannot last because in Coriolanus' Rome the traditional forces of order have become corrupt, self-seeking, intransigent, fickle, or treacherous—senate, tribunes, friends, mother—all except Virgilia his wife. Coriolanus rightly greets Virgilia as his "gracious silence," for in this play the voice of love and grace is muted, and even Menenius the

[27]In view of the "recognition scene" on the heath, where Lear sees Edgar as "unaccommodated man," the words are significant. He might have said, "As I am a king."

moderator is cynical in his moderation. The double vision is lacking
where "each thing meets in mere oppugnancy" not, as the hero con-
tends, because "degree is shaked" but because all are for the party and
none is for the state. For Coriolanus not only Rome but his party
shrinks, as his pride brings about his progressive isolation, to the
dimensions of himself. Lesser men he leaves to their own confusions:

> You common cry of curs, whose breath I hate
> As reek o' th' rotten fens, whose loves I prize
> As the dead carcasses of unburied men
> That do corrupt my air—I banish you.
> And here remain with your uncertainty!
>
> (III, iii, 122–6)

Their praise and their curses he disdains alike, valuing only the good
opinion of the one human being he considers his superior—his mother.
Yet even her praise embarrasses him by making him conscious of
falling short of her heroic expectations.

Again we are presented with the paradox of excessive virtues turned
to defects. Volumnia is so much the noble Roman matron that she is
an unnatural mother, and Coriolanus behaves towards her not with the
deference natural in a son but with servility. In his contacts with others
he makes honesty the excuse for scorn and the symbols of order the
justification for disorder. Like Hamlet, Coriolanus is a perfectionist,
but he lacks Hamlet's breadth of vision and his passion for self-
knowledge. His resentment of his own imperfection is projected outward in the form of contempt for lesser men, but nevertheless it
infects unseen, and drives him to identify himself with the enemies of
his country, that is, of those fellow-citizens he cannot bear to admit as
equals. He is able to overcome this inverted *hubris* only by destroying
himself, by ceasing to be the man he is and becoming again a boy at
his mother's knee, and though in one sense he may be said to save
himself spiritually by becoming as a little child he is not granted rebirth
into self-knowledge. He dies, as he has lived, in a rage, with Aufidius'
taunting "Boy!" ringing in his ears.

In *Coriolanus* the recurrent image of musty grain signifies the
corruption of nature and of natural order. The play opens with First
Citizen's moderate plea that "distribution should undo excess / And
each man have enough":

> What authority surfeits on would relieve us; if they would yield
> us but the superfluity *while it were wholesome* [italics mine], we
> might guess they reliev'd us humanely.   (I, i, 15–19)

But humanity is in even shorter supply than corn in republican Rome. Its "pomp" has not taken physic to "know what wretches feel" and does not favour shaking "the superflux to them" in order to "show the heavens more just." Significantly, Volumnia's harvest image is not one of fertility but of destruction:

> His bloody brow
> With his mail'd hand then wiping, forth he goes,
> Like to a harvest-man that's task'd to mow
> Or all or lose his hire.

> (I, ii, 34–7)

For Coriolanus, to make any concession to the plebeians' demands is to nourish "the cockle of rebellion, insolence, sedition, / Which we ourselves have plough'd for, sow'd and scatter'd" (III, i, 70–1). The citizens themselves are "our musty superfluity" to be vented in the Volscian wars. His old commander, Cominius, returns from his mission in Act V to report that when he begged Coriolanus to spare his fellow countrymen, among whom were his friends and family and former comrades-in-arms, his reply was,

> He could not stay to pick them in a pile
> Of noisome musty chaff. He said 'twas folly,
> For one poor grain or two, to leave unburnt
> And still to nose th' offence.

> (V, i, 25–8)

Menenius throws the speech in the teeth of the tribunes:

> For one poor grain or two!
> I am one of those. His mother, wife, his child,
> And this brave fellow too—we are the grains:
> You are the musty chaff, and you are smelt
> Above the moon. We must be burnt for you.

> (V, i, 28–32)

Yet there is little enough fertility in these grains of seed. It is only the chaff which shows any trace of magnanimity towards political opponents, which sometimes gives credit where it is due and urges the common good of Rome as well as its own interest. Brutus the Tribune is Coriolanus' greatest enemy in Rome—except, of course, for himself—but Brutus' estimate of him, while not wholly just, perhaps, is not an inaccurate one:

> Caius Marcius was
> A worthy officer i' th' war, but insolent,
> O'ercome with pride, ambitious past all thinking,
> Self-loving—

> (IV, vi, 29–32)

This is truth, if not the whole truth.

The high-souled man's inability to come to terms with man's ingratitude is also the theme of *Timon of Athens*, in which both Timon and Alcibiades are separated from their country with good cause to hate their countrymen. Timon's disillusionment corrupts his soul with hate for all mankind, for universal Nature herself. His last prayer is for chaos to come again, his last speech a curse. It is Alcibiades, less noble in nature than Timon but more humane, who shows himself capable of extending to the citizens of Athens the mercy he had formerly, and vainly, urged upon them. He has the last word in this bitterest of plays, and that word is "peace."

> Bring me into your city,
> And I will use the olive, with my sword;
> Make war breed peace, make peace stint war, make each
> Prescribe to other, as each other's leech.
>
> (V, iv, 81–4)

Historically, Alcibiades is a very dubious hero, but in an imperfect world it is perhaps only the imperfect hero, knowing and accepting both good and evil, who can thus reconcile the olive and the sword.

In the three classical plays with which Shakespeare's tragic period concludes, the tragic motivation is his characteristic mingling of chance, character, and fate, in which the hero's downfall is made to seem at once inevitable and the result of free choice. John Palmer's summing up of the final scene between Coriolanus and his mother is applicable to the tragedies as a whole:

He moves to a point determined from the outset by the inexorable play of character and circumstance, and yet contrives to make every step towards his conclusion seem like the adventure of a free spirit. He thus reproduces with fidelity the ultimate paradox of life itself, namely a constant opposition of free-will with necessity.[28]

For his final dramatic synthesis of the themes of disillusionment, estrangement, division, and their opposites, Shakespeare turned to the romance tradition, in itself a double inheritance. The medieval romance of knights and paladins, magicians, jousts, and dragons upheld the codes of courtly honour and courtly love, as embodied in tales of adventure which exemplified the chivalric virtues of loyalty, service, truth to one's pledged word, generosity, and friendship. The classical romance tradition is derived largely from Greek prose fiction of the

[28]*Political and Comic Characters of Shakespeare* (London: Macmillan; New York: St. Martin's Press, 1961), p. 297.

third and fourth centuries. Its plots are equally adventurous but involve persons and incidents of a different sort—princes in disguise, kidnapped maidens whose lineage or identity often is doubtful or hidden, captives sold into slavery, and extensive journeys attended by piracy or shipwreck. Both traditions use the quest frame, but its purpose in classical romance, rather than the releasing of the victim of a magic spell or oppressive tyranny, is usually the search for someone lost—a lover, friend, or relative (often a child) who is at last miraculously or seemingly miraculously restored. The dominating values are courage, persistence, piety, and faith that the lost one will eventually be restored. One of the most famous of Greek romances, Longus' *Daphnis and Chloe*, is a pastoral, and therefore was especially popular with the Elizabethans, who cherished and adapted both traditions, but an aura of pastoral innocence, sometimes bordering on naiveté, surrounds the young hero and heroine of most romances.

Romance plays appealed particularly to the courtly audience, both as celebrating the traditional courtly virtues and as a form of escape entertainment. The middle classes were not long in taking up the courtly vogue, however, and citizen-romances were soon presented in the public theatres and satirized in the private ones. In part, the popularity of the romance represents a reaction in taste against the realistic presentation of moral chaos and the obsessive moral questioning of many earlier Jacobean dramas. Tragi-comedy is the typical form of Jacobean romance plays and it verges on melodrama in that neither the perils of its plots nor its happy endings need be realistic or logically motivated. The accounts of the voyagers, as Spenser at the beginning of Book II of *The Faerie Queene* and Gonzalo in *The Tempest* (III, iii, 43–9) point out, had made the marvellous seem almost probable, and in the fantasy world of romance anything can happen simply because it does happen. This particular romance convention released the playwright's imagination and gave him the poetic freedom of a non-realistic world, but at the cost of diminished seriousness of purpose, psychological subtlety, and universality.

Shakespeare's use of romance materials demonstrates his characteristic desire to have the best of both worlds. He exploits to the full the fashionable taste for music, song, dance, stage effects, and other forms of spectacle without abandoning the seriousness of theme which had pleased "the graver sort." In order to do so he makes extensive use of allegory—a dominant feature of late medieval and Renaissance romances—and employs the restoration theme of the classical romances as a vehicle for the reconciliation of conflict. These he associates closely with the cycle of Nature and with the "whirligig of time" which, in the final plays, brings in not revenges but reunions. Time changes all things, but it is the regenerative rather than the destructive aspects of mutability which are stressed. Without change and decay there can be no continuance of life.

Greek romance plots usually covered a prolonged period of time, and Sidney's comment, during an earlier vogue of romance plays, on their unfitness for drama upholds both the classical unities and the Renaissance view that art, however idealized, should also be true to life, that its illusion should be credible:

Now of time they are much more liberal. For ordinary it is that two princes fall in love; after many traverses she is got with child, delivered of a fair boy, he is lost, groweth a man, falleth in love, and is ready to get another child— and all this in two hours' space; which how absurd it is in sense even sense may imagine, and art hath taught, and all ancient examples justified. . . .[29]

It is just such a plot as this which Shakespeare uses in *The Winter's Tale* and calls in Time himself, as chorus, to justify. Time not only separates but unites persons and events; it is not only *edax rerum* but *artifex rerum*, destroyer and creator.

Allegory lends itself to the presentation of extremes; the cycle of Nature exemplifies the reconciliation of opposites, and the more extreme the opposition the greater the triumph of reconciliation. Thus, while points of polarity in the last plays are sometimes even farther apart than in the middle plays, the emphasis is upon the coming together rather than upon the division of things. Sometimes in persons and events, sometimes in symbols, good and evil, flesh and spirit, art and nature, parents and children, brothers and friends are presented as separated or in conflict and are reunited in harmony. Good and evil are seen as the manifestations of "grace and rude will" rather than as arising from events. Though both "opposed kings" may be encamped within a single breast and the predominance may alternate from one side to the other, the dramatic emphasis is upon the dominant element rather than, as in most of the tragedies, upon the ambivalence. The good man's "dram of evil" may "dout" the whole substance to his own scandal but it is wholly purged by repentance. The absence of logical motivation makes evil take extreme forms, and thus the jealousy of Leontes seems less excusable than that of Othello because Leontes is self-tempted. Similarly, the gullibility of Posthumus in *Cymbeline* is more reprehensible than that of Othello not only because, like Lucrece's

[29]*Defense of Poesy*, ed. A. S. Cook (Athenaeum Press Series; New York: Ginn, 1890), p. 48.

husband, he makes his wife's fidelity a matter for boasting but because he believes against her the circumstantial evidence not of a tried comrade-in-arms with a reputation for unswerving honesty but that of a cynical stranger.

Many of the characters, particularly the minor ones, come from the narrative rather than the dramatic tradition; they are not merely types, but stereotypes, appropriate to the tale rather than the play, and they are presented without explanation and are seldom developed dramatically. The full force of characterization, in contrast to as late a play as *Antony and Cleopatra*, where even the least significant characters are made to appear as individuals, is concentrated upon the central figures, and there is a similar concentration on significant events, the linking material often being narrated with very little if any pretense of dramatization. Folk-tale elements of this kind are part of the romance tradition, but are in evidence as early as *King Lear*, a play which, as already indicated, anticipates the romances in several aspects of theme and characterization.

Another element which differentiates the romances from the earlier plays is that of attitude. Instead of involving the audience in an emotional identification with his characters and their fortunes, Shakespeare here seems to be deliberately holding his material at a distance and inviting the audience to join him in contemplating the phenomena of human behaviour from a similarly detached point of view. In *The Tempest* this distancing is personified in Prospero, and his point of view is the audience's. Related to this handling of dramatic illusion is a manipulation of "planes of reality," to use Tillyard's term,[30] which sometimes blurs, sometimes accentuates the dividing line between appearance and reality, between circumstance and symbol.

In the romances the characteristic materials of the earlier plays are reworked in new colours and in a new pattern. The persistent themes of political loyalty and responsibility, the beneficent and destructive elements of love, the recognition and acceptance of evil, deception and self-deception, the self-destructiveness of self-regard and of revenge, all are there, but a combination of forces restores their seemingly irreconcilable disorder to harmony. In all four romance plays fertility symbolism abounds. In all four the emblem of reconciliation is a daughter and the instruments are Time, Chance, and Change, operating through love to bring good out of evil. The elements of tragedy are

---

[30]*Shakespeare's Last Plays* (London: Chatto and Windus; Toronto: Macmillan, 1938), Ch. III. See also S. L. Bethell, *The Winter's Tale: A Study* (London, 1944), especially "Antiquated Technique and the Planes of Reality," pp. 47 ff.

actively present, but in the broader temporal frame of reference, which is frequently and specifically set in the context of eternity, they are brought, by grace divine and human, to a happy rather than a fatal conclusion.

The unifying force of love is seen as operating in all its aspects—sexual love, the love of parents and children, Christian charity and Divine Providence. Love reconciles through the grace which is capable not only of forgiving those who are penitent but of accepting those who are not, which requires no justification but is self-justifying. It is such grace that Posthumus calls upon in prison:

> Is't enough I am sorry?
> So children temporal fathers do appease;
> Gods are more full of mercy.
> > (*Cymbeline*, V, iv, 11–13)

The pattern of incident in the romances is basically that condemned by Sidney—birth, loss or estrangement, storm, discovery, reconciliation, and reversal—though the management of Time shapes this pattern differently in the various plays. In *Pericles* Shakespeare or his collaborator begins with incest—a perversion of love between father and daughter. This unnaturalness arouses a storm of disillusionment in the hero which is paralleled by a storm in Nature. Yet out of these storms come symbols of continuance; Pericles recovers the armour of his father and gains the love of Thaisa. A second storm appears to destroy the hope of continuance in the "terrible childbed" which brings Marina to birth and Thaisa to supposed death. The play proceeds by a succession of such paradoxes—foster mother turned murderess, purity in a brothel, and the discovery of the lost mother among the virgins of Diana—to the final juxtaposition of opposites in which the news of Thaisa's father's death coincides with the announcement of Marina's coming marriage. With Pericles' discovery of Marina and the birth of love between them the movement from perverse to natural father-daughter relationship is completed. The harvest of the storm in this first of the romances is a mingling of good and evil, of creative and destructive elements, until the balance of Time comes to rest in the harmony of marriage, which is a promise of life's continuance.

It is in *The Winter's Tale* and *The Tempest* that Shakespeare's symbolic patterning of romance conventions is most clearly evident. The difference between their patterns lies chiefly in the management of Time. In the first, action and counter-action are separated by a gap of sixteen years; in the second, the counter-action only is given dramatic representation, the action being narrated. In the first movement of *The Winter's Tale* we see harmony in love and friendship wilfully destroyed by passion and folly. The only traitor at the court of Sicily lodges within the breast of its king, a man as self-willed and perverse as Lear, who comes to self-knowledge only when, as he believes, his wife and daughter as well as his son have become the victims of his intransigence in setting his judgment above that of the gods.

As in *Pericles*, the counter-movement begins with a storm, and again the constructive-destructive dialectic of Nature is emphasized by the juxtaposition of birth and death, as well as by the change of setting from courtly to pastoral and of tone from tragic to comic. From Antigonus' vision of Hermione to his burial on the seacoast of Bohemia, the transition is bold if masterly in its mingling of natural and supernatural, romance and realism, in its exemplification of the cyclic pattern. Hearing the "savage clamour" of the hunt Antigonus turns to flee, only to become the prey of the bear who has given his own pursuers the slip. The pattern is still more firmly sign-posted in the words of the old shepherd, who reflects the comic aspect of the division between generations in his good-natured grumbling about the habits of adolescents. "Now bless thyself," he bids his son after hearing his account of the bear's dinner, "Thou mettest with things dying, I with things newborn." And the ambiguous figure of Time, in the role of Chorus Prologue to Act IV, both accentuates and bridges the division between the two halves of the play:

> I, that please some, try all, both joy and terror
> Of good and bad, that makes and unfolds error,
> Now take upon me, in the name of Time,
> To use my wings.
>
> (IV, i, 1–4)

Time's theme, appropriately enough, is mutability, the insubstantial pageant of this world, the power of Time to "plant and o'erwhelm custom":

> so shall I do
> To the freshest things now reigning, and make stale
> The glistering of this present, as my tale
> Now seems to it.
>
> (12–15)

Yet Time is not an awesome, but a benevolent, even a witty figure in this prologue.

The second movement of the play culminates in the speeches of the lovers at the sheep-shearing feast, speeches in which references to time and change, the cycle of the seasons, and the interrelationships of art, nature and love form an accompaniment to what is said overtly and at times take it upon themselves to carry the melody. Perdita is wholly natural; she is "Flora, peering in April's front," opposed to any sort of artifice, as her colloquy with Polixenes about "gillivors" shows. Florizel, only slightly more sophisticated, embodies the artist's agonizing sense of the transience of physical "grace" in his commendation of Perdita.

> When you do dance, I wish you
> A wave o' th' sea, that you might ever do
> Nothing but that; move still, still so,
> And own no other function.
>
> (IV, iv, 140–3)

The paradox is concentrated in the image of the ever-changing wave of the changeless sea and in the ambiguity of "still" as associated with it.

Florizel desires to control Time, to preserve each of his humble mistress's queenly actions forever. But to keep each graceful gesture "still" in the sense of keeping it always is to make it "still" by robbing it of its essence, which is movement, the evidence of life. It is to turn the living woman into a statue. It is not true love, but love as destructive possessiveness which so regards its object as an object and thus, as the final scene reminds us, turns the beloved to stone. Only liberating love can bring the statue to life. Florizel is aware of this, as indicated by his listing of a variety of actions which arouse this emotion in him. The list shows not only the futility of the desire but his recognition that, in this world, change is essential to beauty as to life. His attitude is not so much that of a boy crying for the moon as that of a poet contemplating a Grecian urn, and it is interesting that Keats should make use of the same play on words in his opening line, "O still unravished bride of quietness."

Perdita's flower-speech which evokes this response in Florizel is also filled with allusions symbolic of the central concepts of the play. Her references to flowers of spring come appropriately enough after the winter of Leontes' discontent and are full of the promise of a new generation, already in process of fulfilment in her love for Florizel. Dis's wagon points forward to another winter of trial to come after the high summer of the present moment, and the situation in Sicilia is glanced at in the reference to rosemary (remembrance) and rue (repentance) which "keep seeming and savour all the winter long." The "flowers of middle summer" which are given "to men of middle age," are all "seasonings," except for the marigold which "goes to bed wi' the sun / And with him rises weeping." Perdita is herself the lost Proserpina who will bring back spring to the court of Sicily and the heart of her mother.

The high-point of harmony and the beginning of discord come together in the course of the shepherd's dance when Polixenes questions the old shepherd about Perdita. This dance, with the interlude of the entrance of Autolycus, the lovable rogue representing both good and evil in the harmony of his songs and the disorder of his pocket-picking, along with the dance of satyrs which follows, gives the scene a masque-antimasque pattern, the antimasque forming the bridge to the third movement. In this, many of the motifs of the first movement are repeated. Polixenes assumes the role of Leontes as the representative of the forces opposed to love and loses a son in consequence of that opposition. Again there is a sea voyage, this time with no storm but "a prosperous south wind friendly" which brings all estrangements and oppositions to reunion, restoration, and reconciliation. Leontes' sixteen years of penance come to an end, and even Paulina, the personified voice of his conscience who has offered to withdraw as out of place in the general exultation—or, as she puts it,

> I, an old turtle,
> Will wing me to some wither'd bough and there
> My mate, that's never to be found again,
> Lament till I am lost—
>
> (V, iii, 132-5)

is rewarded with the hope of a second harvest in marriage to the faithful Camillo.

The Winter's Tale is truly a tragical-comical-pastoral, and there is a bit of burlesque as well in the ironic good-Samaritan overtones of the device by which Autolycus first deceives Perdita's clownish foster-brother. There is also the deliberate breaking of the theatrical illusion in referring to the contemporary Italian painter Julio Romano[31] in a pre-Christian Greek setting. This cannot be due to ignorance, as the clock-striking in *Julius Caesar* may have been, and carelessness of this magnitude in the handling of the delicately balanced final scene is unlikely. It is probable that the reference is a reminder to the

---

[31]An appropriate choice, since Romano was famous, especially, for his painting of the Holy Family and for his illustrations of the licentious poems of Aretino.

audience (as in the "glistering of this present" in the speech of Time) that the world of the play is not the world of the here and now. The inhabitants of the fantasy world of romance may accept, if the audience cannot, such impossibilities as a woman pretending successfully to be a statue, even in the sight of her husband. The non-realistic is similarly pointed up by means of its opposite in Leontes' complaint that the artist has recreated in the statue of his lost Hermione not the woman she was when she died in the bloom of her beauty but the woman she would have been had she lived. This irony reiterates the theme of the transience of beauty in nature and the lifelessness of beauty in art already pointed at in Florizel's speech to Perdita. The intermingling of illusion and reality, nature and art is more fully and more subtly developed in *The Tempest*, which, as I hope to show in a later chapter, carries still farther the extremes and the concentrations of the earlier romance plays. It reiterates, also, the theme that acceptance of life in this world is the necessary prelude to transcending the things of this world, whether in this world or the next.

This brief survey of the nature of Shakespeare's dualities has concentrated on themes and the various ways in which he treated them as best indicating a pattern of development in his attitude toward the dilemmas and contradictions of human existence. But themes alone do not make a poetic dramatist, and in subsequent chapters evidence of similar patterns and attitudes in other aspects of his art will be considered. In order to discover whether his poetic techniques reflect this same preoccupation with duality it seems best to concentrate first on the poetry, and especially on that poetic form which by structure and traditional content lends itself most readily to the expression of ambivalent attitudes. In the Sonnets, the theme of time, of the transience of beauty in nature and hope for its partial preservation in art, which we have noted in the final plays, appears again and again. In Shakespeare's end is his beginning, but the similarity results not from stasis but from movement. The wheel comes full circle.

III

The Poetry of Ambivalence

"With what I most enjoy contented least."
(Sonnet 29)

CRITICISM OF SHAKESPEARE'S SONNETS has suffered from an overemphasis on questions of biographical significance[1] and problems of dating. More recently, however, a larger proportion of scholarly writing on the sonnets has been devoted to the poems as poems, and to poetic relationships between the sonnets and the plays.[2] The particular concern of this chapter, however, is with duality of attitude as reflected in poetic

[1]The identity of the friend is irrelevant to the matters of attitude and technique with which this chapter is concerned. As to date, both internal and external evidence suggest that the greater part of the sequence was written between 1592 and 1597, though some of the sonnets may have been composed before or after these limits. Parallels in theme, language, and situation between the sonnets and such plays as *The Two Gentlemen of Verona, A Midsummer Night's Dream, Love's Labour's Lost, The Merchant of Venice, Romeo and Juliet, Richard II*, and the two parts of *Henry IV*, are frequent. Meres's mention, in *Palladis Tamia*, of Shakespeare's "sugar'd sonnets among his private friends" is testimony that a number of the poems were circulating before 1598, and those included in *The Passionate Pilgrim* (1599) indicate that the sonnets to the Dark Lady were among these. Except for brief periods the theatres were closed because of rioting and the plague from June, 1592 to the Spring of 1594. This may well have been the time of distress referred to as "the spite of fortune" in Sonnet 90.

[2]In addition to G. Wilson Knight's *The Mutual Flame* (London: Methuen, 1954), L. C. Knights's articles in *Scrutiny* 3 (1934–5) and in *Explorations* (1946), and J. B. Leishman's *Themes and Variations in Shakespeare's Sonnets* (London, Hutchinson, 1961), discussions of the poetic qualities of the Sonnets which have been useful for this chapter are to be found in Patrick Cruttwell's *The Shakespearean Moment* (London: Chatto and Windus, 1954), William Empson's *Some Versions of Pastoral* (London: Chatto and Windus, 1935), and *Seven Types of Ambiguity* (2nd edition; New York: Meridian Books, 1955), Joan Grundy's "Shakespeare's Sonnets and the Elizabethan sonneteers" (*Shakespeare Survey* 15, pp. 41–9), J. W. Lever's *The Elizabethan Love Sonnet* (London: Methuen, 1956),

techniques, and especially in ambiguity of language and in the structure and dramatic dialectic of the sequence.

Emotional ambivalence is part of the sonnet tradition. To the Renaissance sonneteer love, his all-pervading theme, is a paradox. Conventionally, it is spoken of in terms of war, its effects in such oxymora as burning ice, freezing fire, poisoned sweet, and honeyed gall. The state of the lover is often described as analogous with or antithetical to one or another aspect of the cyclical pattern of nature, frequently seen as the macrocosm of the lover's fortunes or of his divided disposition. Such comparisons often provide the structural framework of the sonnet. In the Italian form, the paradox, antithesis, irony, or ambiguity of the theme is often reinforced by the division into octave and sestet. The structure of the English sonnet does not lend itself so obviously to the formal reflection of a divided attitude, but it often follows the pattern of thesis, antithesis, and paradox in its three quatrains, the final couplet expressing either the resolution or an epigrammatic summation of the ambivalence.[3]

Since most Renaissance sonnets are tinged, in varying degrees, with Renaissance Neoplatonism, their treatment of the theme of ambivalence is often related to Neoplatonic doctrines about the proper balance and function of fleshly and spiritual desire. In the Platonic concept of love, the senses, and above all the eyes, are the channels by which

---

M. M. Mahood's *Shakespeare's Wordplay* (London: Methuen, 1957), and "Love's Confined Doom" (*Shakespeare Survey* 15, pp. 50–61), F. T. Prince's "The Sonnet from Wyatt to Shakespeare" in *Elizabethan Poetry*, Stratford Upon Avon Studies 2 (London: Edward Arnold, 1960), and Hallet Smith's *Elizabethan Poetry: A Study in Conventions, Meaning and Expression* (Cambridge: Harvard University Press, 1953).

[3]A typical example of the pattern is Sonnet 10 of *Astrophel and Stella*:

Reason, in faith thou art well serv'd that still
   Wouldst brabling be with sense and love in me:
   I rather wish thee climb the Muses' hill,
   Or reach the fruit of Nature's choicest tree,
Or seek heav'ns course, or heaven's inside to see:
   Why shouldst thou toil our thorny soil to till?
   Leave sense, and those which senses objects be:
   Deal thou with powers of thoughts, leave love to will.
But thou wouldst needs fight with both love and sense,
   With sword of wit, giving wounds of dispraise,
   Till downright blows did foil thy cunning fence:
For soon as they strake thee with Stella's rays,
   Reason, thou kneel'dst, and offeredst straight to prove
   By reason good, good reason her to love.

In this instance the resolution occupies the last three lines, the epigrammatic summation the final two. Compare also *Amoretti*, 55 and 57, and Daniel's *Delia*, 6 and 12.

love enters the heart.[4] Physical desire of the physically beautiful is therefore the necessary prelude to the higher, spiritual desire for the spiritually beautiful. "Fancy," as the song in *The Merchant of Venice* asserts (III, ii, 67), "is engend'red in the eyes." But "fancy dies / In the cradle where it lies" (68–9). Only by rising above the physical can the lover experience the ennobling force of true love. The ascent is a perilous one, involving struggle and pain, and in the English sonnet the difficulty of reconciling the claims of flesh and spirit, of time and eternity, is as often the theme as is the ideal of reconciliation toward which the struggle is directed.[5] That harmonious ideal is the ultimate truth, beauty, and goodness which is God, in whom all contradictions are reconciled.

Spenser, who makes the nature and relationships of earthly and heavenly love and beauty the theme of his *Fowre Hymnes,* reconciles the conflict of flesh and spirit in the *Amoretti,*[6] and more specifically in the *Epithalamion,* in the symbolism of Christian marriage. In terms of the Platonic staircase, Spenser's ideal of marriage seems to represent a half-way house appropriate to man's middle state, a resting-place between the earthly and the heavenly which recognizes and enjoys the values of both.

[4]See pp. 7 ff.
[5]For example, *Astrophel and Stella* 71:

> Who will in fairest book of Nature know
> How virtue may best lodged in beauty be,
> Let him but learn of love to read in thee,
> Stella, those fair lines which true goodness show.
> There shall he find all vices' overthrow,
> Not by rude force, but sweetest sovereignty
> Of reason, from whose light those night birds fly,
> That inward sun in thine eyes shineth so.
> And not content to be perfection's heir
> Thyself, dost strive all minds that way to move
> Who mark in thee what is in thee most fair.
> So, while thy beauty draws the heart to love,
> As fast thy virtue bends that love to good.
> But, oh! Desire still cries, "Give me some food."

Here, the strictly Neoplatonic theme of Petrarch's Sonnet 120 is completely reworked. Petrarch's Laura is the Platonic Idea of the good and the beautiful embodied in the "royal raiment" of the flesh, a physical and therefore a mortal form which gives the lover a brief glimpse of the heavenly pattern. Stella's "sovereign light," however, is not her physical beauty but her reason, which controls but cannot destroy the desire of the flesh which is almost irrelevant to Petrarch's theme.
[6]Sonnet III—"The sovereign beauty which I do admire"—is Spenser's adaptation of the same Petrarchan sonnet and is more strictly Neoplatonic than Sidney's. The flesh, however, receives its due of praise elsewhere in the *Amoretti* (e.g. in Sonnets LXXVI and LXXVII) and the reconciliation of the conflict in the *Epithalamion*

Shakespeare's sonnets also make use of the traditional themes as of traditional devices of structure and language, but they wear their Petrarchisms with a difference, and the differences become more frequent and more significant as the sequence progresses.[7] The first of these differences is that the sonnets which are regarded as conventionally "Petrarchan" or "Neoplatonic" are addressed to a young man,[8] as is the greater part of the sequence as a whole. The second is that the sonnets addressed to the mistress are not in the least conventional in their attitude to the beloved. They express neither the despairing fidelity of the courtly nor the philosophical idealization of the Platonic lover, but the violent alternation of infatuation and revulsion.

The extreme ambivalence towards sexual love which is so apparent in the sonnets to the "Dark Lady" and which culminates in Sonnet 129 ("Expense of spirit in waste of shame") is equally evident in the "sex-debates" of *Venus and Adonis* and *The Rape of Lucrece*. In the former, lines 157–216 rehearse the themes and the language of Sonnets 1–17. Venus puts the argument from nature and function, and expatiates on the doctrine of "use," the sterility of narcissism, and reproduction as a duty owed to parents and to posterity. Adonis replies at first with cold disdain, then pleads his unripe years, and finally is driven to formal rebuttal, or rather invective. Love's seeming sweetness is a "deceiving harmony," he insists. Equating the emotion with

---

(published simultaneously with the *Amoretti*) is foreshadowed as early as Sonnet VI:

> Be nought dismayd that her unmoved mind
> Doth still persist in her rebellious pride:
> Such love, not lyke to lusts of baser kynd
> The harder wonne, the firmer will abide.
> The durefull Oake, whose sap is not yet dride,
> Is long ere it conceive the kindling fyre;
> But, when it once doth burne, it doth divide
> Great heat, and makes his flames to heaven aspire.
> So hard it is to kindle new desire
> In gentle brest, that shall endure for ever:
> Deepe is the wound, that dints the parts entire
> With chast affects, that naught but death can sever.
>   Then thinke not long in taking litle paine
>   To knit the knot, that ever shall remaine.

[7]While there is no evidence that the 1609 order of the Sonnets is due to the author's intention rather than the publisher's convenience, I have decided, for the purposes of this discussion, to accept that order, with certain variations to be indicated, as constituting a rough chronological progression.

[8]Shakespeare is not alone in this, several of his sonnets resembling those of Barnfield's *Affectionate Shepherd*, published in 1592. (*See* G. Wilson Knight, *The Mutual Flame*, p. 17.)

its tutelary deity, he accuses Venus of lending "embracements unto every stranger" and of using specious reasoning as "the bawd to lust's abuse." To him, the goddess represents not love, but lust:

> Love comforteth like sunshine after rain,
> But Lust's effect is tempest after sun;
> Love's gentle spring doth always fresh remain:
> Lust's winter comes ere summer half be done.
> Love surfeits not: Lust like a glutton dies.
> Love is all truth: Lust full of forged lies.
>
> (ll. 799–804)

This is illogical in the extreme, since it is the Goddess of Love, not Lust he is addressing and rejecting. The implication, conscious or unconscious, is that the "love" he praises is not, and cannot be, the love of women. Nevertheless, taken out of context, the speech expresses standard moral doctrine. It is disturbingly inappropriate, however, in the context of this particular poem. As a genre, the outstanding characteristic of Ovidian poetry is its evocation and celebration of sensuous beauty. Medieval and Renaissance interpreters might succeed in "moralizing" Ovid himself, but the purpose of his imitators was not primarily didactic but descriptive. In most Ovidian poems the tone is no more than semi-serious, and the attitude to amorous activity, as in pastoral, is one of sophisticated simplicity. In the love-passages of *Hero and Leander*, for example, there is an undercurrent of mirth; the author seems to invite the reader to join him in the urbane and indulgent laughter, half superior, half envious, and yet gentle, of those for whom the innocence of youthful passion is only a memory. Nowhere, however, is love as such the object of attack, cynical or moral.

One of the reasons that Shakespeare's poem is generally regarded as less successful than Marlowe's "fragment" is that the poet's attitude is in conflict not only with his genre but with his material. Marlowe's "chastity debate," in which Leander employs the same arguments for seduction as Venus, and Hero makes the half-hearted resistance to them which maidenly modesty demands, does no violence to his myth. In the myth of Venus and Adonis, however, the goddess (in spite of the biter-bit irony of her situation) is the sympathetic figure. By falling in love with a mortal and suffering the torments of human lovers she may be said to "mediate" (in the words of Socrates' Diotima in *The Symposium*) "between gods and men." Like the story of Eros and Psyche, the myth is an allegory of the dual nature of love—at once divine and human, spiritual and physical. Ovid's Adonis is not a reluctant lover, but in some Renaissance versions he is, like Narcissus, the proud and foolish mortal who in rejecting love finds death, since life is impossible without love. Shakespeare's treatment of the myth, however, inverts both theme and emphasis and thus destroys the allegory.

The opening stanzas of *Venus and Adonis* present not so much a plea for love on the part of Venus as an unsuccessful seduction attempt which threatens to become a rape, were such a thing possible. Since it is generally regarded as impossible, Adonis' impregnable defence against a fate worse than death has a ludicrous effect quite as much at variance with what seems to be the serious intention of the author as with the traditional mood of the Ovidian poem, a contradiction which is intensified by the circumstance that whereas Shakespeare's celebration of sensuous beauty is absent, his evocation of it is not only very much present but is particularly vivid. What is communicated in the first 850 lines of the poem is an ambivalent combination of sexual titillation and moral revulsion.

Obviously what we have here is a case of mistaken identity. Both Shakespeare and Adonis confuse the divine Queen of Love and Beauty with her mischievous son, Eros, though neither of them ever indicates any awareness of the error. Venus is represented as a wanton enchantress, a bird of prey, an insatiable whore who uses all the arts of her trade to corrupt an innocent youth. Adonis, like Burn's prude, damns the faults he has no mind to with such petulant iteration that the reader is tempted to echo Lady Booby's comments on male virtue as expressed in *Joseph Andrews*. Yet this is by no means the response the author demands: the tone of these stanzas suggests that the reader is expected to take Adonis' defence of his chastity as wholly serious and wholly unexceptionable.

The effective theme of *Venus and Adonis* is "desire is death," as Geoffrey Bush asserts,[9] pointing out the "deadly sexual affinity" between Venus and the boar and between Venus and poor Wat, the hare: ". . . in the sweet and fatal warfare of desire, she is both the hunter and the hunted." Shakespeare's inversion of the "moral" leaves him in the dilemma of finding an ending for the poem which will accord with the known events of the source myth without contradicting his theme, and this dilemma he fails to resolve. Instead, once the youth is slain, he quite arbitrarily transfers the reader's sympathies from Adonis to Venus, who suddenly abandons the role of seductress for that of true love bereaved. So far as the reader is concerned, Adonis is dead, and there an end. Venus has all the sympathy and none of

[9]*Shakespeare and the Natural Condition* (Harvard University Press, 1956), p. 25.

the responsibility for the tragic outcome. The crowning contradiction is the final prophecy, or rather curse, in which she falls into Adonis' "idle, over-handled theme" of the opposition of love and lust. Love, she foresees, will become what Adonis had insisted it already was—wrongly, one must now assume. Love will lose the innocence which, in terms of the poem, it never had. The poem ends not with a reconciliation, but with a reiteration of the ambivalence with which it began, except that the antagonist has been converted. In spite of the evocative power of its descriptions and the lyric intensity of many passages, the poem fails to come to terms with the implications of its subject-matter. Shakespeare has decided to treat love in terms of its polarities, and his myth simply does not provide characters which may appropriately be considered the personifications of these polarities.

In the Sonnets the theme of love is again presented in terms of its polarities: the mistress, like Venus, is the heavenly flesh that leads men to hell; nor, any more than in *Venus and Adonis*, is there any attempt to resolve the dilemma of flesh and spirit in the heterosexual context of the Renaissance Neoplatonic tradition. Instead, these diverse aspects of love are regarded not as complementary but as separate and conflicting forces, and the conflict is resolved not by reconciliation but by rejection. Like Plato's unfortunate charioteer, the lover is driving the two horses of love—one white, one black—which do not constitute a team:

> Two loves I have, of comfort and despair,
> Which like two spirits do suggest me still;
> The better angel is a man right fair,
> The worser spirit a woman colour'd ill.
>
> (Sonnet 144)

The morality-play allusion is an indication that however autobiographical the story the sonnets tell, however painfully personal the emotions they express, the poet has attempted to place them in the context of allegory, perhaps in order to achieve the aesthetic distance necessary to effective poetic composition. Sometimes the allegorical framework breaks down and the distance is annihilated by intensity of feeling until the pen falters and at last must be laid aside:

> O, know, sweet love, I always write of you,
> And you and love are still my argument;
> So all my best is dressing old words new,
> Spending again what is already spent. . . .
>
> (Sonnet 76)

The poet's muse is "sick," "tongue-tied," "dumb," commonplace and outmoded; love itself is all his "art."

> This silence for my sin you did impute,
> Which shall be most my glory, being dumb;
> For I impair not beauty, being mute. . . .
>
> (Sonnet 83)

Reinforcing the dichotomy which casts the friend as the good, the mistress as the evil angel, is a second and related level of allegory in which the spiritual and physical elements of love are similarly personified. For the purposes of the Sonnets Shakespeare seems to have accepted Plato's contention that the love of women could not rise above physical desire and that the higher love was therefore restricted to relationships with men. Quite apart from any possible implications of homosexual attitudes in the Sonnets there is something very Greek in the pattern of the relationship between the older man and the youth as it evolves in the course of the sequence. The poet is at first the counsellor, then the accepted servant, the admiring and approved friend, and finally is admitted into the intimacy of "undivided loves" in a "marriage of true minds."

In eschewing the Renaissance compromise between classical and courtly attitudes which invested heterosexual love with the Platonic ideal of a relationship which could embrace both physical and spiritual values in their proper proportion and function, Shakespeare was no doubt consulting his own predispositions as much as the authority of Plato and the precepts of Cicero's *De Amicitia*. The ambivalence towards physical desire indicated in his treatment of the myth of Venus and Adonis and expressed in Sonnet 129 is reflected in the thematic division of the sonnet sequence. What his heart cannot reconcile, his mind chooses to separate, and as in the earlier plays he is here more concerned to point out the contradictions of life than to reconcile them. He is not yet able to rest in the riddle of things. Love is a union of souls in the sonnets to the fair youth, a tyranny of the body in those to the Dark Lady.

Shakespeare follows the sonnet tradition, however, in seeing in his friend's physical beauty, as in the aspects of external nature to which it is so often compared, the heavenly light of universal truth, and he praises his friend's charms, in the early sonnets particularly, in the conventionally hyperbolic terms. But however intense the longing for acceptance, however acute the fear of loss, neither yearning nor despair is expressed in terms of physical desire. Where the Petrarchan lover begs his mistress to be "kind," Shakespeare, in the same sort of language, urges his friend to marry. His attitude resembles that of the proud possessor of a masterpiece who is willing to allow others to share in the enjoyment of his treasure but not in its ownership. There is a certain naïveté, which seems incompatible with a homosexual passion, in the playfully rueful lament of Sonnet 20 that this marriage of minds cannot become a marriage of bodies also, that his friend possesses all the physical and spiritual attributes of the ideal mistress— save (or perhaps, rather, plus) one. If the tone of the sonnet is incompatible with overt homosexuality, it is, however, strictly compatible with the sexual revulsion indicated by the structural division of the sequence.

These Sonnets accord to love-in-friendship the position Petrarch accords to the dead Laura, Dante to Beatrice, Spenser to love-in-marriage.[10] It is the great ennobler (Sonnet 29), the great healer (Sonnet 30). The beloved is an amalgam of every aspect of nature's best, of all beauties and all loves of all time (Sonnets 105, 106); he is the embodiment of that beauty which is a joy forever—or as long as the memory of it is preserved in "powerful rhyme." But unlike Spenser, Shakespeare does not abstract personal experience into the universal; rather he sees in his friend the universal become particular, given a local habitation and a name in the immediacy of personal love. In the sonnets as in the plays, the focus always returns from the universal and the eternal to the here and now. It is in loving *him*, in showing *him* kindness that the youth both emanates and inspires that universal love which encompasses all loves:

> Thy bosom is endeared with all hearts
> Which I by lacking have supposed dead,
> And there reigns love and all love's loving parts,
> And all those friends which I thought buried. . . .
> Thou art the grave where buried love doth live,
> Hung with the trophies of my lovers gone,
> Who all their parts of me to thee did give;
> That due of many now is thine alone.
>   Their images I lov'd I view in thee,
>   And thou, all they, hast all the all of me.
>
> (Sonnet 31)

[10]The concepts of courtly love and of Neoplatonic love in relation to Shakespeare's plays (but not, specifically, to the sonnets) are discussed in John Vyvyan's *Shakespeare and the Rose of Love* (London: Chatto and Windus, 1960) and *Shakespeare and Platonic Beauty* (London: Chatto and Windus, 1962). The "un-Platonic Platonism" of the sonnets is commented upon in J. B. Leishman's *Themes and Variations in Shakespeare's Sonnets*. Leishman points out that Shakespeare's treatment of philosophical concepts in these poems differs from that of the middle plays (pp. 117–8) but since he favours a late date for the sonnets he does not take into account the very similar attitudes expressed in the plays written between 1592 and 1597.

For Shakespeare the pattern of beauty is not laid up in heaven but has its habitation on earth in the person of his friend, whose death would be for him, "truth's and beauty's doom and date" (Sonnet 14). For Shakespeare the Platonic staircase becomes not only a means by which the lover may climb to spiritual union with truth and goodness, but the means by which truth and goodness may descend to the world of men, repeating, for every true lover, the miracle of the Incarnation.

> Let not my love be call'd idolatry,
> Nor my beloved as an idol show,
> Since all alike my songs and praises be
> To one, of one, still such, and ever so.
> Kind is my love to-day, to-morrow kind,
> Still constant in a wondrous excellence;
> Therefore my verse, to constancy confin'd,
> One thing expressing, leaves out difference.
> 'Fair, kind, and true' is all my argument,
> 'Fair, kind, and true' varying to other words;
> And in this change is my invention spent,
> Three themes in one, which wondrous scope affords.
> Fair, kind, and true, have often liv'd alone,
> Which three, till now, never kept seat in one.
>
> (Sonnet 105)

Thus Shakespeare uses the Platonic Trinity to invert the Neoplatonic thesis. For him, the individual beloved represents not merely a single aspect of the elements of that trinity of goodness, truth, and beauty, but the totality; his personal love is not merely a part of universal love but its microcosm. He differs from Plato, also, in seeing love as an integration of similitudes rather than as a harmony of differences. But he has not resolved the whole dilemma of humanism. He has seen the world in a grain of sand, but not eternity in an hour. The here and now is subject to Time, and in the Sonnets Time is not the healer and restorer who brings about the resolutions of the final plays but the devourer, and his daughter is not Truth but Oblivion. Time is the Goliath against whose relentless force the poet fights to make the immediate eternal, to immortalize his beloved in that "little moment" of perfection which comes to "everything that grows." As his use of the phrase indicates, Shakespeare's mind recognizes that change and transience are inseparable from life, but his heart cannot yet accept the imperfection of impermanence. Having invested his love with the universality he would also invest it with the eternity of perfection, or at least with the temporal permanence of art. That this can be "eternal" only in the context of this world does not greatly matter, since he is concerned with the human, and indeed the personal validity of the true, the good, and the beautiful (Sonnet 18).

But the poet's embodied image of perfection is not only mortal—he is all too human. Time, the defacer of monuments and delver of parallels in beauty's brow, stains goodness also, and destroys not only the memory of factual truth but the "truth" which is fidelity. Change and transience become matters of present rather than future significance in Sonnet 33, in which the first cloud of disillusionment dims the uncertain glory of love's spring. The remainder of the sequence deals, among other things, with Shakespeare's progress—through doubt, denial, evasion, excuse, sophistry, cowardice, self-deception, rejection, withdrawal, return, and forgiveness, to the acceptance of imperfection. It is a path subsequently followed, in whole or in part, by not a few of his characters.

From Sonnet 33 on, the internal conflicts are reinforced by external ones, soliloquies begin to take on the characteristics of one side of a dialogue, and additional characters appear; good and evil, as personified in Sonnet 144, struggle for possession of the poet's soul. The pattern of the sonnet-drama is the characteristic tragi-comic one of the morality play, in which the central figure is progressively isolated from his world, but strengthened by trial at last wins through to victory. The forces of separation are possessiveness, self-distrust, self-abasement, envy, suspicion, disillusionment, lust, and sexual jealousy. The higher love may be free of the ambivalence of flesh and spirit, but where the spiritually destructive forces enter it is not, Shakespeare finds, any freer than sexual love of the "civil war" of "love and hate" (Sonnet 35).

The process of separation is slow and painful. It begins with physical absence, during which Shakespeare finds reason to suspect that the friend's outward and physical beauty may not be a wholly trustworthy index of a state of inward and spiritual grace. His friend appears to have turned aside from the higher to the lower love. This blow seems to coincide with a personal and crippling misfortune—either illness or disgrace, or both—which adds to the poet's sense that he is unworthy of his friend's love. In Sonnet 40 it becomes clear that the "wantonness" which had tarnished the image of his friend was not merely one of the "petty wrongs that liberty commits" (Sonnet 41) but the seduction of the poet's mistress (whether the Dark Lady or another). There is, however, a temporary reconciliation, followed by further doubts, reassurances, and jealousies, along with a resentment, on Shakespeare's part, of the tyranny of love (Sonnets 57, 58). This time it would appear to be Shakespeare, rather than his friend, who turns aside from the higher love to pursue the satisfactions of the flesh (Sonnet 56), but a deeper source of conflict is the friend's favouring of a rival poet, one whom Shakespeare admits to be his superior in art, but one who, he insists, is his inferior in love. The conflict of art and nature again becomes a theme, but now the issue is that of sincerity rather than immortality, and Shakespeare changes sides to become the proponent of nature's superiority to art, as well as artifice. The highest reaches of human wit may hope to imitate, but not to excel Nature's master-piece, whose excellence is not an imitation but the sum of universal beauty.

> In whose confine immured is the store
> Which should example where your equal grew?

It is the subject of his rival's poems which lends grace to his art, not the reverse:

> Let him but copy what in you is writ,
> Not making worse what nature made so clear,
> And such a counterpart shall fame his wit,
> Making his style admired everywhere.
>
> (Sonnet 84)

Like Cleopatra, his beloved "outstrips all praise, and makes it halt behind" him.

> There lives more life in one of your fair eyes
> Than both your poets can in praise devise.
>
> (Sonnet 83)

Yet Sonnet 84's assertion that the beloved is the perfection of Nature is followed, in the final couplet, by recognition that absolute perfection cannot occur in nature. The friend who, for Shakespeare, is Spenser's "sovereign light" of heavenly beauty, shares with Lucifer the only sin of which angels are capable—vanity.

> You to your beauteous blessings add a curse,
> Being fond on praise, which makes your praises worse.

The attempt to compartmentalize love, to treat good and evil, in the context of human emotion, as absolutes, fails because these elements are in conflict in the spirit as in the flesh. In poetry as in life their conflict must be acknowledged. This identity of difference is symbolized, in the Sonnets, by the juxtaposition and linking of two triangular relationships—poet-friend-rival poet, and poet-friend-mistress. As in many of the plays, sub-plot reinforces main plot. Rivalry in friendship is paralleled by rivalry in sexual love, in which the mistress is both prize

and enemy. In both love and friendship appearance and reality are at
odds; neither friend nor mistress "do the thing they most do show,"
both make shame "lovely" (Sonnet 95), and both are "common" in
bestowing their favours. The serpent invades Eden, lilies fester, and
the angel descends into hell.

The poet's ultimate disillusionment, his ultimate humiliation, is
expressed in his recognition of this conjunction of good and evil, of
flesh and spirit, and his identification of himself with that coming
together in an involvement with both sides from which he cannot
escape.

> So now I have confess'd that he is thine,
> And I myself am mortgag'd to thy will;[11]
> My self I'll forfeit, so that other mine
> Thou wilt restore to be my comfort still.
> But thou wilt not, nor he will not be free,
> For thou art covetous, and he is kind.[12]
> He learn'd but surety-like to write for me
> Under that bond that him as fast doth bind.
> The statute of thy beauty thou wilt take,
> Thou usurer that put'st forth all to use,
> And sue a friend came debtor for my sake;
> So him I lose through my unkind abuse.
>   Him have I lost; thou hast both him and me;
>   He pays the whole, and yet am I not free.
>   (Sonnet 134)

Desire is death, and the friend-redeemer has taken upon himself the
poet's sin, but the harrowing of the hell of lust cannot be completed
until the "bad angel fire my good one out" (Sonnet 144). The poet has
become Everyman, and, as with Lear, his acceptance of his humanity
marks both the low point of his degradation and the beginning of his
restoration through self-knowledge and self-acceptance. But the other
side of the coin remains to be considered.

If in one sense the sonnets to the Dark Lady represent an extreme
form of Platonic puritanism, in another they represent Platonism turned
upside down. Petrarch, Tasso, Sidney, Spenser, and Shakespeare himself in his sonnets to the fair youth had accepted the thesis that "the
soul is form and doth the body make" and celebrated those they loved
as exemplifying "how virtue may best lodged in beauty be." The Dark
Lady, however, is vice lodged in beauty, and in nothing but her colour-

[11]"Will" as her desire and as himself (Will) desiring her. This sonnet immediately precedes the well-known punning "will" sonnet in which the various senses
of the word are played upon.

[12]"Kind" in both senses, of course—as meaning generous, and as possessing the
natural desires of a man.

ing is the nature of her soul reflected in her outward form. Sonnet 130 makes it plain that her beauty is earthly rather than heavenly and, along with other conventional hyperbolic comparisons, rejects the sun as the correlative of her eyes. The heavenly beauty which emanates throughout the universe as light is perceived by the soul through the medium of the senses, but this love, though sensual to excess, is not "engend'red in the eyes" but in the heart (Sonnet 141). Like the conventional Petrarchan lover Shakespeare speaks of his mistress in images of the sea, but her "bounty," though "boundless as the sea" cannot be regarded in the same sense as Juliet's. Her love resembles rather that apostrophized by Duke Orsino which,

> notwithstanding thy capacity
> Receiveth as the sea, nought enters there,
> Of what validity and pitch so'er,
> But falls into abatement and low price
> Even in a minute!
>
> (*Twelfth Night*, I, i, 10–14)

This is a love not of the good and the true but of falseness, a love which corrupts reason and sees as particular what is all too universal (Sonnet 137), and when "the lover compareth his state to a ship," his mistress is "the bay where all men ride."

Yet to this wholly un-Platonic union of two faithless souls centred upon their "sinful earth" is applied the Platonic metaphor of harmony. It is applied ironically, however, for this music which is the "food of love" feeds not the soul, but the body, as Sonnet 128 makes clear. The instrument upon which his mistress plays is the only "virginal" thing about her, and the "concord" her fingers evoke "confounds" the hearer with desire, not for the harmony, but for the flesh. Earthly and heavenly love come together in an oblique allusion to the vision of Saint Cecilia in the reference to the "blessed wood," doubly "blessed" in being caressed by the fingers of the poet's "music."

When the sonnets to the Dark Lady conclude, the poet is still the unwilling prisoner of his will. He is still unable to resolve the paradoxes of a relationship in which love is sin, and hate is virtue (Sonnet 142), in which the "rebel powers" of the flesh (Sonnet 146) are still able to persuade him to "betray / My nobler part to my gross body's treason" (Sonnet 151); he is still thinking foul, fair (Sonnet 147), and still swearing that a lie is truth (Sonnet 152).

There is no account of the medicine which restored to sanity the reason Shakespeare thought "past cure" because "past care" (Sonnet 147). In learning to know good by experiencing evil the patient has, in a sense, ministered to himself (Sonnet 118). Cured he was, however, and Sonnets 108–26 chronicle and celebrate his return to grace in friendship by way of the traditional three stages of repentance, confession, and amendment. Frank as the confession is, there is no undue self-abasement about it, nor any suggestion that there has not been guilt on both sides. "Uncertainties now crown themselves assured" (uncertainties of both good and evil, hope and fear) in a new relationship of love which is not Time's fool, and the service of which is not servility but perfect freedom. The transience of nature, the lifelessness of art are accepted, and thereby defied (Sonnet 123) along with the "necessary wrinkles" of age. In its death and resurrection (Sonnet 108) love has demonstrated its own immortality, which is not the static immortality of art, but the immortality of growth, growth not destroyed but nurtured into new life by change (Sonnets 115–26). Sonnets 113 and 114 recognize the friend not merely as the totality of goodness, truth and beauty, but as the totality of the universe, which, with all its contradictions, is the image of divine love. Along with time and change Shakespeare is at last ready to accept the double vision of good and evil, reconciling its contradictions in the harmony of human love which also reflects the divine image.

> Since I left you, mine eye is in my mind,
> And that which governs me to go about
> Doth part his function . . .
> For if it see the rud'st or gentlest sight,
> The most sweet favour or deformed'st creature,
> The mountain or the sea, the day or night,
> The crow or dove, it shapes them to your feature.
>
> (Sonnet 113)

> . . . shall I say mine eye saith true,
> And that your love taught it this alchemy
> To make of monsters and things indigest
> Such cherubins as your sweet self resemble,
> Creating every bad a perfect best
> As fast as objects to his beams assemble?
>
> (Sonnet 114)

It is the wisdom, not the folly of love which "sees Helen's beauty in a brow of Egypt," "a soul of goodness in things evil." The single vision which saw only absolutes he now admits to have been the vision of self-delusion,

> Applying fears to hopes, and hopes to fears,
> Still losing when I saw myself to win!
> What wretched errors hath my heart committed,
> Whilst it hath thought it self so blessed never!

> How have mine eyes out of their spheres been fitted
> In the distraction of this madding fever!
>
> (Sonnet 119)

But, through mutual forgiveness, mutual guilt (Sonnet 120) has proved a *felix culpa*, redeeming loss and building stronger what it had destroyed.

> O benefit of ill! Now I find true
> That better is by evil still made better;
> And ruin'd love, when it is built anew,
> Grows fairer than at first, more strong, far greater.
>   So I return rebuk'd to my content,
>   And gain by ill thrice more than I have spent.
>
> (Sonnet 119)

The sonnet sequence traces the progress of love-in-friendship from confidence, through self-distrust, rejection and despair to rehabilitation; it also traces a similar and often parallel progress in the poet's attitude to his art. Accompanying the latter is a gradual change of style, particularly in the use of images and still more specifically in the employment of paradox and ambiguity.

In the earliest sonnets (the "invitation to marry" group) the poet appears to be emotionally detached from his theme and displays no ambivalence. The paradoxes in these sonnets, therefore, are those which arise from the conventions of the "fertility argument," and however effectively they may develop theme, they are external to mood. Usually they are ornamental rather than structural. Paradoxes and ambiguities are nevertheless frequent, the cycle of the seasons with its equation of womb and tomb, the battle of summer and winter, the parable of the talents, and the Aristotelian concept of natural function providing the bulk of them. Derivative as they are, occasionally a special emphasis or an unusual twist of application invests them with a characteristically Shakespearean flavour. Such is the condemnation of the youth's refusal to marry as unproductive narcissism. The sin of self-love is a theme which recurs frequently in the sonnets,[13] and it is a failing which is later to motivate many of the tragedies. All of the recurrent figures mentioned are carefully worked into the opening sonnet:

> From fairest creatures we desire increase,
> That thereby beauty's rose might never die,

---

[13]For example, in 54, 62, and 94. On this point see Edward Hubler, "The Economy of the Closed Heart," in *The Sense of Shakespeare's Sonnets* (Princeton University Press, 1952).

But as the riper should by time decease,
His tender heir might bear his memory;
But thou, contracted to thine own bright eyes,
Feed'st thy light's flame with self-substantial fuel,
Making a famine where abundance lies,
Thyself thy foe, to thy sweet self too cruel,
That thou art now the world's fresh ornament
And only herald to the gaudy spring,
Within thine own bud buriest thy content,
And, tender churl, mak'st waste in niggarding.
    Pity the world, or else this glutton be,
    To eat the world's due, by the grave and thee.

Yet even here, among such obvious figures, we find a hint of the concealed wordplay, the buried but pregnant pun characteristic of Shakespeare's mature expression. Whether we read "content" as còntent or contènt—as the seed of the potential child, as the happiness of having one's children about one in maturity, or as physical satisfaction —it makes equally good sense in the context, and the line lends itself to the suspicion of other connotations as well.

Similar subtleties underlie the opening lines of Sonnet 2:

When forty winters shall besiege thy brow
And dig deep trenches in thy beauty's field,
Thy youth's proud livery, so gaz'd on now,
Will be a tatter'd weed of small worth held.

Notice the interrelationship of the ideas of winter and war (destruction), heraldry (preservation—of lineage and famous deeds) and agriculture (creation for productive consumption). "Field" is first the land eroded by the winter wind, then the battle field, then the "field" of a banner or coat-of-arms, and last, the farmer's field trenched but unseeded. Similarly "weed" is first the livery of youthful beauty now worn and tattered, then the worthless ragweed which has taken possession of the fallow field. "Gaze" suggests "graze"—the young man's beauty feeds the eyes of all beholders, and the connotations coalesce in the "deep-sunken eyes" of the old man whose gaze has fed on his own beauty, and who therefore, like the unprofitable steward who buried his treasure in a "field," is ashamed to answer when asked where "all thy beauty," "all the treasure of thy lustful days" lies.

But such felicitous boldness of complication is rare in the early sonnets, and where the attempt is made to compress multiple significance into a single image it is more than likely to "crack the wind of the poor phrase." Typical is the eyes-stars, poet-almanack-maker analogy of Sonnet 14, of which only the two final lines appear to be personally meaningful. Though Sonnet 15 is more successful, it is still a standard conceit-sonnet elaborating an analogy between man and vegetative nature, as is the better-known Sonnet 18 ("Shall I compare thee to a summer's day?"). But in the latter the note of subtlety is heard once more. "Summer's lease" gains additional vividness and depth when it is remembered that "lease," in Elizabethan pronunciation, is homonymic with "lace." And in the lines,

> And every fair from fair some time declines,
> By chance, or nature's changing course, untrimm'd,

"untrimm'd" may modify "fair," meaning that beauty's ornaments have been stripped away, or "course," in which case it picks up the connotation of "chance" in suggesting that nature's course is not purposefully "trimmed" but drives on before the winds of chance and change. The second "fair," in this marine image, may be understood as in "fair stood the wind for France," tying in with the "rough winds" of line 3. Or "untrimm'd" may be understood to mean "uncurtailed": in the course of nature, beauty must decline if it is not cut off by death in the springtime of its flowering.

Though Sonnet 18 is the first in which the note of personal emotion is heard, its complexities are intellectual rather than emotional. M. M. Mahood's comment on the relationship of ambiguity and ambivalence in the Sonnets displays her usual sensitivity:

The nature of the wordplay in the sonnets varies according to whether Shakespeare is too remote or too near the experience behind the poem or whether he is at a satisfying distance from it. When he is detached, the wordplay is a consciously used, hard-worked rhetorical device. When his complexity of feeling upon the occasion of a sonnet is not fully realized by him, the wordplay often reveals an emotional undercurrent which is perhaps hidden from the poet himself. But in the best sonnets the wordplay is neither involuntary nor wilful; it is a skilfully handled means whereby Shakespeare makes explicit both his conflict of feelings and his resolution of the conflict.[14]

The first seventeen sonnets are certainly detached, their rhetoric conscious though sometimes effective. With the onset of love, however, Shakespeare gives poetic expression to literary as well as emotional self-analysis and becomes increasingly conscious of the problems of style.

The wholehearted admiration for the young man expressed in Sonnet 18 is accompanied by a confident assertion of the life-giving efficacy of his "powerful rhyme":

> So long as men can breathe, or eyes can see,
> So long lives this, and this gives life to thee,

[14]*Shakespeare's Wordplay*, p. 89.

and is followed by the still more confident challenge to "Devouring Time" with which Sonnet 19 concludes:

> Yet, do thy worst, old Time. Despite thy wrong,
> My love shall in my verse ever live young.

In Sonnet 21 he rejects the artificial rhetoric of graceful compliment as inappropriate to the sincerity of his feeling for his friend. In lines which anticipate those of the better-known Sonnet 130 he abjures the whole catalogue of Petrarchan hyperbolic comparisons:

> So is it not with me as with that Muse,
> Stirr'd by a painted beauty to his verse;
> Who heaven itself for ornament doth use,
> And every fair with his fair doth rehearse,[15]
> Making a couplement of proud compare
> With sun and moon, with earth and sea's rich gems,
> With April's first-born flowers, and all things rare
> That heaven's air in this huge rondure hems.
> Oh, let me, true in love, but truly write,
> And then believe me, my love is as fair
> As any mother's child, though not so bright
> As those gold candles fix'd in heaven's air.
>   Let them say more that like of hearsay well:
>   I will not praise that purpose not to sell.

No more than Sidney was Shakespeare able to observe, consistently, the injunction, "Look in thy heart, and write," but the incidence of purely ornamental figures does decline from this point on. Metaphor is integrated with structure, and the tone becomes more conversational, fulfilling the promise of Sonnet 23 to write what, "like an unperfect actor," the poet is too self-conscious and too timid to speak. When he gets into difficulties with the structural analogies of this section of the sequence, it is usually because having found an original but not wholly appropriate comparison he has made it "conceited" by wrenching and forcing the emotion to fit its every aspect. Failures of this sort, resulting from errors of "invention" rather than from emotional detachment, are Sonnet 24 ("Mine eye hath play'd the painter . . .") and Sonnet 46 ("Mine eye and heart are at a mortal war"). The latter gives what is perhaps the tritest of sonnet comparisons an original twist by turning the "war" into a law case, but the result is far from happy. It is perhaps of such poems as these that Shakespeare is thinking when he laments, in Sonnet 76, his inability to use "compounds strange."

[15]Cf. Mercutio's mockery of "the numbers that Petrarch flowed in"—"Laura, to his lady, was a kitchen-wench . . . Dido, a dowdy; Cleopatra, a gypsy, Helen and Hero, hildings and harlots . . ." (*Romeo and Juliet*, II, iv, 42–5).

Less awkward but still not entirely effective is Sonnet 26, in which the wordplay on "conceit" as figure of speech and as opinion recognizes the stylistic difficulty for what it is, that "conceit of foil" which results from the attempt to give expression to the ideal, and which troubled the mind of Shakespeare as it did the "senses" of Tamburlaine.[16]

> Lord of my love, to whom in vassalage
> Thy merit hath my duty strongly knit,
> To thee I send this written embassage,
> To witness duty, not to show my wit;
> Duty so great, which wit so poor as mine
> May make seem bare, in wanting words to show it,
> But that I hope some good conceit of thine
> In thy soul's thought, all naked, will bestow it;
> Till whatsoever star that guides my moving
> Points on me graciously with fair aspect,
> And puts apparel[17] on my tattered loving
> To show me worthy of thy sweet respect.
>   Then may I dare to boast how I do love thee;
>   Till then not show my head where thou mayst prove me.

Shakespeare returns frequently to the defence of the plain style as evidence of sincerity of feeling, but as Sonnet 26 and several of the sonnets of the rival-poet group indicate, he was not wholly convinced by his own argument, the less so when his friend began to bestow his patronage on another and "worthier" pen. "True, plain words" might tell the bare truth, but they did not adequately communicate either the depth of his affection or the greatness of its object. They were honest, but limited, lacking the richness and beauty of outward form which should image the richness and beauty of the theme. In poetry also, the body is the form of the soul. Sometimes, therefore, he has recourse to the conventional figures, and often profitably so, especially when the "not entirely realized" emotional undercurrent of which Miss Mahood speaks gives the comparison additional complexity and depth. Sonnet 33 illustrates the way in which involuntary ambiguities express a recognized but explicitly rejected ambivalence:

> Full many a glorious morning have I seen
> Flatter the mountain-tops with sovereign eye,
> Kissing with golden face the meadows green,
> Gilding pale streams with heavenly alchemy;
> Anon permit the basest clouds to ride
> With ugly rack on his celestial face,

---

[16] *I Tamburlaine*, V, ii.

[17] The dictum that "language is the dress of thought" is a commonplace of Renaissance criticism. Compare the "noted weed" of Shakespeare's "invention" in Sonnet 76.

> And from the forlorn world his visage hide,
> Stealing unseen to west with this disgrace.
> Even so my sun one early morn did shine
> With all triumphant splendour on my brow;
> But out, alack! he was but one hour mine,
> The region cloud hath mask'd him from me now.
>> Yet him for this my love no whit disdaineth;
>> Suns of the world may stain when heaven's sun staineth.

The disdain which the couplet denies is expressed, with cumulative emphasis, in the connotations of falseness and deceit conveyed by such words as "flatter," "gilding," "stealing," and "masked" and the word-play, "disdain—dis-stain." "Sovereign" and "golden face" are perhaps intended to suggest financial patronage, as "Gilding pale streams with heavenly alchemy" is undoubtedly an allusion to Shakespeare's inferior birth as much as to his poetry. But, as Jonson's play demonstrates, the alchemist was regarded as a charlatan perhaps even oftener than as a magician or philosopher, as a trickster who flattered the desires of his "gulls" and deceived them with glowing promises. In this sense there is ironic bite in the inversion by which the sovereign sun flatters[18] the subject mountain-tops, his countenance investing the green hopes of the meadows with the golden illusion of harvest. The "sensual fault" referred to in Sonnet 35 may be glanced at in "ride," as associated with "basest clouds" and contrasted with the "kissing" of the meadows. "Rack" may be not only the mass of clouds but the "wrack" of the heavenly beauty stained by its darkness, as well as the torture which disillusionment inflicts on the deserted friend, the "forlorn world" of line 7. The connotations of the expletives "out" and "alack" add to the force of "He was but one hour mine." Latent and overt ambiguities combine to invest lamentation and excuse with the bitterness of unacknowledged accusation.

Sonnet 73 is another example of the successful use of a number of the "ornaments" rejected in Sonnet 21. Here again, one side of the ambivalence is expressed overtly, the other gradually communicated by progressively more insistent connotative suggestion of its opposite. The difference is that the undercurrent is here deliberate and skilfully managed. In contrast to Sonnet 33, the identification of the poet with his subject-matter precedes the development of the comparison (or, in this instance, comparisons) and the tone is therefore consistently

---

[18]Similarly, Gaveston, in *Edward II*, speaks of flattering the three despised poor men who offer him their services: "I'll flatter them and make them live in hope" (I, i, 43 of Tucker Brooke's edition of *The Works of Christopher Marlowe* [Oxford: Clarendon Press, 1910]; all references to Marlowe's plays are to this edition).

maintained throughout rather than achieving its emphasis by contrast as Sonnet 33 does. The elegiac mood is introduced in the opening statement and reinforced by the slow, monosyllabic movement of the verse. Mind and body are equated with a late autumn landscape which is wholly dreary in atmosphere until the mention of "birds" in line 4 reminds us that winter is followed by spring. In view of what follows it is perhaps not straining too much to see in those yellow leaves an allusion to Virgil's golden bough, the talisman plucked in the grove of Cumae to enable the poet to return from the underworld of death. There may be an association with the sacred grove in the "bare ruin'd choirs" into which the yellowed boughs are transmuted, since, in terms of the analogy, the songs of praise of the departed birds must be those of the poet. The imagery has moved swiftly from the body, through "nature," to the soul—from one decayed temple of the Holy Spirit to another. From this point on, the cyclical pattern of the images becomes more marked. Sunset is followed by sunrise, and night's blackness, "Death's second self" in a phrase originally applied by Seneca to sleep, "seals up all in rest," the great restorer. In the Phoenix allusion of the final quatrain, the death-resurrection duality becomes explicit:

> In me thou seest the glowing of such fire
> That on the ashes of his youth doth lie,
> As the death-bed whereon it must expire,
> Consum'd with that which it was nourish'd by,

and the compensations of loss are given overt statement in the couplet:

> This thou perceiv'st which makes thy love more strong,
> To love that well which thou must leave ere long.

The group of sonnets on the ending of love by death (to which Sonnet 73 is central) immediately precedes the "rival poet" group in which Shakespeare laments the sickness of his Muse. The reference to "Bare ruin'd choirs where late the sweet birds sang" serves as a link between them. Love and the poetic skill which love emboldened to hurl defiance at Time have alike become Time's victims. Body, mind, and spirit are alike subject to decay. Sonnet 76, the first in which Shakespeare analyses his dissatisfaction with his art, looks at the coin the other way round, however. His difficulty is, he feels, that he has not changed, and that therefore he is behind the times:

> Why is my verse so barren of new pride?
> So far from variation or quick change?
> Why, with the time, do I not glance aside
> To new-found methods and to compounds strange?

His "invention" continues to wear "a noted weed," so that

> . . . every word doth almost tell my name,
> Showing their birth, and where they did proceed.

In Sonnet 78 his poetry is the product of "rude ignorance," it is "tongue-tied" and a "saucy bark" far inferior to the rival's tall ship in Sonnet 80. In Sonnet 82, he excuses his friend's desire to seek "some fresher stamp of the time-bettering days," a stamp which in Sonnet 85 takes the form of "richly compil'd" comments of praise, and "precious phrase by all the Muses fil'd." His own poems are "unlettered"; they lack "polish'd form" in comparison with the rival's style, which he sometimes envies, sometimes criticizes as "strained" rhetoric, but which he admits to be strong, rich, varied, learned, carefully wrought, and above all new.

Shakespeare's dissatisfaction with his art increases, paralysing his pen until he is unable to write anything but excuses for not writing (Sonnets 100–3). The admission of failure comes in Sonnet 103:

> O, blame me not, if I no more can write!
> Look in your glass, and there appears a face
> That over-goes my blunt invention quite,
> Dulling my lines, and doing me disgrace.
> Were it not sinful then, striving to mend,
> To mar the subject that before was well?

The references to three years' "process of the seasons" (Sonnet 104), to absence and estrangement (Sonnets 109, 110) and to alteration (Sonnet 116) suggest that Sonnet 103 marks the severing of the relationship, and that the sonnets to the Dark Lady might have been inserted here were the order of the sonnets identical with the order of composition. Most of the sonnets between 104 and 127 allude, directly or indirectly, to a reconciliation.

Whatever disturbances of heart and mind Shakespeare may have suffered from his infatuation with the Dark Lady, its fever rekindled the fire of his Muse, and potions of siren tears proved a more efficacious draught than the Pierian Spring. Not even Shakespeare complains of any lack of variety in the sonnets to the Dark Lady. Their tone shifts from tenderness to cynicism, tolerant playfulness, anguished protest, revulsion and condemnation, reflecting, perhaps, the lady's fickleness as well as the bitter conflict of reason and passion in her lover. The whole sonnet armory of ambiguity—puns, witty or conceited, paradoxes, analogies, antitheses, every sort of wordplay—is employed with varying effectiveness. What emerges out of the turmoil of soul and the exercising of old skills in a new context is a new kind of control, in which involvement and detachment are balanced. This is particularly evident in the "playful" sonnets such as 138 ("When my love swears that she is made of truth"), which accept the satisfactions and dissatisfactions of the situation without self-deception and without overt bitterness.

One of these is Sonnet 151, which plays with the conflict of appetite, will, and reason in a manner not unlike that of Donne's early poems.

> Love is too young to know what conscience is;
> Yet who knows not conscience is born of love?
> Then, gentle cheater, urge not my amiss,
> Lest guilty of my faults thy sweet self prove.
> For thou betraying me, I do betray
> My nobler part to my gross body's treason.
> My soul doth tell my body that he may
> Triumph in love; flesh stays no farther reason,
> But, rising at thy name, doth point out thee
> As his triumphant prize. Proud of this pride,
> He is contented thy poor drudge to be,
> To stand in thy affairs, fall by thy side.
> > No want of conscience hold it that I call
> > Her 'love' for whose dear love I rise and fall.

Here the ambivalence of flesh and spirit is expressed through the manipulation of concepts associated with the fleshly and spiritual connotations of the word "conscience." "Love" is variously Cupid, desire, the sexual act, the poet's devotion, and his mistress, who is also his "soul." Since he is a child, the God of Love cannot fully comprehend "conscience" as either physical awareness or the moral sense, and Eros (sensual love) is therefore innocent. Yet enhanced physical awareness[19] is the fruit of love and enhanced spiritual awareness of the good arises from the senses' perception of physical beauty.[20]

This paradoxical logic brings reason into the conflict, but too late to influence will, which has taken its direction from appetite, the poet's "soul" (that is, his mistress) having betrayed his spiritual soul[21] by permitting his body to triumph in the conquest of her body, which is also the conquest of reason. "Conscience" then takes on the further

[19]According to the doctrines of courtly love, all the senses are revitalized and given heightened awareness by the power of love. See *Love's Labour's Lost*, IV, iii, 323–49 on love's ability to give "every power," whether physical or mental, "a double power."

[20]See the discussion of the function of the senses in Platonic love, pp. 7 ff.

[21]The conventional three-fold division of the soul into appetite, reason, and will assumed that the reason, the controlling and judicial function, evaluated the impulses of the appetite stimulated by the senses and directed the will to follow or to disregard these impulses. In a state of order, the three functions of the soul worked together in harmony. In a state of disorder, appetite might be directing the will, by either by-passing or posing as reason. "Rude will," in Friar Laurence's phrase, is will that does not listen to reason. In this instance, will, with the usual pun on Shakespeare's name, is all too likely to make the voice of desire its guide rather than that of reason.

connotation of integrity in the sense of allegiance and "rise," "stand," and "fall" are played upon in this context as well as in the ceremonial and the sexual, as the "prize" of conquest suggests the battlefield and the standard. The pride of conquest goes before a fall, however, both spiritually and physically, and both soul and body become enslaved by the captive. But the couplet returns to the concept of innocence with which the sonnet began, since such faithful service, such prompt response to command cannot be regarded as want of "conscience" in either the physical or the spiritual sense.

Witty and wryly humorous as the tone of this sonnet is, it has its serious undertone which almost breaks through the surface in the oblique allusion to the fall of the angels through the sin of pride. Lust in action is still a descent into hell for all the tongue-in-cheek casuistry and equivocation about its innocence.

The sonnets of reconciliation with the friend also demonstrate this ability to combine sincerity of feeling, depth and subtlety of expression, and poetic detachment. In these poems Shakespeare still, from time to time, deprecates his poetic style as lacking in variety (Sonnets 105, 108) and in skill (Sonnet 106), but neither in his appreciation of love restored nor in his regret that his art is unable to give that love complete expression do we find the fear of loss so poignantly expressed in the earlier sonnets. In poetry as in personal relationships Shakespeare appears to have gained new confidence through learning to accept imperfection as an element of the human condition. The attitude towards the contradictions of life expressed in the Sonnets follows a similar pattern of development to that expressed in the plays. It moves from the search for absolutes, through the recognition of difference and preoccupation with divisions and inversions of value to acceptance of the interdependence of opposites. The Sonnets do not achieve a complete fusion of ambivalences, however, but only a partial one. Sex and spirit are left in a state of armed truce, if not of civil war. It is to the plays written at the same period or shortly afterwards that we must turn for the terms of peace between them.

Echoes of the sonnet story may be found in the dark heroines and threatened friendships of several of the early comedies, but it is in *Love's Labour's Lost* that the two sonnet themes of truth in poetry and truth in love receive their fullest dramatic exposition. Navarre and his courtiers are guilty of their initial folly in dedicating themselves for three years[22] to intellectual and spiritual concerns alone. The

---

[22]That this should be precisely the time-span of Shakespeare's relationship with his friend, as mentioned in Sonnet 104, is perhaps something more than mere coincidence.

unnaturalness of such a dedication is revealed when, no sooner than they have taken their oaths, they are betrayed by their "gross body's treason." Their second folly is to regard the love of women as that treason and nothing more, and the Princess and her ladies must convince them that false love is as reprehensible as rejection of love. Berowne pleads for all the lovers that, once brought into the sunshine of the ladies' favour, the false oaths and "three-piled hyperboles" of false love will purify themselves and turn to grace expressed in "honest, plain words." His "blazon" in praise of love is the heir of both Renaissance traditions— the courtly and the Platonic. Love, he insists, is the heavenly harmony which stimulates the mind as well as the senses and inspires the "fiery numbers" of the poet. Love is "first learned in a lady's eyes," and they

> . . . are the books, the arts, the academes,
> That show, contain, and nourish all the world.
>
> (IV, iii, 348–9)

So much of *Love's Labour's Lost* is taken up with the parodying of various sorts of literary affectation that it is not the play which most clearly reveals Shakespeare's new poetic style, though it is clear enough as to what he rejected of the older literary fashions. It is *Romeo and Juliet,* his first tragedy of love, which presents sexual love not as the destroyer but as the restorer of order, and does so in the language of his poetic maturity. Desire still brings death, since this is a tragedy, but the victory is not the grave's, but love's.

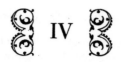

IV

The War of the Elements:
Imagery in *Romeo and Juliet*

"Does not our life consist of the four elements?"
(*Twelfth Night*)

But all subsists by elemental strife,
And passions are the elements of life.
(Pope, *Essay on Man*)

REFERENCES TO THE DIALECTIC of the four elements are almost as abundant in Shakespeare as parallels between macrocosm and microcosm, and indeed such parallels often make use of the frame of reference of this universal dialectic. The best known, perhaps, is Antony's tribute to Brutus, in whom the elements of human nature were "so mixed . . . that Nature might stand up / And say to all the world, 'This was a man!'" Cleopatra uses the same metaphor to describe not only the dissolution of her physical elements in death but her transmutation of character into Roman and tragic dignity: "I am all fire and air; my other elements / I give to baser life." Sonnets 44 and 45 deal with the four elements as the components of life and love.

The theory of the elements postulates the fundamental irony that only through the action-reaction functioning of opposed elements, physical or spiritual, can harmony be achieved and order maintained. It is this concept of order established or restored through conflict, which provides theme, conflict, and resolution in *Romeo and Juliet*. The elements with which this play is concerned are those of human passion; their disorder is the result of an excess of one element which only a compensating excess of its opposite can correct. But the conflict of human passions is displayed against the cyclic pattern of the physical universe, and the correspondences between macrocosm and microcosm are stressed over and over again in the imagery of the play as well as in direct and allegorical statements. Its focus is on the point of balance at which contraries meet and part, and its tragedy is that the order of reconciled oppositions is attainable only by means of sacrifice.

In the Prologue to Act I this basic dialectic is stated as the interaction of the opposed forces of love and hate:

> Two households, both alike in dignity,
> In fair Verona, where we lay our scene,
> From ancient grudge break to new mutiny,
> Where civil blood makes civil hands unclean.
> From forth the fatal loins of these two foes
> — A pair of star-cross'd lovers take their life;
> Whose misadventur'd piteous overthrows
> Doth with their death bury their parents' strife.
> The fearful passage of their death-mark'd love,
> And the continuance of their parents' rage,
> Which, but their children's end, nought could remove,
> Is now the two hours' traffic of our stage. . . .

The paradoxical nature of the theme is underlined by the interweaving of paradox and ambiguity in language. Our attention is repeatedly directed to the juxtaposition of opposites such as birth and death, love and hate, in images which reinforce the irony of situation in which hate gives birth to love. With equal irony tragic death, caused by the original hate acting upon the love, results in the destruction of that hate and the restoration of civil harmony. The ambiguities of language and situation are as insistent as the ironies. Though the households are alike in dignity of position, dignity is the very quality they lack when they first appear on stage involved in public strife. Lady Capulet finds the sight of the two old men fighting so ridiculous that she cannot refrain from the jibe, "A crutch! a crutch! Why call you for a sword?" The second "civil," in line 4 of the Prologue, is both ironic and ambiguous. It is Romeo's civility in attempting to put an end to the "civil strife" between Mercutio and Tybalt which results in Mercutio's death and in the soiling of his own hands with the blood of Tybalt, his fellow citizen and kinsman by marriage. Again, the "star-cross'd lovers" "take their life" from the "fatal loins" of "these two foes," but it is part of their star-crossed destiny that "the continuance of their parents' rage" shall cause them to take their own lives.

The tragic theme thus introduced in the Prologue is restated by implication in the opening scene. Here the dialectic of birth, death, love, and hate is intensified by the sexual connotations of such terms as "stand," "fall," and "die," as well as by more overt references to cutting off the heads of maids. Opposed forces are brought together in more ways than one. The scene begins on a comic and ends on a tragic note. The bawdy wordplay of the servants develops not only the exposition of the feud between the two houses but also the underlying love-death motif.

Throughout the play, the theme of unity in diversity, of harmony achieved through discord, is reflected not only directly in the dialogue but indirectly in its dominant imagery. In *Romeo and Juliet* imagery is used in all the characteristically Shakespearean ways[1]—to create atmosphere, to portray and individualize character, to emphasize ironies of situation, and often, by foreshadowing and reminiscence, to bind together elements of plot. But its particular function is to reinforce the theme of order in disorder. Many of the recurring images are concerned with parallels between macrocosm and microcosm and with the elemental divisions of matter: earth, air, fire, and water. In considering the dialectic of the elements as the "expanded metaphor" of the play, therefore, it is both logical and convenient to organize our examination of thematic imagery into the categories represented by the four elements.

The recurring celestial or aetherial images of *Romeo and Juliet* reflect the original paradox of creation, that the first step in the setting-up of an ordered universe was to establish the opposites of light and darkness. Contrast and harmony, whether cosmic or human, are interdependent. The light of the stars is made visible by the presence of darkness, and Juliet is said to hang "upon the cheek of night / As a rich jewel in an Ethiop's ear" (I, v, 43).

The sea, in common with other symbols of the universal order, is eternally changing yet eternally unchanged, and Juliet's love is "as boundless as the sea . . . for both are infinite" (II, ii, 133).

Fire is, of course, the symbol of passion. As love, like its source the

[1]This chapter shares in the general indebtedness of recent studies of Shakespeare's imagery (see M. C. Bradbrook, "Fifty Years of Criticism of Shakespeare's Style," *Shakespeare Survey* 8, 1–13) to the pioneering work of Caroline Spurgeon, W. H. Clemen, and G. Wilson Knight. E. A. Armstrong (*Shakespeare's Imagination*, London: Lindsay Drummond, 1946), Patrick Cruttwell (*The Shakespearean Moment*, London: Chatto and Windus, 1954; New York: Random House Modern Library ed., 1960), and M. M. Mahood (*Shakespeare's Wordplay*; London: Methuen, 1957) have contributed valuable insights into Shakespeare's attitudes and techniques. Among previous studies of the imagery of *Romeo and Juliet*, E. C. Pettet's "The Imagery of Romeo and Juliet" (*English* VIII, Autumn, 1950, pp. 121–6) considers some of the points dealt with in the present discussion, and in particular the star and pilot images, but does so from a different point of view. The star imagery is also examined in Roy Walker's "The Celestial Plane in Shakespeare" (*Shakespeare Survey* 7, pp. 109–17).

sun, it is the creator of life; as rage, it is the executioner, Death. It is a force most hazardous to the unwary, the rash, and the inexperienced, and the black and white horses of the allegory of love in Plato's *Phaedrus* are no steeds for Phaetons.

Earth, as the centre of the physical universe and the seat of the "paragon of animals," man, demonstrates the pattern of divine order in its ceaseless cycle of birth and death.

Of these four divisions of created nature, earth provides the greatest number of individual and recurring images. Thirty are drawn from the pattern of ordered conflict in the human life cycle alone. These life-in-death ambivalences are to be found in every moment of dramatic tension and on the lips of every major character. Take, for example, Capulet's first conversation with Paris on the subject of Juliet's marriage:

> Earth hath swallowed all my hopes but she;
> She is the hopeful lady of my earth.
>
> (I, ii, 14–15)

Here is a double ambiguity. The grave has devoured all of Capulet's other children; they have returned to the dust of which all flesh is made, leaving only this one daughter as the promise of his "earth" both as his world—the centre of his personal universe—and as the issue of his clay.

A similar pattern of implication lies beneath the surface of the Nurse's idle prattle about Juliet's age. Susan, the Nurse's own daughter and Juliet's foster sister, is "with God," the old gossip tells us as she recalls Juliet's weaning. This first step towards self-sufficiency is taken, appropriately enough, with the assistance of "wormwood." The Nurse recalls that when Juliet began to walk alone she tumbled, and the commonplace incident is associated in her memory with a deviation from the cosmic order. There was an earthquake, and the cotes of the doves, symbols of peace and purity, were shaken. The last link in the chain of association of birth, growth, marriage, and death is provided by the jest of the Nurse's husband, a merry man but, like his child, now dead. "To see, now, how a jest shall come about!" comments the Nurse on hearing that the County Paris has made an offer for Juliet's hand, and continues with an ejaculation reminiscent of Simeon's:

> Thou wast the prettiest babe that e'er I nurs'd;
> An I might live to see thee married once,
> I have my wish.
>
> (I, iii, 61–3)

The first meeting of the lovers calls forth another such association.

Here the obvious foreshadowing carries an undertone of irony, since the condition necessary to fulfilment of the unconscious prophecy is contrary to the fact, unless we interpret Juliet's words as meaning, "if he should ever be married":

> Go, ask his name.—If he be married,
> My grave is like to be my wedding-bed.
>
> (I, v, 132–3)

These ironic associations of grave and marriage-bed are frequent, and especially so in the climactic third act. On hearing of Tybalt's death and Romeo's banishment Juliet cries out:

> I'll to my wedding-bed;
> And death, not Romeo, take my maidenhead!
>
> (III, ii, 136–7)

The passage is echoed in Lady Capulet's subsequent outburst against her daughter's stubborn refusal to marry Paris: "I would the fool were married to her grave!" (III, v, 140) and in Capulet's lament over the seeming fulfilment of that wish (IV, v, 25 ff.). Juliet pleads with her mother to

> Delay this marriage for a month, a week;
> Or, if you do not, make the bridal bed
> In that dim monument where Tybalt lies.
>
> (III, v, 200–2)

Shakespeare often uses an image early in a play for purposes of foreshadowing or of ironic contrast with the same image as seen in the context of later developments, a device which occurs frequently in *Romeo and Juliet*. For example, "temp'ring extremities with extreme sweet" (Prologue, Act II) recalls Tybalt's vow that "this intrusion shall, / Now seeming sweet, convert to bitt'rest gall" (I, v, 89) and also anticipates "Death, that hath suck'd the honey of thy breath" and the other ambivalent references to death as the agent of fertility in the last act of the play.

It is chiefly to the earlier marriage-death associations, however, that these Janus-like functions are assigned. Rather than marry Paris Juliet would prefer Friar Laurence to

> hide me nightly in a charnel house,
> O'er-cover'd quite with dead men's rattling bones,
> With reeky shanks and yellow chapless skulls;
> Or bid me go into a new-made grave,
> And hide me with a dead man in his shroud. . . .
>
> (IV, i, 81–5)

This bit of Senecan horror not only anticipates the ordeal which the Friar is to impose upon her, as well as her own wild imaginings before drinking the potion (IV, iii, 30–58), but also glances backward to her plea to Lady Capulet in the previous scene, quoted above. Similarly, Juliet's comment when her mother attempts to assuage her supposed grief for Tybalt by vowing vengeance on Romeo, combines verbal irony[2] with the irony of foreshadowing:

> Indeed I never shall be satisfied
> With Romeo till I behold him—dead.
>
> (III, v, 93–6)

This speech is in turn echoed in Friar Laurence's words to Juliet when she wakens in the tomb: "Thy husband in thy bosom there lies dead" (V, iii, 155) and both are echoes of Juliet's premonition:

> O God, I have an ill-divining soul!
> Methinks I see thee, now thou art below,
> As one dead in the bottom of a tomb.
>
> (III, v, 54–6)

"Well, Juliet, I will lie with thee tonight," the grim promise which Romeo makes on hearing of his wife's supposed death, again associates death with love, as the Friar's use of the word "bosom" in the line previously quoted links the love-death association with maternal sustenance, the beginning of life. Paris, as well as Romeo, desired to "set up his rest" (IV, v, 6) in Juliet's bosom, and he shares with Romeo "a triumphant grave" (V, iii, 83).

Linked in a pattern as persistent and almost as complex as the death–marriage-bed references are the images in which Death exercises the *droit du seigneur* of forestalling the bridegroom, having "a greater power than we can contradict." Friar Laurence describes the effects of the potion:

> ... in this borrow'd likeness of shrunk death
> Thou shalt continue two and forty hours,
> And then awake as from a pleasant sleep.
> Now, when the bridegroom in the morning comes
> To rouse thee from thy bed, there art thou dead.
>
> (IV, i, 104–8)

A few lines later he tells Juliet that he and Romeo will "watch thy waking," thus pointing up the irony of the previous passage. As prospective bridegroom, Paris does find Juliet, as he thinks, dead when he comes to rouse her from her slumbers on the wedding-morn, but Romeo, who should have come to watch her waking two-and-forty hours later, in fact comes to join her in what he supposes to be death.

[2]Both "satisfied" and "dead" have, of course, sexual connotations.

There, he charges Death with being enamoured of Juliet. With the same image, Capulet reveals his loss to Paris:

> O son, the night before thy wedding day
> Hath Death lain with thy wife. There she lies,
> Flower as she was, deflowered by him.
> Death is my son-in-law, Death is my heir;
> My daughter he hath wedded; I will die,
> And leave him all; life, living, all is Death's.
>
> (IV, v, 35–40)

In terms of the imagery of the play, Capulet's concluding statement is literally true. Every aspect of the life cycle, from the prelude to birth[3] to the hope of life hereafter is closely linked with death. Life is indeed "not life, but love in death" (IV, v, 58). The birth of a new love is spoken of as the death-bed vigil of the old in the Prologue to Act II:

> Now old desire doth in his death-bed lie,[4]
> And young affection gapes to be his heir.

Friar Laurence replies to Romeo's reminder, "And bad'st me bury love," with, "Not in a grave / To lay one in, another out to have" (II, iii, 83). In begging the Friar to marry him to Juliet, Romeo bargains with Death:

> Then love-devouring death do what he dare;
> It is enough I may but call her mine.
>
> (II, vi, 7–8)

He fulfils that bargain at Juliet's tomb when his lips seal "a dateless bargain to engrossing death" (V, iii, 115). Death is again "love-devouring" in the lines Romeo speaks as he forces his way into the tomb:

> Thou detestable maw, thou womb of death,
> Gorg'd with the dearest morsel of the earth,
> Thus I enforce thy rotten jaws to open,
> And, in despite, I'll cram thee with more food!
>
> (V, iii, 45–8)

This is not the only occasion on which death is a symbol of fertility as well as of destruction. Friar Laurence will later (V, iii, 151) refer to the vault as "that nest of death." A few lines earlier death had been the bee which nourishes itself by closing the life-cycle of one flower while commencing that of another:

---

[3]For example, "the fatal cannon's womb" (V, i, 65) and "womb of death" (V, iii, 45).

[4]Again the sexual connotation. "Gapes" suggests both the yawning of the vigil-keeping heir and his eagerness to inherit.

> O my love! my wife!
> Death, that hath suck'd the honey of thy breath,
> Hath had no power yet upon thy beauty.
>
> (V, iii, 91–3)

Death is in love with both lovers. Friar Laurence commiserates with Romeo as one "wedded to calamity," and Romeo marvels at the freshness of the supposedly dead Juliet's beauty, asking whether he should believe

> That unsubstantial Death is amorous,
> And that the lean abhorred monster keeps
> Thee here in dark to be his paramour?
>
> (V, iii, 103–5)

The obvious allusion to the myth of Proserpina emphasizes the love-death-rebirth motif.

Most of the images so far noted have been concerned with the encroachment of death upon life. But in the final act Shakespeare, in his attempt to create a mood of reconciliation, makes use of images in which death is a restoration to life eternal. Romeo dreams,

> . . . my lady came and found me dead. . . .
> And breath'd such life with kisses in my lips
> That I reviv'd, and was an emperor.
>
> (V, i, 6–9)

The dream has a partial fulfilment when Juliet kisses Romeo as he lies dead in her arms. Searching for some "friendly drop to help me after" to that death which is the gate of life, she murmurs,

> I will kiss thy lips;
> Haply some poison yet doth hang on them,
> To make me die with a restorative.
>
> (V, iii, 164–6)

It is this constant association of love with death, far more than direct insistence on the over-riding force of destiny or the frequency of ironies of circumstance, which gives this tragedy its atmosphere of fatality. For Juliet and her lover are not to be regarded as merely the puppets of a malignant fate. The "extremities" natural to youth help to bring about their catastrophe. It is the language of the play which gives us the impression that they are caught up in the cyclic sweep of that universal dialectic by which any excess—even excess of love—either destroys the balance of order or, in being destroyed, restores it.

The interdependence of life and death is reiterated in a second group of images drawn from the cycle of vegetable nature.

The earth that's nature's mother is her tomb;
What is her burying grave, that is her womb.

The theme has its formal analysis in Friar Laurence's speech on the participation of herbs in the duality of all nature (II, iii, 9–30). A good Thomist, he explains that in the spiritual as in the physical worlds there are no moral absolutes. Nothing in nature is wholly good or wholly bad; everything must be evaluated in terms of balance, function, and ends. In an ideal world medicine might always prevail over poison in plants, and grace over rude will in the souls of men, but in this imperfect existence the best we can hope for is a truce between these opposed kings. In such a world as ours even this best does not always prevail. Sometimes, for example, the fittest do not survive, but die young.

As elsewhere in Shakespeare, this thought finds expression in the metaphor of the blighted blossom.[5] In the Friar's opening speech death is a canker which attacks the rose of life. In separating the combatants in Act I, the Prince refers to both peace and hate as "cankered" in different senses of the word. The citizens' swords have been "cankered" (warped) by disuse and must now be wielded to part "cankered" (cancerous) hate. Juliet is frequently referred to as a flower blasted by death. Paris (I, iii, 77) and Romeo (II, v, 44 and III, ii, 73) are both likened to flowers, and the guests at Capulet's ball are called "fresh female buds" (I, ii, 29). Romeo's father complains that the secret of his son's melancholy is

So far from sounding and discovery,
As is the bud bit with an envious worm,
Ere he can spread his sweet leaves to the air,
Or dedicate his beauty to the sun.

(I, i, 148–51)

Death is said to lie on Juliet,

. . . like an untimely frost
Upon the sweetest flower of all the field.

(IV, v, 28–9)

It is against the background of such references, conventional though they may be, that we can discern the thematic implications of spring-summer-harvest associations in less obvious allusions. One such is Juliet's hope that

This bud of love, by summer's ripening breath,
May prove a beauteous flow'r when next we meet.

(II, ii, 121–2)

[5]See Caroline Spurgeon, *Shakespeare's Imagery* (Cambridge University Press, 1952), pp. 46, 88, 91, 292–3.

Another is Capulet's intention to

> Let two more summers wither in their pride
> Ere we may think her ripe to be a bride.
>
> (I, ii, 10–11)

There is obvious ironic intention in the words, "wither," "pride," and "ripe" in this juxtaposition. The intention is underlined by Paris's reply, "Younger than she are happy mothers made," and by Capulet's retort, "And too soon marr'd are those so early made."

By associating the tragic lovers with the universal pattern, this reiterated linking of love and death, growth and decay, arouses awe. To arouse pity the imagery shifts its emphasis from the cosmic and universal to the microcosmic and particular—to the blighted bud, the untimely frost, the golden harvest which is doomed to die at the moment of its fruition, and the green of springtime which is one with "Tybalt green and festering in his shroud."

The aspects of the cyclic process so heavily stressed in the images of earth are echoed in the imagery of the celestial or aetherial plane of being. Here the emphasis falls upon the contrast and mingling of light and darkness: the streaks of dawn marking the transition from night to day and from joy to woe, the stars sparkling against the midnight sky, the flash of lightning across a storm-cloud. Love is light, hate darkness; knowledge is light, ignorance darkness; life is day, death night. Beauty also is light in darkness.

At the Capulets' ball Juliet, in Romeo's eyes at least, outshines all the other "earth-treading stars that make dark heaven light" (I, ii, 23).

> O, she doth teach the torches to burn bright!
> It seems she hangs upon the cheek of night
> As a rich jewel in an Ethiop's ear—
> Beauty too rich for use, for earth too dear!
> So shows a snowy dove trooping with crows
> As yonder lady o'er her fellows shows.
>
> (I, v, 41–7)

In keeping with the Petrarchan tradition Juliet is the sun, but she is also a light in the darkness of the grave (V, iii, 84). In the macrocosmic analogy she is the earth, the centre of the Ptolemaic universe (II, i, 1). She is the light of true love as contrasted with the "artificial night" (I, i, 138) of Romeo's love for Rosaline. "Being but heavy, I will bear the light," says Romeo on the way to the ball, contrasting the light of the torch with this self-induced spiritual darkness (I, iv, 12).

Romeo's sudden recognition of the light of true love expressed in the "torches" speech is contrasted with the darkness of the fiery

Tybalt's hate, which is itself set off against the genial tolerance of the hospitable Capulet. He tries to quiet his truculent kinsman and play the jovial host at the same time:

> Be quiet, or—More light, more light!—For shame!
> I'll make you quiet.
>
> (I, v, 85–6)

The light he calls for is intended as much for Tybalt, in one sense, as for the dancers, in another. Nature herself frowns at night, and smiles with "the gray-ey'd morn" (II, iii, 1).

Although both hate and the wrong kind of love are dark or darkness-loving, theirs is the darkness of ignorance rather than of conscious evil. Even Tybalt behaves correctly according to his misguided notions of a code of honour, and Romeo insists to Tybalt that his hate is due to ignorance of love (III, i, 66, ff.). The result of actions motivated by ignorant rage is the darkness of sorrow, contrasted with light in the parting speeches of the lovers:

> JUL.:   O, now be gone! More light and light it grows.
> ROM.:   More light and light—more dark and dark our woes!
>
> (III, v, 35–6)

The darkness of false love is also due to ignorance: it "did read by rote that could not spell," and, lacking enlightenment as to the true nature of love, it did not "love for love allow" (II, iii, 86, 88). Such lovers wear the "vestal livery" of the "envious moon," and "none but fools do wear it" (II, ii, 9). Romeo casts off the reflected love-light of the cold, fruitless moon when he calls upon Juliet, as the sun, to "arise . . . and kill the envious moon, / Who is already sick and pale with grief," (II, ii, 4–5). He has recognized the symbol of chastity as the symbol of death.

Juliet also disclaims the moon as a symbol of love, though for other reasons:

> O, swear not by the moon, th' inconstant moon,
> That monthly changes in her circled orb,
> Lest that thy love prove likewise variable.
>
> (II, ii, 109–11)

Though Juliet's eyes are stars, the light of her beauty would "shame those stars, as daylight doth a lamp," and her tribute balances Romeo's. His beauty is such that were his body "cut out . . . in little stars" it would "make the face of heaven so fine / That all the world will be in love with night," paying "no worship to the garish sun" (III, ii, 22–5).

At the close of the balcony scene the image of love as light in darkness is repeated:

> JUL.: A thousand times good night!
> ROM.: A thousand times the worse, to want thy light.
>
> (II, ii, 154–5)

Love desires darkness only as a shield against the eyes of an unenlightened world, and for true lovers the light of "their own beauties" is sufficient illumination. By such light, "true love acted" is but "simple modesty," Juliet proclaims, concluding her epithalamion with the summons to Romeo, "Come, thou day in night!" (III, ii, 17).

In the *aubade*, the lovers lament the coming of the light of day, which cannot but be envious of their surpassing light of love. But "Night's candles are burnt out," and the lovers, who have illumined the night with the beauty of love, have also reached their consummation.[6] Though the comparisons of love to light usually bear a favourable connotation they do not escape completely the universal duality. The lightning-flash which streaks across the darkness of night, or storm, or death is ominous as well as transient, and Juliet recognizes the possibility of danger, as well as loss, in love when she says,

> I have no joy of this contract to-night:
> It is too rash, too unadvis'd, too sudden;
> Too like the lightning, which doth cease to be
> Ere one can say 'It lightens.'
>
> (II, ii, 117–20)

In the many passages in which the element of fire is the correlative of passion the most interesting and the most frequent references are those which liken excessive emotion to gunpowder. Here the natural properties of fire serve as a vivid illustration of the action-reaction process. Since the function of gunpowder is to fulfil its purpose in destroying itself, its explosion symbolizes not only the self-destructiveness of passion but the cyclic process of birth and death. Friar Laurence, the voice of spiritual "measure" in the play, warns the lovers that,

> These violent delights have violent ends,
> And in their triumph die; like fire and powder,
> Which, as they kiss, consume.
>
> (II, vi, 9–11)

On a later occasion he uses the same image to emphasize the need for control of despair by reason:

[6]Cf. Donne's "The Canonization," line 21: "We are Tapers too, and at our owne cost die."

> Thy wit, that ornament to shape and love,
> Misshapen in the conduct of them both,
> Like powder in a skilless soldier's flask,
> Is set afire by thine own ignorance,
> And thou dismemb'red with thine own defence.
>
> (III, iii, 130–4)

The image occurs again when Romeo, ignorant of the true state of affairs in Verona, demands from the apothecary "a mean of death,"

> A dram of poison, such soon-speeding gear
> As will disperse itself through all the veins
> That the life-weary taker may fall dead,
> And that the trunk may be discharg'd of breath
> As violently as hasty powder fir'd
> Doth hurry from the fatal cannon's womb.
>
> (V, i, 60–5)

In the opening scene of the play Benvolio alludes to one of the medical applications of the theory of balanced forces; fevers are reduced by the application of heat, and a counter-irritant can be used to make the pain of a wound bearable:

> Tut, man, one fire burns out another's burning,
> One pain is less'ned by another's anguish.
>
> (I, ii, 45–6)

Benvolio is equating physical fire and pain with the spiritual fire and anguish of love, but new love, as well as driving out the old, also burns out the fire of hate, and the pain inflicted upon the Montagues and Capulets by the death of their children destroys the anguish inflicted upon the state by their strife.

Fire provides another thematic image in the familiar lines:

> Gallop apace, you fiery-footed steeds
> Towards Phoebus' lodging; such a waggoner
> As Phaethon would whip you to the west,
> And bring in cloudy night immediately.
>
> (III, ii, 1–4)

The Phaeton image is always ominous. In Marlowe's plays and in Shakespeare's early Histories[7] it exemplifies the glories and dangers of the aspiring mind, in other words, of *hubris*. In Juliet's speech the sun and Romeo are equated, but she has no patience with the progress of either. The sun's waggoner should be Phaeton, the reckless youth who destroyed himself by underestimating the forces he aspired to control

---

[7] For example, Richard II's "Down, down I come like glist'ring Phaethon,/Wanting the manage of unruly jades" (III, iii, 178–9).

and guide. Such was the fate of the lovers, as set forth in Brooke's comment on their story in his *Romeus and Juliet*.

The sea imagery of *Romeo and Juliet* is as varied as the watery element itself. The traditional identifications of the sea with life and with love are present, and the varying moods of the sea are used to differentiate characters or to indicate their development. Love promises the treasures of Eldorado to those who are willing to risk their all in the voyage into unknown seas. True and fancied love are distinguished by association with opposed aspects of the eternal and ever-changing sea. Romeo's love for Rosaline is, "Being vex'd, a sea nourish'd with loving tears" (I, i, 190). Capulet tries to tease his daughter out of her grief by comparing her, in a fully developed conceit, to a storm at sea:

> In one little body
> Thou counterfeit'st a bark, a sea, a wind;
> For still thy eyes, which I may call the sea,
> Do ebb and flow with tears. The bark thy body is,
> Sailing in this salt flood; the winds thy sighs,
> Who, raging with thy tears, and they with them,
> Without a sudden calm will overset
> Thy tempest-tossed body.
>
> (III, v, 130–7)

The "sudden calm" which he has arranged in order to save Juliet from being swamped by grief is, of course, the projected marriage to Paris which precipitates the catastrophe. But Capulet misunderstands his daughter as much as her situation, for her emblem is not the storm-tossed sea but the sea as provider of life. She "cannot sum up the sum of half" her love, and can compare it only to the sea:

> My bounty is as boundless as the sea,
> My love as deep: the more I give to thee
> The more I have, for both are infinite.
>
> (II, ii, 133–5)

To Romeo, his mistress embodies all the romance and riches of the new world:

> I am no pilot; yet, wert thou as far
> As that vast shore wash'd with the farthest sea,
> I should adventure for such merchandise.
>
> (II, ii, 82–4)

There is an ironic ambiguity in the lyric intensity of these lines, for the "vast shore wash'd with the farthest sea" is not only the *Terra Incognita* of the sea-discoverers; it is also the shore of "that undiscover'd country" to which Romeo will venture rather than live without his love. Love is a ship in the metaphor in which Romeo refers to the rope-ladder as the "tackled stair,"

> Which to the high top-gallant of my joy
> Must be my convoy in the secret night.
>
> (II, iv, 183–5)

Romeo is particularly fond of sea imagery. On the way back to Verona he speaks of his grief-stricken soul as "betossed"; on his arrival at the tomb he describes his passion as "savage-wild,"

> More fierce and more inexorable far
> Than empty tigers or the roaring sea.
>
> (V, iii, 38–9)

Romeo's development toward maturity and fatal independence is reflected in his various uses of the "pilot" metaphor and in his other references to supernatural guidance. While still the victim of the self-induced hypnosis of love-melancholy he shakes off a sense of impending doom with the conventionally pious ejaculation:

> But He that hath the steerage of my course
> Direct my sail!
>
> (I, iv, 112–13)

As true love changes him from a worshipper of darkness to a lover of light, so it rouses him from apathy to activity. He moves from boyhood to manhood, a process which is completed at Juliet's tomb when he addresses Paris as "boy," for Paris, who speaks his love "by the book" is the "double" of Romeo's former self. Romeo's wooing of Rosaline had similarly followed the course laid down by the code of courtly love; to win Juliet, however, he needs no seaman's skill, no chart of shoals or soundings. Love is guide enough.

> With love's light wings did I o'erperch these walls,
> For stony limits cannot hold love out;
> And what love can do, that dares love attempt.
>
> (II, ii, 66–8)

"By whose direction found'st thou out this place?" asks Juliet. "By love, that first did prompt me to enquire." Later in the same scene Romeo's "I am no pilot" confesses inexperience but again proclaims the self-sufficiency of love. The change is a sudden one. The Romeo of the first act is a weak-willed adolescent who indulges in emotional hypochondria and is a nuisance to himself, a worry to his family, and a jest to his friends. The Romeo of Act II is on his way to becoming a new man; he has undergone a conversion from the "religion" of the eye to the religion of the heart.

"Call me but love, and I'll be new baptiz'd (II, ii, 50) is perhaps not merely a witty response to Juliet's "Wherefore art thou Romeo?" but an unconscious recognition that he has been born again in love. Love may conquer all things, but in merging his whole identity with love, in regarding even such an earthly love as this not as a means to but as the equivalent of that perfect love which is heavenly, Romeo is guilty of something approaching a *hubris* of love. What he lacks is a sense of proportion, and Juliet shares in this excess. She is his "saint," he her "pilgrim" whose "rude hand" is blessed by her touch. He is the "god" of her "idolatry." Habitually, the lovers use the terminology of religion in speaking of their love. In defying death (II, vi, 7) and the stars (V, i, 24) Romeo also defies the gods. Friar Laurence warns him repeatedly that even virtuous passion must be guided and controlled by reason, the image of God in the soul of man. In asserting that love needs no pilot, Romeo casts off reason, the pilot of the will, and his shipwreck is therefore inevitable. It is an unconscious choice which is implied by the use of the pilot image in the balcony scene. In the next such reference, however, Romeo deliberately casts aside love in favour of rage as his guide to conduct, and in so doing he chooses the course of action which is certain to bring down disaster upon himself and Juliet. When the civility he has tendered to her cousin Tybalt has cost him his honour and his dearest friend his life, he cries out,

> Away to heaven respective lenity,
> And fire-ey'd fury be my conduct now!
>
> (III, i, 120–1)

In the last use of the pilot image, despair, symbolized by the poison, has become the guide. As he lifts the fatal draught to his lips, Romeo invokes it thus:

> Come, bitter conduct, come, unsavoury guide.
> Thou desperate pilot, now at once run on
> The dashing rocks thy sea-sick weary bark.
>
> (V, iii, 116–18)

The major images drawn from the spheres of influence of earth, air, fire, and water are gathered up and woven, with variations, into a contrapuntal accompaniment to the catastrophe. Paris sounds the opening note with his "Sweet flower, with flowers thy bridal bed I strew," as Romeo enters bringing with him the poison which is to operate as "violently as hasty powder fir'd / Doth hurry from the fatal cannon's womb." Romeo then attempts to force the "jaws" of the tomb, that "detestable maw," that "womb of death." When Paris attempts to restrain him they fight, and Paris is slain. When Romeo discovers that his *alter ego* is one "writ with him in sour misfortune's book," he promises him the only atonement in his power:

> I'll bury thee in a triumphant grave.
> A grave? O no! A lantern, slaught'red youth;
> For here lies Juliet, and her beauty makes
> This vault a feasting presence,[8] full of light.
> Death, lie thou there, by a dead man interr'd.
> How oft when men are at the point of death
> Have they been merry! Which their keepers call
> A lightning before death. O, how may I
> Call this a lightning?[9] O my love! my wife!
> Death, that hath suck'd the honey of thy breath,
> Hath had no power yet upon thy beauty.
> Thou art not conquer'd; beauty's ensign yet
> Is crimson in thy lips and in thy cheeks,
> And death's pale flag is not advanced there. . . .
> . . . Ah, dear Juliet,
> Why art thou yet so fair? Shall I believe
> That unsubstantial Death is amorous,
> And that the lean abhorred monster keeps
> Thee here in dark to be his paramour? . . .
> . . . here will I remain
> With worms that are thy chambermaids. O, here
> Will I set up my everlasting rest,
> And shake the yoke of inauspicious stars
> From this world-wearied flesh. Eyes, look your last.
> Arms, take your last embrace. And, lips, O you
> The doors of breath, seal with a righteous kiss
> A dateless bargain to engrossing death!
> Come, bitter conduct, come, unsavoury guide.
> Thou desperate pilot, now at once run on
> The dashing rocks thy sea-sick weary bark.
> Here's to my love! O true apothecary!
> Thy drugs are quick. Thus with a kiss I die.[10]
>
> (V, iii, 83–120)

[8]The "lantern," a tower with openings on all sides, was usually the highest portion of the main body of the church building, in contrast to the underground crypt where the great were usually buried. Frequently, the lantern was located directly over the transept crossing, where, in front of the roodscreen, mass was customarily served to the laity. "Feasting presence" may, therefore, be taken as an allusion to the "real presence" of the body of Christ in the mass-bread, especially as the play exhibits, throughout, the usual Renaissance fusion of Christian and Platonic concepts of "heavenly love." A reference to the presence chamber of the queen, to which only the favoured were admitted, is also a possibility.

[9]The words recall Juliet's "too like the lightning" (II, ii, 119).

[10]The line contains a double equivocation. The first is an allusion to the "quick and the dead": the apothecary's drugs are "quick" in bringing death. The second is the usual sexual pun, as unmistakable here as in the "I must be gone and live, or stay and die" of the *aubade*.

Juliet's final speech, in keeping with her contention that "Conceit, more rich in matter than in words, / Brags of his substance, not of ornament" (II, vi, 30), is briefer than Romeo's though equally paradoxical in its imagery. The Friar sees her stir, then wake. She addresses him as "O comfortable friar!" though all the comfort he can give her is the sorrowful summons,

> . . . Lady, come from that nest
> Of death, contagion, and unnatural sleep;
> A greater power than we can contradict
> Hath thwarted our intents. Come, come away;
> Thy husband in thy bosom there lies dead.
>
> (V, iii, 151–5)

But Juliet turns to the body of her husband with the words,

> What's here? A cup, clos'd in my true love's hand?
> Poison, I see, hath been his timeless end.
> O churl! drunk all, and left no friendly drop
> To help me after? I will kiss thy lips;
> Haply some poison yet doth hang on them,
> To make me die with a restorative.
>
> (V, iii, 161–6)

Interrupted by a noise outside the tomb, she stabs herself with Romeo's dagger and dies.

The long coda which conveys the tragic reconciliation brings us round again to the theme announced in the Prologue to Act I. It is formally stated by the Prince, who is the spokesman of civil as the Friar is of spiritual order. Having called upon those present to

> Seal up the mouth of outrage for a while,
> Till we can clear these ambiguities,
> And know their spring, their head, their true descent,[11]
>
> (V, iii, 215–17)

he learns from the Friar that the rival houses have as he had foretold (I, i, 91) quenched the fire of their "pernicious rage" with "purple fountains issuing from" their "veins"—in other words, have quenched

---

[11]The upward and downward connotations of "spring" and "descent" are in keeping with the death-resurrection tone of the final scenes, and there may be a suggestion of the regenerative power of "spring" also. Shakespeare is never the one to miss a chance at a paradox combined with a triple meaning at the risk of tautology.

their "blood"[12] with the blood of their own "blood."[13] He then summons the fathers:

> Where be these enemies? Capulet, Montague,
> See what a scourge is laid upon your hate,
> That heaven finds means to kill your joys with love!
>
> (V, iii, 290–2)

The repentant Capulet then uses the terminology of a marriage contract to indicate that love, in destroying their "joys," has also destroyed their hate:

> O brother Montague, give me thy hand.
> This is my daughter's jointure, for no more
> Can I demand.
>
> (V, iii, 295–7)

Montague's offer to erect a golden statue of Juliet as a monument to their reconciliation is countered by Capulet's offer of a "dowry":

> As rich shall Romeo's by his lady's lie—
> Poor sacrifices of our enmity!
>
> (V, iii, 302–3)

The key word is sacrifice, for the play can indeed be regarded as an adaptation of the archetypal myth in which youth and maiden are sacrified for the peace and fertility of the state. Such an interpretation is supported by the ubiquitous fertility imagery, by the prevalence of overt and latent sexual ambiguities, and by the religious imagery of the lovers, as well as by the emphasis on the forces of life and regeneration in the death scene. In this view of the play, Friar Laurence becomes the officiating priest who administers the sacrificial draught. Inadvertently, a priest is also responsible for Romeo's drinking of the fatal hemlock, and Juliet's seizing of Romeo's knife makes complete the voluntary acquiescence of the victims which was considered essential to the efficacy of the rite. The ceremony concludes with the Prince's acceptance of the sacrifice on behalf of the community.

But the play's imagery also exemplifies the maintenance of order by means of conflict and the paradoxes which that process involves, as it demonstrates Shakespeare's concern with the interrelationships of private and public order and with the interaction of good and evil in the microcosm of the individual, the larger world of the state, and the universal macrocosm. The innocent victims of private enmity and

[12]In the sense of Othello's "My blood begins my safer guides to rule" (II, iii, 197).

[13]In the sense of the Prince's "My blood for your rude brawls doth lie a-bleeding" (III, i, 186).

public disorder are indeed star-crossed in that these forces, though not directed against them, cause the opposed forces of love and order to be "misapplied" in such a way as to bring about their downfall. Every well-meaning action of parents, priest, and prince has disastrous consequences for them. Romeo's interference in the duel and Juliet's refusal to marry Paris are similarly fated. Yet this is only one side of the general paradox. Out of these private evils the "greater power" which thwarted human intents has brought about, by means of the love which Plato termed "the mediator between gods and men," the general good.

Though the "elemental strife" of matter and of external nature dominates the thematic imagery of the play, other elements are at war in it also; in particular, opposed views of love and of art, and the oppositions of art and artifice, love and fancy, are often juxtaposed. This is often overlooked, and the critical estimation of the play suffers from the widespread assumption that an early tragedy which treats of the woes of immature lovers must itself be immature. Derek Traversi's attitude is typical. He dismisses the play as "a tragedy at once 'literary,' artificial, and profoundly sentimental," in which "Formal considerations . . . prevail over the full development of emotion, and the elaborate verbal pattern corresponds to considerations that are primarily literary and rhetorical, and only in a very secondary sense personal."[14] "Profoundly sentimental" is a paradox worthy of Shakespeare himself; how does one reconcile the profundity with the sentimentality? Part of our difficulty in expressing an unequivocal evaluation of *Romeo and Juliet* is that all the words we have to describe the particular sort of love which it celebrates are tarnished by overuse. "Simplicity," and "sentiment," and "romance" no longer mean what they once did; they are debased coinage and we have nothing to replace them. For the Elizabethan audience, the love of Romeo and Juliet represented an ideal already familiar to them from the poems of Spenser. It was a love which reconciled the opposition of flesh and spirit in Christian marriage. Like so many sixteenth-century ideals, however, it also represents a realistic reaction against traditional ideals—in this instance the artificial and exaggerated idealizations of the code of courtly love and the excessive spiritualization of sexual relationships in the more extreme versions of Platonic love. It represents a reaction, also, against the strictly practical attitude in which, with complete disregard for the emotions of the individuals concerned, marriage became an instrument of financial, political, or social "policy." In spite of protests against

[14]See *An Approach to Shakespeare* (London: Sands and Co., 1937, 1957), pp. 17, 18.

"the miseries of enforc'd marriage" it was still true that most matches between young persons of any consequence were arranged by their parents on a basis of supposed mutual advantage rather than personal inclination.

It is perhaps appropriate to consider briefly here Shakespeare's treatment of love in this play and elsewhere. As matter is compounded of the four basic elements of earth, air, fire, and water, and the body of the four humours, so love has its fourfold composition. For Shakespeare the four elements of love would seem to be passion, devotion, reason, and faith, each of which has its characteristic manifestation of excess and defect. The excess of passion is lust, the defect frigidity; the excess of devotion servility, the defect neglect; the excess of reason "policy," the defect folly; the excess of faith "fondness" or "doting," the defect jealousy. In perfect love these elements are found in perfect balance, though true love is not incompatible with a slight excess or defect of one element or another, provided that the imbalance is not such as to produce serious disorder. Whether in their own loves or in their attitude to the loves of others, Shakespeare's characters illustrate many of the possible combinations of these elements.

The division into types is most marked in *As You Like It*, where Silvius demonstrates servility, Phebe scorn or neglect; Touchstone and Audrey lechery, somewhat mitigated in Touchstone's case by "policy," which is in turn restrained by Jacques' reason. Rosalind's love approaches something like an ideal combination of elements, and in the marriage of Oliver and Celia the "policy" is Shakespeare's rather than the lovers. Leontes is an obvious example of defective, Desdemona of excessive faith; Hamlet's attitude towards the physical aspect of love is one of revulsion, while to Iago love is nothing but "a lust of the eye and a permission of the will." Parents are usually representatives of "policy" in their attitude to love. The characteristic imbalances of love appear also in *Romeo and Juliet*. Romeo's first love is excessive in devotion to one who would not "love for love allow," his second somewhat defective in reason. The Nurse's bias is indicated by her consoling remark to Juliet regarding Paris's marriage proposal:

> Your first is dead, or 'twere as good he were
> As living here and you no use of him.
>
> (III, v, 225–6)

Capulet, who as the fond father of Act I had recognized the importance of his daughter's inclination in choice of a husband, changes his ground in Act III when piqued by her rejection of his carefully planned surprise. He makes a statement of the "politic" view of marriage:

God's bread! it makes me mad:
. . . and having now provided
A gentleman of noble parentage,
Of fair demesnes, youthful, and nobly train'd,
Stuff'd, as they say, with honourable parts,
Proportion'd as one's thought would wish a man—
And then to have a wretched puling fool,
A whining mammet, in her fortune's tender,
To answer, 'I'll not wed, I cannot love,
I am too young, I pray you pardon me'!

                                                    (III, v, 176–87)

The lovers are not idealized into perfection; they are human beings with human weaknesses. Romeo is rash, sometimes silly, and occasionally weak. Juliet is impatient, and on occasion can be saucy, stubborn, and inconsiderate. They are very young people very much in love—or, from another point of view, self-willed adolescents rebellious against all authority. This latter was the view of their story which Arthur Brooke inherited and enshrined in the preface to his poem, but forgot about when he began to tell the tale of their tragic love.

Young as they are, it should not be forgotten that, in any but strictly chronological terms, they are not as young as they would be in the twentieth century, as Paris's "Younger than she are happy mothers made" and Lady Capulet's "I was your mother much upon these years / That you are now a maid" make clear. When the play opens Romeo is old enough to be considered a responsible human being who comes and goes as he sees fit, and Juliet grows into maturity during the course of it. To regard the lovers, star-crossed though they are, merely as pathetic children who are the pawns of destiny, to ignore the implications of Juliet's impatience with time and Romeo's headlong rashness, is to do less than justice to this paradoxical tragedy in which the intensity of passion contributes to the catastrophe, but in conquering the opposed passion of hate makes the grave, in Romeo's word, "triumphant."

The charge that *Romeo and Juliet* is "at once literary and artificial" is more difficult to refute, but again the question is one of purpose. It is obvious to the most casual reader that there are two poetic styles in this play and that one of them is literary and artificial in the extreme. The other takes two forms which are closely related but not identical— the lyric and the tighter, more swiftly-paced dramatic. A similar mingling of lyric and dramatic styles is found in *Richard II*, where it is equally appropriate to the theme. It is the emotionally heightened language of the lyric passages and the conscious over-elaboration of the rhetorical ones which are incongruous with each other. I find it difficult to believe that Shakespeare's ear was so defective as not to know that they were incongruous, and there is ample indication that the incongruity was intentional, its purpose to satirize affectation in language and in love. We have seen this double target attacked before —in *Love's Labour's Lost*.

To be certain that the ancient devices of oxymoron and hyperbolic conceit are being satirized we have only to notice where they are to be found. They appear, as they continue to do in the later plays, in the formal speeches and proclamations of rulers, to whom the dignity of a traditional style is appropriate. They appear, as in Lady Capulet's comparison of Paris to a book (I, iii, 82–93), and her husband's comparison of Juliet's grief to a storm at sea (III, v, 130–7), in the speeches of older people who fancy themselves as having had a pretty turn of phrase when they "heard the chimes at midnight" some twenty or thirty years previously, of people who may be expected to be out of sympathy with the new ways—in language or in love. They also appear in the early speeches of Romeo, where their artificiality is an outward and audible sign of the inward and spiritual sterility of his infatuation with Rosaline. They fade away slowly in the first conversation of Romeo and Juliet at the ball, where they are suited to the formality of the occasion. But once Romeo "loves and is loved again" he discards most of his rhetorical mannerisms. He suffers a brief relapse, to be sure, when, after Tybalt's death and his own banishment, despair has momentarily undermined the maturity he has found in Juliet's love. Here his excesses of speech are a sign of emotional disorder, as Juliet's are when she hears the news of the same events. That such language is to be regarded as the reverse of admirable is indicated by the fact that both the Nurse and the Friar berate Romeo for speaking in a style unbecoming a "man." Juliet, who has never been the victim of a self-induced, artificial passion, never uses the artificial language appropriate to such emotion except when, at the ball, she shows that she can match Romeo at his own game of conversation on a high poetic level, and when she too is plunged into despair at the news of Tybalt's death. Almost immediately, however, she recovers her native good sense and accuses herself of disloyalty in having so "mangled" her husband's name. Romeo's change of language is so complete once he knows that his love is returned that Paris must be brought in to play the part, and speak the speeches, of the young man in love with love. Throughout the serious scenes of the play—for the wit-combats of Mercutio and his friends must be excepted—"strain'd touches" of rhetoric and "precious phrase" are associated with the inferior, the artificial, and especially the outmoded.

Mercutio has been neglected in this discussion but on this point he is the witness whose testimony should prove decisive. For all his scintillating wit, his extravagant flights of fancy, Mercutio is the realist, even, as Enobarbus is in *Antony and Cleopatra*, the "ironist" of the play. One of his functions is to make fun of affectation, and especially of affectation in love and war. In the early scenes, the chief target of his wit is Romeo's callow infatuation with Rosaline: he is not aware of Romeo's love for Juliet, and his "A plague on both your houses!" has reference only to the feud between them. It is the artificiality of Romeo's speech which seems most to amuse Mercutio and, from his comments, we may conclude that the excessive use of rhyme, and the insertion of whole sonnets into the dialogue in the earlier scenes of the play are a part of the conscious burlesquing of such artificiality. The first of these taunts comes in the well-known conjuration speech:

> Romeo! humours! madman! passion! lover!
> Appear thou in the likeness of a sigh;
> Speak but one rhyme and I am satisfied;
> Cry but 'Ay me!' pronounce but 'love' and 'dove';
> Speak to my gossip Venus one fair word,
> One nick-name for her purblind son and heir,
> Young Adam Cupid, ...
>
> (II, i, 7–13)

In Act II, scene iv, Romeo is still being sought for, and until he appears Mercutio contents himself with mocking Tybalt's affectations of speech. On seeing the young lover approach, however, he returns to his favorite subject:

> Now is he for the numbers that Petrarch flow'd in. Laura, to his lady, was a kitchen-wench—marry, she had a better love to berhyme her; Dido, a dowdy; Cleopatra, a gypsy; Helen and Hero, hildings and harlots; Thisbe, a gray eye or so, but not to the purpose.
>
> (II, iv, 38–42)

The devices of style we may expect to be burlesqued, therefore, are hyperbole, excessive or inappropriate use of rhyme, stock rhymes, stock epithets and stock classical allusions, and the Petrarchan conceit.

If we accept the view that the highly artificial style found in the early scenes of the play is intended as satiric parody, we must ask ourselves in how far the style of the rest of the play can be acquitted of the charge of being "literary." In the passage cited Traversi uses the term as meaning that poetic effects do not arise naturally out of character or situation. It must be admitted that even in the later scenes of *Romeo and Juliet* Shakespeare is occasionally guilty of "fine writing." But did he ever free himself completely from this weakness? Polonius' precepts, even if they are taken from the commonplace books, make pretty good practical sense for a "wretched, rash, intruding fool," and "honest" Iago's dissertation on the theme of "Who steals my purse steals trash . . . " cannot be said to come from the heart. Certainly contemporary audiences did not expect complete consistency in these matters, and Shakespeare had the best possible literary precedent and critical authority for putting fine speeches into the mouths of characters with whose natures the views expressed are inconsistent. In his commentary on *The Iliads*, Chapman defends the practice of Homer in giving speeches of "good sentence" to foolish Menelaus:

Nor useth our most inimitable imitator of nature (Homer) this cross and deformed mixture of his (Menelaus') parts, more to colour and avoid too broad a taxation of so eminent a person, than to follow the true life of nature, being often, or always, expressed so disparent in her creatures. And therefore the decorum that some poor critics have stood upon to make fools always foolish, cowards at all times cowardly, etc., is far from the *variant order of nature, whose principle being contrary, her productions must needs contain the like opposition.*

Such licence would amply cover such minor aberrations as Romeo's moralizing advice to the apothecary, one of the passages open to criticism as a piece of "fine writing" out of character. As for his description of the apothecary's shop, regarded as an extraneous intrusion into a dramatic moment, this is surely nothing more than verbal scene-painting.

Clemen[15] finds Juliet's pre-potion imaginings distressingly over-elaborate. But surely this elaboration is something more than a survival of Senecan sensationalism. In that it is justifiable under the circumstances of Juliet's situation and indeed arises directly from them, this premonition of horrors and the heightened language in which it is expressed are "dramatic" rather than "literary." "He jests at scars that never felt a wound!" Emphasis here is not only completely in character with the vivid imagination of the adolescent under stress, but is dramatically necessary. "My dismal scene I needs must act alone." Where is the victory if the scene does not seem to her very dismal indeed?

[15]*The Development of Shakespeare's Imagery* (London: Methuen, 1951), p. 73.

Nor, with the possible exception of Romeo's star-conceit in II, ii, 15, is the language of the love-scenes "ornamental" in the earlier "rhetorical" style. The substance of these scenes is the "overflow of powerful feelings," to which the emotionally heightened language of the lyric style is perhaps more appropriate than the realistic intensity of the dramatic. As for Juliet's "take him and cut him out in little stars . . . ," although a fully-developed conceit the speech is appropriate to the emotion of the speaker. To Juliet, Romeo is all "fire," the supreme element. Even after death, when the air of breath and the "fire" of the soul have left the "earth" and "water" of the body, that body will still retain so much of the radiance of Romeo's spirit that the most minute particles of it would out-dazzle the very stars. And how well the juxtaposition of images in this passage illustrates the precise state of Juliet's development at this moment—standing with anything but reluctant feet "where the brook and river meet": the "little stars" reminiscent of the little girl cutting pretty patterns out of discarded bits of cloth, companioned by the summoning of the matron, Night, to teach the initiatory rites of "true love acted."

Yet even in the love-scenes—for all their conscious lyricism—more often than not the images appear to have the Shakespearean "inevitability," to arise naturally from the situation and from the character of the speaker, to be, in other words, integrated with the dramatic action. As previously noted, Romeo's apostrophes to Juliet as "the sun" and as "bright angel" are not just examples of exaggerated sonnetese; they point up, respectively, the contrast between the darkness and artificiality of the old love and the radiant truth of the new one, as well as underlining the almost religious intensity of Romeo's adoration. Similarly the Phaeton image, though trite, as used by Juliet is the perfect symbol of her impatience, her youth, and the fatal issue of the play. The lyric tone of such passages is not that of the conventional Petrarchists or of Shakespeare's own earlier sonnets; it is the vivid, strongly connotative, often equivocal tone of the later ones, the note of Shakespeare's maturity.

Often we find this lyric imagery associated with the homely and familiar but nonetheless vivid imagery of the later dramatic style, the contrast intensifying the effectiveness of both. A classic instance is Hamlet's protest against his mother's "frailty" in remarrying within

> A little month, or ere those shoes were old
> With which she followed my poor father's body,
> Like Niobe, all tears. . . .

(I, ii, 147–9)

A similar contrast occurs in the "epithalamion," where the "stars" passage is followed immediately by the lines:

> O, I have bought the mansion of a love,
> But not possess'd it; and though I am sold,
> Not yet enjoy'd. So tedious is this day
> As is the night before some festival
> To an impatient child that hath new robes,
> And may not wear them.
>
> (III, ii, 26–31)

The final image is completely appropriate to the speaker's character, her age, and her situation, and expresses with the utmost vividness the eagerness and impatience of her love; yet it is neither elaborate nor decorative, but homely and intimate.

According to Shakespeare,[16] the function of the imagination—for the Elizabethans still, literally, the image-making faculty—is to bring together things disparate in nature; to associate the abstract with the concrete, the rare with the commonplace, the remote with the familiar, the intellectual with the physical. In so doing, the image illuminates and intensifies meaning by presenting it from a new point of view or in a new light, by setting the particular in the context of the universal and giving immediacy to the universal in terms of the particular. This two-way movement is strongly in evidence in *Romeo and Juliet*. Not only does the dominant imagery reflect the duality of general Nature in particular events; many individual images demonstrate the process in reverse, describing general phenomena in terms of the daily life of the individual. In the epithalamion, Juliet calls upon night not as a dark queen who presides over mysteries, but as if she were issuing an hospitable invitation to a familiar and respected guest:

> Come, civil night,
> Thou sober-suited matron, all in black,
> And learn me how to lose a winning match,
> Play'd for a pair of stainless maidenhoods;
> Hood my unmann'd blood, bating in my cheeks,
> With thy black mantle, till strange love, grown bold,
> Think true love acted simple modesty. . . .
> Come, gentle night, come, loving black-brow'd night,
> Give me my Romeo.
>
> (III, ii, 10–21)

This addressing of night as a respectable matron, a kind of preceptress in the rites of marriage, though abating no whit of Juliet's eagerness, gives it a kind of social *cachet*, takes away from it any imputation of

[16] *A Midsummer Night's Dream*, V, i, 7–17.

lasciviousness; it fits perfectly the mood of "true love acted simple modesty." The effect is similar to that of Cleopatra's use of the simple epithet in her death cry,

> Husband, I come.
> Now to that name my courage prove my title!
>
> (V, ii, 285–6)

Similarly vivid and intimate effects are achieved by the use of simple and homely images in such lines as:

> . . . fleck'led darkness like a drunkard reels
>
> (II, iii, 3)

and

> Night's candles are burnt out, and jocund day
> Stands tiptoe on the misty mountain tops.
>
> (III, v, 9–10)

Juliet, awaiting the Nurse's return, marks the length of her vigil with

> Now is the sun upon the highmost hill
> Of this day's journey; and from nine to twelve
> Is three long hours, ...
>
> (II, v, 9)

It is a simple, even a commonplace image on the surface, but, like so many of Shakespeare's images, it has subtle overtones of meaningful suggestion. It is not only the noon of day but also the noon of love for Juliet—the high point of anticipation immediately preceding the realization of marriage, the "little moment" for which love, in common with "everything that grows," "holds in perfection." In Sonnet 60, Shakespeare associates the progress of the sun with the cycle of life from birth to death:

> Nativity, once in the main of light,
> Crawls to maturity, wherewith being crown'd,
> Crooked eclipses 'gainst his glory fight,
> And Time that gave doth now his gift confound.

Similarly, Donne compares the course of love to the daily course of the sun in the lines:

> Love is a growing, or full constant light;
> And his first minute, after noone, is night.
>
> ("A Lecture upon the Shadow")

Noon is, therefore, a symbol of mixed connotations: it is the high point of achievement and the portent of inevitable decline and death.

Juliet finds that her wedding-day "crawls to maturity," as her life has been a slow progress to the maturity of fulfilment in marriage; her use of the "noon-highmost hill" image is one of Shakespeare's ways of preparing the mood of his audience for the "crooked eclipses" and the brief afternoon to come.

Not only cosmic phenomena but the most intense of human emotions are expressed in metaphors drawn from the familiar activities, the sports and pastimes of everyday life. The Prologue, giving the "argument" of Act II, tells us that the lovers will "steal love's sweet bait from fearful hooks," reminding us of Donne's elaboration of a similar conceit in his reworking of the "Come Live with Me . . ." theme of Marlowe's pastoral lyric in "The Bait." On her second visit to the Friar, the desperate Juliet pleads:

> Give me some present counsel; or, behold
> 'Twixt my extremes and me this bloody knife
> Shall play the umpire, arbitrating that
> Which the commission of thy years and art
> Could to no issue of true honour bring.
>
> (IV, i, 61–5)

Here again is the characteristic note of Shakespeare's mature style, the expression of emotional intensity or intellectual complexity in terms of the concrete object or the familiar experience—the "local habitation" and the "name."

One cannot pretend that the imagery of *Romeo and Juliet* is consistently mature. Certainly Juliet's "O serpent heart, hid with a flowering face!" (III, ii, 73) belongs with "O tiger's heart wrapt in a woman's hide!" After Greene's jibe at that line, however, Shakespeare could hardly have written the words, or the formal catalogue of opposites which follows them, without his tongue in his cheek. Then why does he give to Juliet, in a high dramatic moment, a speech (III, ii, 43–84) which parallels in style the obvious parody of Romeo's

> Why then, O brawling love! O loving hate!
> O anything, of nothing first create!
> O heavy lightness! serious vanity!
> Mis-shapen chaos of well-seeming forms!
> Feather of lead, bright smoke, cold fire, sick health!
> Still-waking sleep, that is not what it is!
>
> (I, i, 174–9)

It is frequently a trait of Shakespeare's characters that they change their style of speech under emotional stress. Hamlet babbles nonsense-jingles and applies disrespectful epithets to his father's ghost. The

plausibly devious Claudius becomes forthright, the tongue-tied Gert-
rude and the heavy-tongued Horatio wax lyrical, and the modest
Ophelia tosses off bawdy speeches. Even the blunt, cynical wit of
Enobarbus gives way to sheer poetry on occasion, notably when he
describes "The barge she sat in . . ." and addresses the moon as "sovran
mistress of true melancholy." When the Nurse informs Juliet of Tybalt's
death we have already heard her speak as the witty Juliet, the forthright Juliet, and the lyric Juliet, as the dramatic situation has required.
How else than by the artificiality of her language can Shakespeare
show that she has, for the moment, lost touch with the reality of love,
that her emotions are not, at this point, well-tempered but bitterly at
war, and that disappointment and despair have won out, temporarily,
over reason, that she is not, in other words, herself. The Friar's comments on Romeo's excessively emotional speeches in the next scene
explain in part these violent changes of style. He who goes to such
extremes of language is temporarily insane, he has lost the use of his
reason.

> Hold thy desperate hand.
> Art thou a man? thy form cries out thou art:
> Thy tears are womanish; thy wild acts denote
> The unreasonable fury of a beast. . . .
> Thou hast amaz'd me. By my holy order,
> I thought thy disposition better temper'd. . . .
> Why railest thou on thy birth, the heaven, and earth?
> Since birth, and heaven, and earth, all three do meet
> In thee at once; which thou at once wouldst lose.
> Fie, fie! thou sham'st thy shape, thy love, thy wit;
> Which, like a userer, abound'st in all,
> And usest none in that true use indeed,
> Which should bedeck thy shape, thy love, thy wit.
>   (III, iii, 108–25)

In these, as in the opening scenes of the play, excessively heightened
language is not an attempt to give poetic expression to intense and
sincere emotion by means of the sheer weight and mass of rhetorical
flourishes, but the representation in language of a lapse from the
emotionally good, true, and beautiful.

Romeo and Juliet is a play of transition not because it mingles new
and old styles but because it shows us, in conjunction, the death of the
old and the birth of the new. "The date is out of such prolixity" says
Shakespeare, with Benvolio (II, iv, 3), and with Juliet, "Conceit, more
rich in matter than in words, / Brags of his substance, not of ornament"
(II, vi, 30–1). This play is his declaration of independence, in which

he publicly casts off the old, familiar, but no longer adequate tradition and indicates the course he intends to follow in shaping a new one. Approaching the noon of life and dissatisfied, as the Sonnets show, with the achievement of its morning, Shakespeare sets out in *Romeo and Juliet* to write a new kind of tragedy in a new poetic style, a romantic tragedy involving not royal or politically important figures but the upper or upper-middle class lovers he had used in comedy. It is a tragedy based on contrasts: the old tradition is set off against the new in both love and poetry; youth is opposed by age, new love by old hate. Everywhere allegiance is given to the new, the old expressly repudiated. It is a tragedy of paradoxes and contradictions, of the "spite of fortune," of the strange compounds of the warring elements of nature and of life expressed in the "compounds strange" of the new poetic style. It reflects the composition of matter and the riddles of life in being itself a compound of contrasting tones and moods—the tragic and the comic, the lyric and the satiric, the romantic and realistic, the sentimental and the philosophical. This is no isolated experiment in sentimental tragedy, but one of the upper reaches of the main stream of Shakespeare's tragic comment on man, life, and nature. In *Romeo and Juliet* the sun of his poetic and dramatic achievement has begun to climb the crest of the "highmost hill of his day's journey" and is a growing, if not yet a "full, constant light."

V

Twelfth Night in *Twelfth Night*

To every thing there is a season, and a time to every
purpose under the heaven.

(Ecclesiastes 3:1)

THE "NOON" OF SHAKESPEARE'S COMEDY, after which "the first minute" is
the "night" of tragedy, is represented by *Twelfth Night*. John Dover
Wilson's estimate of it as "the most exquisite of all Shakespeare's
comedies"[1] echoes the consensus of generations of readers, critics, and
audiences. Yet the play's theme, like that of its nearest rival for pre-
eminence, *The Tempest*, is the inversion of values and of appearance
and reality which is also the dominant theme of the tragedies, and the
links between this, perhaps the happiest of the comedies, and *King
Lear*, perhaps the most sombre of the tragedies, are many.

As has been indicated in an earlier chapter, Shakespeare's dramatic
and poetic approach to the contraries of human existence is, in the
poems and early plays, to define such oppositions and stress the conflict
between them. Usually, harmony is restored only when one excess
destroys another. In the middle plays, however, the thematic emphasis
lies not only upon those inversions of nature which are unnatural and
therefore monstrous, but also upon the necessity of accepting, as essential to the harmony of the whole, those elements physical and emotional
which are conventionally denigrated as inferior to the rational and
spiritual, if not as wholly subversive of order. In these plays the
divisive attitude of the Sonnets is gone; flesh and the passions must be
recognized as having their place in man's nature and as contributing to
his well-being. Man's felicity may depend upon his control of these
instincts but he denies them at his peril. "Banish plump Jack and

[1]*Shakespeare's Happy Comedies* (London: Faber and Faber, 1962), p. 163.

banish all the world!" Reason should guide, not suppress emotion, and should allow it to exercise its proper functions as a citizen of the human microcosm, lest the soul suffer "the nature of an insurrection," fatal unless the parties can be reconciled, as Hamlet and Othello discover.

One method of control is provided by the "safety-valve" mechanism. Occasionally the lower classes of man's inner commonwealth must be provided with circuses as well as bread, must be indulged as well as dieted, for balances can be restored by purgation through excess as well as by restraint, and this is the purpose of all festivals.

Even if we must render a Scottish verdict of "not proven" on J. Leslie Hotson's contention that *Twelfth Night* received its first performance at court on January 6, 1600–1,[2] it seems wholly appropriate that Shakespeare should give to his comic treatment of the theme of inverted values a title which reminds his audience that once a year, at least, "rude will" is licensed to take precedence over "grace" and disorder to rule with the full approval of the whole company of revellers, including the audience. C. L. Barber's *Shakespeare's Festive Comedy* draws attention to the Saturnalian associations of comedy from its beginning and establishes the persistence of the tradition in Elizabethan drama: "The saturnalian pattern appears in many variations, all of which involve inversion, statement and counter-statement, and a basic movement which can be summarized in the formula, through release to clarification."[3] Many of these "variations" appear in *Twelfth Night*, as the action moves from disorder to order through a succession of inversions—social, sexual, intellectual, emotional, and ethical—of which the discomfiture of Malvolio, the spokesman of conventional order, is only one. But Shakespeare's awareness of the implications of his title and its appropriateness to his theme is not limited to the carnival concept of tolerated misrule, though repeated allusions to the various seasonal festivals[4] associated with one or another form of "misrule" make his consciousness of this aspect obvious. Twelfth Night, however much its observance in sixteenth-century England may have reflected the excesses of the Roman winter festivals and earlier pagan rites associated with the December solstice, is the Christian feast of the Epiphany as well as a Christmas carnival. As a religious festival it celebrates, at the

---

[2]*The First Night of Twelfth Night* (London: Rupert Hart-Davis, 1954).
[3]*Shakespeare's Festive Comedy* (Princeton University Press, 1959), p. 4.
[4]For a full description of the customs associated with such festivals, and especially with their dramatic aspects, see E. K. Chambers, *The Medieval Stage* (Oxford: Clarendon Press, 1903), vol. I, Book II, pp. 89–390.

departure of the world's sun, the double revelation of the "Light of the World" in Christ's baptism and his "showing forth" to the Kings of the East guided to his birthplace by the light of the Star of Bethlehem. This aspect of the festival is stressed in the "clarification" towards which the romantic action of the play moves and which is a revelation of love. The themes of disorder and love, and of disorder in love, are set in a seasonal frame of reference. Repeated allusions to time and season and to light and darkness, along with a pervasive if half-realized undertone of gentle melancholy which sets off the mirth by its foil, remind the audience that if "there is a time for laughter" at the follies of disorder there is also "a time for weeping"—but not yet. Not until "our play is done."

By the end of the sixteenth century some of the traditional Twelfth Night revels had begun to fall into disuse, partly because of the general decay of lavish "housekeeping," partly because of Puritan attacks upon them as pagan survivals. It is perhaps with that opposition in mind that Shakespeare makes Maria refer to Malvolio as "sometimes . . . a kind of Puritan" (II, iii, 131). Among the Saturnalian customs the most persistent was the turning upside down of the social hierarchy to obliterate, for one day or more, the distinction between master and servant.[5] The Roman King of the Saturnalia has as his descendant the medieval and Renaissance "Christmas Lord" or "Lord of Misrule," who reigned at court until the accession of Mary, and in country and town houses, university colleges, and inns of court until well into the next century.[6] The reign of the Lord of Misrule extended throughout the Christmas season, and in the inns of court and the universities might be prolonged until Candlemas, a festival which, like Christmas, has its origins in a pagan festival of the sun, and which, like Twelfth Night, was celebrated with masques, mummings, disguisings, plays, and pageants. It was at such a revel at the Middle Temple that the first recorded performance of *Twelfth Night* took place on February 2, 1602. The office of the Prince of Christmas was distinct from that of the Master of the Revels,[7] whose duty it was to see that licence did not exceed the extremely liberal limits of tolerance as well as to act as master of ceremonies and producer of a variety of entertainments. The

[5]It is still customary, in the great houses of England, for the master and his family to dance with the servants at the annual Staff Party held for them on Boxing Day. My publisher's reader comments: "I have stayed at two large urban hotels in the west of England where, on Old Christmas Day, the owners and management served the employees and catered at a dance and feasting."

[6]See Chambers, *The Medieval Stage*, I, 403–19.

[7]*Ibid.*, p. 405.

Lord of Misrule directed the mummings and more boisterous kinds of foolery, with the privilege of imposing forfeits upon any rebellious subject who might refuse to obey his commands. He was invested "with that title," according to Sir Thomas Urquhart "to no other end, but to countenance the Bacchanalian riots and preposterous disorders of the family where he is installed."[8] In the play, his role is assigned to Sir Toby Belch as Twelfth Night King, with Maria as his Queen, Feste the clown being cast as Master of the Revels, as his name implies. The chief function of the Lord of Misrule was to add to the festive mirth by "befooling" every member of the company in one way or another, and, what with love and disguises, false challenges and forged letters, Feste, Sir Toby, and his companions manage to prove most of the characters in the play fools before the play is out.

Another folk amusement laid under contribution in *Twelfth Night* is the popular debate between Summer and Winter, which takes literary form in Nashe's pageant-play *Summer's Last Will and Testament*. Here, "Summer" is not merely the season, but also the ghost of Will Sommers, the famous clown of Henry VIII's court, played, at the first performance, by an actor named Toy.[9] Shakespeare's familiarity with the folk-customs which inspired Nashe, if not with Nashe's play itself, is attested by the pageant of Winter and Spring presented by Armado in *Love's Labour's Lost*, and by the seasonal songs of winter ("When icicles hang by the wall") and of spring ("When daisies pied and violets blue") with which the play ends. The seasonal songs in *Summer's Last Will and Testament* resemble them closely. The dates of both works are doubtful, but both are usually assigned to 1592 or 1593. In 1600 Nashe was recently dead of the plague, a circumstance which may account for the echoes in *Twelfth Night* of the hauntingly beautiful songs of his seasonal pageant in praise of Summer and Folly. The first line of its best-known stanza, from "Litany in Time of Plague," is quoted by Feste (I, v, 46):

> Beauty is but a flower
> Which wrinkles will devour,
> Brightness falls from the air,
> Queens have died young and fair,
> Dust hath closed Helen's eye.
> I am sick, I must die,
> Lord have mercy on us.

[8] See Hazlitt's edition of Brand's *Antiquities*, II, 370, as cited in Barber, *Shakespeare's Festive Comedy*, p. 26 and n.

[9] Barber (p. 62) identifies the actor but does not mention specifically the probability of an allusion to his name in the final song of *Twelfth Night*.

Feste's first song (II, iii, 39 ff.) echoes, in its "youth . . . will not endure" theme, the song with which Will Sommer's part opens:

> What pleasure lasts? No joy endures:
> Summer I was, I am not what I was;
> Harvest and age have whitened my green head.
>
> (ll. 123–5)

In the course of the play two killjoys are rebuked for refusing to keep Christmas, and Summer is knighted by Bacchus, with the words, "Rise up, Sir Robert Tosspot." These circumstances make unmistakable the link with Feste's final song, when we take into account the fact that the name of the actor who played Sommer was "Toy."

> When that I was and a little tiny boy,
>   With hey, ho, the wind and the rain,
> A *foolish thing* was but a *toy*,[10]
>   For the rain it raineth every day. . . .
> But when I came unto my beds,
>   With hey, ho, the wind and the rain,
> With *toss-pots* still had drunken heads,
>   For the rain it raineth every day. [italics mine]

Feste's impersonation of Sir Topas the curate may owe its inspiration to yet another traditional celebration of folly associated with Twelfth Night. The Church also had its Lord of Misrule, the mock abbot or bishop who presided over the Feast of Fools held in many of the cathedrals of western Europe including Lincoln and Beverley. The feast was celebrated on different days in different places, but always on one of the holy days of Christmastide, Epiphany being most commonly chosen. According to Chambers' account,[11] these clerical revels paralleled in many respects the secular gaieties of Twelfth Night. The inferior clergy, dressed in the brief authority of the festival, put on fools' costume, abused their superiors, indulged in orgies of eating, drinking, dancing, and singing, and played such fantastic tricks before high heaven as conducting a mock mass in front of the altar and doing honour to an ass (possibly in commemoration of the flight into Egypt). Feste, of course, reverses the rite: the fool plays the curate, not the curate the fool, but the transition, as his rapid alternation of roles indicates, is an easy one. As he says, donning the parson's gown, "Well, I'll put it on and I will dissemble myself in't; and I would I were the first that ever dissembled in such a gown" (IV, ii, 4–6).

---

[10] The allusion to Nashe's clown does not, of course, negate the sexual interpretation suggested by Hotson (*First Night*, pp. 167–70) and others.

[11] *Medieval Stage*, II, 274–335.

A set speech in praise of folly was a common feature of Christmas celebrations. Most of the direct praise of folly in the play centres, naturally enough, upon Feste, who garners tributes, as well as tribute, from almost everyone but Malvolio. Viola is warm in her admiration for this fool who does not wear "motley in his brain":

> This fellow is wise enough to play the fool;
> And to do that well craves a kind of wit.
> He must observe their mood on whom he jests,
> The quality of persons, and the time;
> And, like the haggard, check at every feather
> That comes before his eye. This is a practice
> As full of labour as a wise man's art;
> For folly that he wisely shows is fit;
> But wise men, folly-fall'n, quite taint their wit.
>
> (III, i, 57–65)

Indirectly, however, Sir Toby's justification of his turning night into day, the Duke's glorification of his foolish love, Olivia's soliloquy of love for Cesario, and Malvolio's of self-admiration, are also instances of the praise of folly by fools. The titular fool is wiser; he appreciates praise but knows its dangers. His friends, he asserts,

> . . . praise me and make an ass of me. Now my foes tell me plainly I am an ass; so that by my foes, sir, I profit in the knowledge of myself. . . . (V, i, 15–18)

Other seasonal observances alluded to are the Morris Dance and the St. George play. May Day was the preferred festival for Morris Dances, but they had their place in Christmas gambols also. Sir Toby admits that he rides Sir Andrew as if he were a "hobby horse," addresses Maria as "Marian," and calls on his dupe for a "caper," the characteristic leaping step of the Morris Dancers. When Sir Andrew obliges, Sir Toby commends him by asking, "Why dost thou not go to church in a galliard and come home in a coranto?" perhaps in recollection of Philip Stubbes's description of the Morris Dancers in the 1584 edition of his *Anatomy of Abuses*:

> . . . all the wildheads of the parish . . . choose them a grand captain . . . whom they ennoble with the title of my "Lord of Misrule", and he chooseth twenty . . . or a hundred lusty guts like to himself to wait upon his lordly majesty. . . . Then . . . these men he investeth in his liveries of green, yellow, or some other light wanton colour, and . . . they tie about either leg twenty or forty bells. . . .
> . . . then they have their hobby horses, dragons, and other antics, together with their bawdy pipers and thundering drummers to strike up the devil's dance withal. Then march these heathen company towards the church and

churchyard. . . . And in this sort they go . . . into the church (though the minister be at prayer or preaching) dancing and swinging their handkerchiefs over their heads . . . like devils incarnate, with such a confused noise that no man can hear his own voice. ("Lords of Misrule in Ailgna")

The Morris Dance was a strange medley of many things, among them a folk-masque of Robin Hood the outlaw, imported, appropriately enough, into an immemorial fertility rite which had persisted as an accompaniment of disorderly feasting long after its ceremonial function had been forgotten. Morris Dancers wore a variation of the fool's costume, and Feste the Fool has them in mind when he enters singing "Hey, Robin, jolly Robin, tell me how thy lady does," to visit Malvolio the Madman. Echoes of the mummers' play may be found in the mock combat which turns into a real one when St. George-Sebastian, restored to life, lays low the Turkish Knight, Sir Toby, who then calls for a doctor, one of the stock characters of the folk-play. In the combat of wits, on the other hand, the role of the clerical healer who is to restore to mental health that stout champion of virtue, Malvolio, is played by Feste.

The licensed "misrule" of the sub-plot is disorder in its traditionally festival aspect. When the play begins, however, the forces of disorder are generally, if temporarily, in the ascendant. Family ties have been broken by death and shipwreck; both Olivia and Viola have lost a brother and a father. Elysium is confounded in Illyria. Its ruler is

> Unstaid and skittish in all motions else
> Save in the constant image of the creature
> That is belov'd.   (II, iv, 17–19)

Viola's grief is new and sharp, but she is queen over her passion. Olivia's bereavement is of longer duration but is kept "in season" in the brine of her tears. The mature mind of Orsino has been rendered opalescent by indulging itself in the adolescent fantasies of courtly love. His love-melancholy is as unseasonable as Olivia's grief, and both are inappropriate to the season of mirthful folly, however foolish they may be. They must therefore be surfeited by additional, and purged by opposite follies—Olivia's grieving denial of love by the grief of love denied, Orsino's mistaken love by mistaken hate—that the appetite for such foolishness may sicken, and so die.

These disorders are "natural" in origin, and the unnatural behaviour which arises from them is largely the result of mistaken identity, not of unnatural impulse. Viola's inversion of both sexual and social order in disguising herself as a boy and becoming a servant is made natural by her circumstances. As a forthright person it is unnatural for her to conceal her love for the Duke, and still more unnatural for her to act as his ambassador of love to Olivia. All this involves her in cruelty to a woman with whom she sympathizes, in a most unnatural duel in which the opposed parties are neither angry nor eager, and in being charged with ingratitude and disloyalty—weaknesses utterly foreign to her nature. But Viola does not oppose herself to the necessities of the time, and wisely leaves these knots for Time to unravel. Like Sebastian she can rest in the riddle of a mad world.

The naturalness of Olivia's disordered household is repeatedly stressed. Its oppositions are like the red and white of her beauty, "laid on" by "Nature's own sweet and cunning hand." Sir Andrew Ague-cheek is a "natural" fool, a born gull; Maria the spirit of wit, and Sir Toby unregenerate human nature, whose "cunning" is not always accompanied by sweetness. Only Malvolio is "denatured," and therefore irredeemable.

The gulling of Malvolio is the focus of the "praise of folly" theme, but in discussing it there is danger of losing sight of the carnival atmosphere and falling into Malvolio's own error of mistaking bird-bolts for cannon bullets. He is, as most of the characters admit, "notoriously abused," but the abuses of the feasts of folly were as notorious as they were traditional, and they were directed against authority and wisdom (in the medieval sense of prudence or restraint), of which Malvolio is the self-constituted spokesman. As his name indicates, he is also the spirit of ill-will, which must be exorcised[12] from the Christmas feast of love. He charges the revellers with having "no respect of place, persons, nor time" (II, iii, 89), yet he himself sins against all three, and his particular virtues are as out of season as the "midsummer madness" of his smiling behaviour to Olivia in Act III, scene iv—behaviour which is natural enough, however, in the circumstances of his deception and self-deception.

Virtues, in anything but the carnival frame-of-reference, Malvolio certainly has. He is a devoted, responsible, and competent administrator of Olivia's large household. She would not have him miscarry for the half of her dowry. But good sense divorced from good nature is not enough. No doubt Olivia would not have Sir Toby (to whom she is kin if "nothing allied to his disorders") miscarry for the other half of her dowry. Malvolio's attempt to "confine" the revellers "within the

---

[12]See Frye, "Argument of Comedy," English Institute Essay, 1948, ed. D. A. Robertson, Jr. and *An Anatomy of Criticism* (Princeton University Press, 1957), sections on "The Mythos of Spring—Comedy" and "The Scapegoat."

bounds of civil rule" is only seasonally reprehensible, but if his gravity
and decorum are not wholly blameworthy his ill-nature is. As Sir Toby
points out, Malvolio does not merely desire to ration the cakes and
ale; at heart he is opposed to them altogether, and such total opposition
to the natural is unnatural. More serious sins, however, are his self-
love and his ambition, which are instances of "evil desire," another
possible rendering of his name. It is through these sins that the forces
of folly, since they cannot defeat him, gull him into joining them by
making a fool of himself.

The punishment therefore fits the crime. While attempting to put a
stop to one form of holiday licence in others, he is tricked into yielding
to his wish to take advantage of another form of it himself, and what
is worse, to make that advantage permanent, not seasonal. By marrying
Olivia he hopes to turn the master-servant inversion of holiday play
into an everyday reality. It is important to remember that he has these
ideas before Maria encourages them by dropping the forged letter:

> There is example for't: the Lady of the Strachy married the
> yeoman of the wardrobe. . . .
> Having been three months married to her, sitting in my state—...
> And then to have the humour of state; and after a demure travel
> of regard, telling them I know my place as I would they should
> do theirs, to ask for my kinsman Toby—

All this and much more before he sees the letter at line 76 of Act II,
scene v! It is important also to remember that in his reveries there is
no word of his love for Olivia; we hear only the reasons why it should
be appropriate for her to love him.

Since Malvolio refuses to give the devil his due and pay the seasonal
tribute to mirth, since he will not admit that he is like other men and
that "all nature . . . [is] mortal in folly,"[13] he must be made to give
outward form to his inward state by donning the yellow stockings
which are part of the fool's costume. Since he opposes mirth in season
he must be made to smile out of season; since he opposes the nocturnal
misrule[14] of the Twelfth Night King he must pay his forfeit by
suffering imprisonment in total darkness. And so, the whirligig of time
brings in its revenges. The other fools admit their errors and are
pardoned or given prizes at the end of the play. But since he cannot
love anyone but himself, Malvolio is out of tune with the spirit of

[13]*As You Like It*, II, iv, 51–2.
[14]Barber points out (p. 25) that the Duchess of Malfi rallies her steward,
Antonio, whom she has secretly married, by calling him a "Lord of Misrule."
Antonio replies (III, iii, 9), "True for my reign is always in the night."

comedy as much as with the spirit of festival, and he cannot, therefore, share in the final redemption of folly through love, nor in its clarification through self-knowledge. He knows only that he has been made a fool of, not that he has been a fool, and goes out unrepentant and unforgiving. There is no compromise in this self-righteous exponent of the single vision of righteousness.

The first words of Act V, "Now, as thou lov'st me" are its keynote. That they are spoken by Fabian to Feste in the context of folly's triumph does not make them the less significant, for this long scene of resolution moves by means of repeated enlightenments from the holiday mood of its beginning to the mood of "every day," the words with which it ends, and these enlightenments are epiphanies of love. The first is the declaration by Antonio of his love for Sebastian, a love which has proved faithful almost unto death, but which he mistakenly thinks Sebastian has betrayed in order to possess himself of Antonio's purse:

> That most ingrateful boy there by your side
> From the rude sea's enrag'd and foamy mouth
> Did I redeem; a wreck past hope he was.
> His life I gave him, and did thereto add
> My love without retention or restraint,
> All his in dedication; for his sake,
> Did I expose myself, pure for his love,
> Into the danger of this adverse town. . . .
>   (V, i, 71–8)

In their parallels with the Scriptural accounts of divine love's gift of eternal life through Christ, and of his betrayal by Judas and denial by Peter in the "adverse town" of Jerusalem, the words recall to the audience the serious side of the Christmas festival, as does the Duke's "I'll sacrifice the lamb that I do love," when he hears Olivia's declaration of love for Cesario. She counters his threat by claiming an interest in the youth which takes precedence over the authority of master over servant and sovereign over subject, an interest conferred by the law of God:

> Father, I charge thee, by thy reverence,
> Here to unfold—though lately we intended
> To keep in darkness what occasion now
> Reveals before 'tis ripe—what thou dost know
> Hath newly pass'd between this youth and me.
> PRIEST: A contract of eternal bond of love.   (V, i, 145–9)

The language of religion is maintained as Sir Andrew interrupts Viola's protestations with, "For the love of God, a surgeon! Send one presently

to Sir Toby," disappears while the truth about Sebastian is brought to
light, and returns in Feste's apology for his delay in giving Olivia
Malvolio's letter:

> . . . as a madman's epistles are no gospels, so it skills not much
> when they are deliver'd.   (V, i, 278–80)

Viola's declaration recalls sun-festivals older than Christmas, and that
first of all epiphanies in the Book of Genesis: "Let there be light!":

> DUKE: Boy, thou hast said to me a thousand times
>   Thou never shouldst love woman like to me.
> VIOLA: And all those sayings will I overswear;
>   And all those swearings keep as true in soul
>   As doth that orbed continent the fire
>   That severs day from night.
>   (V, i, 259–64)

The Duke is not long in accepting the fruits of his enlightenment,
being almost as quick in "receiving" as Viola herself. All that he had
said about woman's love has been proved wrong:

> There is no woman's sides
> Can bide the beating of so strong a passion
> As love doth give my heart; no woman's heart
> So big to hold so much; they lack retention.
> Alas, their love may be call'd appetite—
> No motion of the liver, but the palate—
> That suffer surfeit, cloyment, and revolt. . . .
>   (II, iv, 92–8)

Having been proved wrong about women in love, he is willing to
accept that proof at the cost of proving equally wrong in what he had
said about the love of men, and especially about the eternal constancy
of his love for Olivia. His declaration to Viola is couched in language
appropriate to the seasonal rite of exchanged services:

> Your master quits you; and, for your service done him,
> So much against the metal of your sex,
> So far beneath your soft and tender breeding,
> And since you call'd me master for so long,
> Here is my hand; you shall from this time be
> Your master's mistress.
>   (V, i, 308–13)

Jest becomes earnest as the Feast of Folly gives place to the Feast of
Love.

The revels now are ended, the masquers are unmasked, and the Fool

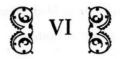

VI

The Laws of Ethical Polity
and the Meanings of "Measure"

Of government the properties to unfold
Would seem in me t' affect speech and discourse,
Since I am put to know that your own science
Exceeds, in that, the lists of all advice
My strength can give you.
(Measure for Measure, I, i, 3–7)

DUKE VINCENTIO'S GRACEFUL COMPLIMENT to his old counsellor, Escalus, may have served not only to announce the theme of the play but also to acknowledge the fame of the studies of "the wisest fool in Christendom," James I, before whom the play was performed on December 26, 1604. The allusions to the Duke's (and James's) distaste for crowds suggest that the play may have been written expressly for this performance, as does its emphasis on tolerance, which was one facet of the royal self-image. On his accession, James had chosen as his motto, "Blessed are the Peacemakers" (Matthew 5:9),[1] and in the early years

[1]The themes and frequently the language of the plays are closely linked with "The Sermon on the Mount" as recorded in Matthew: 5–7 and with St. Paul on law, grace, and justice (especially Romans 3: 24–6).

The relationships of *Measure for Measure* with the Christian Ethic as expounded in the Gospels and in St. Paul's Epistles have been variously interpreted by a number of recent critics, notably by G. Wilson Knight (*"Measure for Measure* and the Gospels," *The Wheel of Fire,* Oxford University Press, 1930; New York: Meridian Books, 1957) and by R. W. Chambers ("The Jacobean Shakespeare and *Measure for Measure,*" British Academy Lecture, 1937) whose essay is a salutary reminder that Isabella, in particular, should be regarded in the light of seventeenth-rather than twentieth-century ethical and theological criteria. Raymond Southall (*"Measure for Measure* and the Protestant Ethic," *Essays in Criticism,* X, pp. 10–33) also discusses the play in terms of Jacobean ethical concepts. S. L. Bethell

of his reign hopes that he might institute a policy of religious toleration ran high, though subsequent events were to dispell them. If in this play Shakespeare was indeed going beyond showing "Virtue her own feature, scorn her own image, and the very age and body of the time his form and pressure" and presuming to advise his learned sovereign on "the properties of government," he would certainly not do so without making himself familiar with his subject, and that is perhaps why *Measure for Measure* echoes so many of the ethical, political, theological, and philosophical commonplaces of the Renaissance.

For this play is a mirror not only of nature but of Shakespeare's intellectual eclecticism, an eclecticism which gathers and selects and adapts, which does not blindly accept contradictions but examines and seeks to reconcile them, and where they cannot be reconciled is content to withhold judgment. There is no need to search for specific indebtedness to printed sources in order to establish Shakespeare's familiarity with concepts which formed part of the intellectual heritage of the educated men and women of his time, a heritage to which Plato, Aristotle, Plotinus, Cicero, Boethius, and their Medieval and Renaissance commentators were major contributors. That the Aristotelian elements in *Measure for Measure* need not be taken as proof that Shakespeare had read the *Nicomachean Ethics* and the *Politics*, nor the Platonic ones that he had read the *Timaeus* and the commentary on it published in Philemon Holland's translation of Plutarch's *Morals* in 1603, does not make them less Aristotelian and Platonic. Nor does their presence diminish the significance of the play's Christian elements. Echoes of St. Matthew's Gospel are particularly unmistakable and

---

(*Shakespeare and the Popular Dramatic Tradition*, 1944) distinguishes between the representational and the symbolic as diverse aspects of the same character, regarding the role of the Duke as played on two levels, the human and the divine. R. W. Battenhouse ("*Measure for Measure* and the Christian Doctrine of the Atonement," *P.M.L.A.*, 1964) discusses the play as an allegory, while L. C. Knights ("The Ambiguity of *Measure for Measure*," *Scrutiny*, X, 1942) sees it as reflecting not so much the dilemma of Christian justice as that of sexual ambivalence. He is opposed by F. R. Leavis ("Measure for Measure," *The Common Pursuit*, London: Chatto and Windus, 1952) who regards the play as an allegory of Divine Providence with the Duke in the title role, in which the author has achieved "inclusive and delicate complexity distinguished from contradiction, conflict and uncertainty. John Vyvyan (*The Shakespearean Ethic*, London: Chatto and Windus, 1959, chs. 6 and 7) discusses the play as a treatment of regeneration through love, N. D. H. Parker (*The Slave of Life: Shakespeare's Idea of Justice*, London: Chatto and Windus, 1955) as an epiphany of Justice and subsequently of Mercy. Of full-length treatments, one of the most stimulating if not the most conclusive, is Mary Lascelles' approach through a thorough comparison of the play with its sources and analogues in *Shakespeare's Measure for Measure* (London: Athlone, 1953).

insistent, and only less so are the allusions to the allegory of the reconciliation of the four daughters of God[2]—Justice, Mercy, Truth, and Peace—based on Psalm 85:

> I will hear what God the Lord will speak: for he will speak peace unto his people, and to his saints: but let them not turn again to folly. Surely his salvation is nigh them that fear him: that glory may dwell in our land. Mercy and truth are met together; righteousness[3] and peace have kissed each other. Truth shall spring out of the earth and righteousness shall look down from heaven. Yea, the Lord shall give that which is good: and our land shall yield her increase.

Though Shakespeare might have gained his familiarity with classical theories of ethics and politics from many sources other than specific books, it would have been strange if, as a schoolboy, he had not read that almost universal textbook on civic responsibility, Cicero's *De Officiis*, and equally unlikely that he would have grown to manhood in ignorance of Boethius' *De consolatione Philosophiae* or have considered writing a play on law and government without consulting Elyot's *The Governor, The Mirror for Magistrates*, and at least Book I of Hooker's *Laws of Ecclesiastical Polity*. He may have derived his Platonism[4] from More's *Utopia*, Castiglione's *The Courtier*, from Spenser, from any or all of a number of less well-known sources or merely from the climate of opinion. What is significant for the purposes of this discussion, however, is not the precise sources of the various concepts of justice, temperance, responsibility, and love which are woven into the fabric of *Measure for Measure*, but the ways in which Shakespeare gives all points of view—Stoic and Epicurean, Christian and pagan, Platonic and Aristotelian, Old and New Testament—literally their day in court, using what he finds relevant in them as the basis of theme and

---

[2]The various treatments of the allegory of the Four Daughters of God in medieval and Renaissance art and literature are discussed in Samuel C. Chew, *The Virtues Reconciled, an Iconographical Study* (University of Toronto Press, 1947), and (with particular application to *Measure for Measure*) in H. M. V. Matthew, *Character and Symbol in Shakespeare's Plays* (Cambridge University Press, 1962, ch. III, sec. 4, pp. 108–18), and in Bernard Spivack, *Shakespeare and the Allegory of Evil* (London: Oxford University Press, 1958, pp. 69–70). In its usual form, the allegory is a debate before the heavenly throne in which Justice and Truth, Mercy and Peace argue the fate of mankind. The opponents are reconciled by Christ's offer to take Man's punishment upon himself, the "remedy" which "he that might the vantage best have took" found out.

[3]Chew (*Virtues Reconciled*, p. 36) notes that the word is "Justicia" in the Vulgate.

[4]See John Vyvyan, *Shakespeare and Platonic Beauty* (London: Chatto and Windus, 1961), ch. 2 and *passim*, also Virgil K. Whitaker, *Shakespeare's Use of Learning* (San Marino, Cal.: Huntington Library, 1953), pp. 206–9.

conflict, and as the material of characterization, structure, irony, and purposeful ambiguity of language.

The ambiguities begin with the play's title, an immediately identifiable allusion to Matthew 7:2:

For with what judgement ye judge, ye shall be judged: and with what measure ye mete, it shall be measured to you again.

Superficially the theme of the play, the text is reiterated in one form or another nearly a dozen times[5] before the denouement which negates it. If in Act V all "taste . . . the cup of their deservings" they are not required to drain it, and if this be a morality play its moral is not the *lex talionis* but the far more characteristic one of salvation by grace. But "measure" has other meanings, some of which are also appropriate to the theme. It can mean "moderation" or "proper proportion," as it does in the opening lines of *Antony and Cleopatra*,[6] or "meter" as the rhythmic pattern of poetry, music, and dance, as in "We'll measure them a measure and be gone" (*Romeo and Juliet*, I, iv, 10). Or these meanings may be combined, as in

> Play, music; and you brides and bridegrooms all,
> With measure heap'd in joy, to th' measures fall,
>   (*As You Like It*, V, iv, 172–3)

or in "justice always whirls in equal measure" (*Love's Labour's Lost*, IV, iii, 380). From here it is an easy associative leap (easy for Shakespeare) to the cosmic dance of universal order as presented in Sir John Davies' *Orchestra* or to the numerical concept of harmony in Plato's *Timaeus*. There is an interesting bit of wordplay on "meter" in that only seemingly inconsequential conversation between Lucio and his disorderly companions in Act I, scene ii. From the topics of peace and prayer they have moved on to grace:

LUCIO: . . . I think thou never wast where grace was said.
2 GENT.:   No? A dozen times at least.
1 GENT.:   What, in metre?
LUCIO: In any proportion or in any language.
1 GENT.:   I think, or in any religion.
LUCIO: Ay, why not? Grace is grace, despite of all controversy,
           as, for example, thou thyself art a wicked villain,
           despite of all grace.

                                                        (ll. 19–26)

In addition to the Christian concepts of grace and mercy, it is Aristotle's general justice as superior to retributive justice which is

---

[5]For example, I: ii, 114–17; II: i, 27–31; ii, 75–9; iv, 141–2; III: ii, 243–64; IV: i, 66–8; ii, 75–81.
[6]See below, p. 194.

Shakespeare's concern in *Measure for Measure,* and for Aristotle the principle on which justice, like the other virtues, is founded, is "measure" or moderation. His concept of general justice includes equity, restitution, and the maintenance of good order in government. He describes it as "perfect virtue because it practices perfect virtue," and goes on to define the qualities of its perfection:

. . . it is perfect in a special way, because the man who possesses justice is capable of practising it towards a second party and not merely in his own case. . . . So the saying of Bias, "Office will prove the man" has found favour with the world. For to accept office is to enter into relations with others and to become one member of an association. And for just this reason—that a relation is established with others—justice is the only virtue which is regarded as benefiting someone else than its possessor.[7]

This is very close to the Duke's words in the expository scenes of Act I (scenes i and iii) and especially to his charge to Angelo:

> . . . Thyself and thy belongings
> Are not thine own so proper as to waste
> Thyself upon thy virtues, they on thee.
> Heaven doth with us as we with torches do,
> Not light them for themselves; for if our virtues
> Did not go forth of us, 'twere all alike
> As if we had them not.
>
>   (I, i, 30–6)

The speech moves on from this allusion to the injunction against hiding one's light under a bushel to refer to the parable of the talents, thus demonstrating in true humanist fashion the parallels between the classical and Christian views of the good life.

Justice is for Aristotle a public rather than a private virtue. It is one aspect of man's functioning as a social animal: the word "justice," he insists, cannot properly be applied except where men have a law to appeal to. To the operation of the principle of the mean in private matters Aristotle gives the name of Temperance, though he does not always distinguish altogether precisely between temperance as moderation in all things and temperance as a specific, self-regarding virtue. It is in the general sense that the word is used in the first of two quotations which may serve to illustrate the currency of the concept in the popular literature of Shakespeare's time. This is from John Higgins' Preface to his edition of *The Mirror for Magistrates*:

The propertie of Temperaunce is to covet nothing which may bee repented; not to exceade the bandes of measure, and to keepe desire under the yooke of Reason. . . . Yet sither there are three other Cardinall vertues which are

---

[7]*Ethics,* tr. J. A. K. Thomson (Penguin Books), Book V, ch. 1, pp. 141 ff.

requisite in him that should be in authoritie: that is to saye, Prudence, Justice, and Fortitude . . . yet shall you finde that for wante of Temperaunce, those which were counted the wisest that ever were, fel into wonderful reproche and infamie. Yea and though Justice that incomparable vertue, as the aunctent Civilians define hir, be a perpetuall and constant will which giveth to every man his right. Yet if she be not constant, which is the gift of fortitude, nor equal in discerning right from wrong, wherein is prudence: nor use proportion in judgement and sentence which pertaineth to temperaunce, shee can never be called equitie or justice, but fraude, deceate, injustice, and injurie. . . . I will . . . lastly set downe, the definition of Temperaunce, according to Cicero his opinion,[8] Temperaunce (saith he) is of reason in lust and other evill assaultes of the minde, a sure and moderate dominion and rule. This noble vertue hath three partes, that is continence, clemencie and modestie. . . .[9]

Yet the tragedies of Higgins' own composition included in this collection are largely concerned with that other sense of "measure" in which the punishment fits the crime, with what we call "poetic justice" rather than with temperance. It is possible that Shakespeare was more disturbed by this contradiction between precept and illustration than the author.

Temperance in the over-all sense is the frame of reference of a popular collection of "sentences" entitled *Keepe within Compasse OR The Worthy Legacy of a Wise Father to his beloved Sonne, teaching him how to live richly in this World and eternally happy in the World to come*, published by I. Trundle in 1619. The "sentences" included in this commonplace book must, of course, have been current much earlier. The chapter on "Direction for a Good Life" includes the following passage:

> Who is a false Judge, one day must appeare
> So to bee judged as hee hath judg'd here.
> All delight in pleasure take
> In the dust thou must lye,
> Till the last trumpe thee awake:
> Therefore all is lost and spended
> That to Vertue is not intended. . . .
> If thou wilt backe into thy Compasse get,
> Beate downe the evill: raise the just:
> Learn best thyself to know:
> Hold holy Writ; and counsel peace:
> Be patient in thy woe.   (Sigs. B1, B1ᵥ)

[8]Other authorities named are Aristotle and Plotinus. For Cicero's discussion of Justice and Prudence (Wisdom) see *De Officiis*, Book I; of Fortitude and Temperance, Book III, especially chapters x and xi.

[9]"Address to the Nobilitie and all other in office" prefaced to *The Firste parte of the Mirour for Magistrates, containing the falles of the first unfortunate*

Here again we have listed (in addition to the themes of *Measure for Measure*) Aristotle's four virtues of the good citizen—justice or righteousness, temperance, fortitude, and prudence, that practical wisdom for a man's self which is based upon self-knowledge. There are, then, two sets of four civil virtues in Renaissance political thought: the biblical Truth, Justice, Mercy, and Peace, and the classical Justice, Temperance, Prudence, and Fortitude. According to Psalm 85, the Kingdom of God will be established on earth when Justice, Mercy, Truth, and Peace are no longer at variance. According to Aristotle, the best of all possible states is that in which the citizens uphold the virtues of the mean—Justice, Temperance, Prudence, and Fortitude. *Measure for Measure* shows its audience all eight of these virtues (and their concomitant excesses and defects) in action. It poses certain questions regarding them, and in the end denies that "measure," in the sense of "an eye for an eye" or in that of the moderation which is a balance between opposites can suffice to create the *ideal* harmony of peace, order, and good government. Ultimate peace, for state or individual, is the liberal gift of that Mercy which is not "strain'd" to conform to any set "measure" and which is exemplified in the one supreme virtue which is not a mean but an excess. Only the love which is beyond measure, which, like Mariana's, goes beyond reason and justice, can mirror, on earth, the abounding grace which restores all losses and frees all faults. (For the general pardon at the end of Act V includes even Lucio, though he may not think so. But more of his case hereafter.) The golden mean is an ideal appropriate to a social ethic; hence its appeal for Aristotle is as the measure of the proper operation of the laws of man, as balanced oppositions provide the principle on which the laws of nature operate. It is a goal which imperfect man may hope to attain. But in Christ the old law is superseded and fulfilled by the law of love, and His kingdom is of this world only so far as it is within us. For Aristotle the supreme virtue is unselfish justice, for the Christian it is unselfish love, but in the social context pagan and Christian are in agreement in seeing the virtue of the individual citizen as the measure of the extent to which the ideal polity may be achieved. In his dramatic examination of the properties of government, therefore, Shakespeare does not merely involve his characters in a conflict which

---

Princes of this lande: From the coming of Brute to the incarnation of our saviour and redemer Jesu Christe, as cited in Lily B. Campbell, *Shakespeare's Tragic Heroes, Slaves of Passion* (Cambridge University Press, 1930; New York: Barnes and Noble, 1960), pp. 7–8.

illustrates some of the problems of government, but gives them characteristics which are, in microcosm, the elements of that conflict, and as far as possible, he achieves its resolution in both Aristotelian and Christian terms.

Of the four "daughters of God" as the virtues of ethical polity Shakespeare is most concerned in this play with Justice and Mercy, though Peace and Truth are not neglected; of the Aristotelian virtues he stresses Justice and Temperance, though Prudence and Fortitude are also touched upon. Justice (in both Christian and classical connotations), Mercy and Temperance form the focus of the theme, but questions are raised about other aspects of government also, notably about the nature of law and about responsibility for its administration. Certain contradictions are pointed out—between law in theory and in practice, between the decrees of law and the dictates of justice, between the nature of the office and the nature of the office-holder.

Of the three central concepts of Justice, Mercy, and Temperance, priority in this discussion of the play will be given to Temperance as the one which has received the least critical attention, and one which, once its importance has been recognized, helps to account for if not to resolve many of the problems of the play. One of these is its "unpleasantness." While recognizing that Temperance may be thought of as a general principle and pointing out that it operates in various spheres of action as Justice, Prudence, and Fortitude, Aristotle discusses it as a *particular* virtue almost entirely in terms of the physical appetites and draws most of his illustrations from sexual relations. In this particular sense he defines Temperance as the mean between the excess of overindulgence and the defect of insensibility, both of which he recognizes as opposed varieties of intemperance, though he later applies that term to a particular kind of overindulgence or licence. Temperance is the moderate gratification of natural physical appetites in the proper way and at the proper time and in the proper place. The reason dictates what these proprieties are, and in the temperate man the will obeys the reason and is not controlled by appetite. Licence is defined in the *Ethics* as having two sub-categories, intemperance proper and incontinency. Incontinency is a less serious departure from the mean than intemperance, since it is an occasional lapse to which the reason does not assent. It arises from a temporary ascendance of appetite over reason, a lust of the blood and permission of the will of which the reason does not approve.[10] Intemperance proper, on the

[10]Iago's discussion of the operation of appetite and will is Aristotelian: "If the balance of our lives had not one scale of reason to poise another of sensuality,

other hand, is not only incurable but is an excess which is so much a part of the individual's natural composition as to be largely an unconscious habit. The intemperate man's reason does not tell him that licence is wrong, and therefore he feels no guilt and has no incentive to mend his ways. If his intemperate behaviour causes injury to others the principle of Justice must operate to ensure that he acknowledges his responsibility and makes restitution. The incontinent man must strive to establish the habit of temperance, and if he succeeds he is more virtuous than the insensible man, though he may seem less consistently temperate, since in achieving restraint he has overcome a natural disposition to excess of passion, while the insensible man who refrains from overindulgence has merely followed his own bent and done nothing to remedy the deficiencies of his disposition. Such a man is not truly temperate, therefore, however free he may be of licentiousness.

It is not to be wondered at that Shakespeare should dramatize the problems of Temperance in sexual terms, since these were the terms in which his audience was accustomed to having them presented[11] and would expect them to be presented. But in *Measure for Measure* it is not the sexual problem alone which is presented in terms of Temperance in the larger sense, nor is the sexual problem treated solely from that point of view. The administration of the law is seen as following, at its best, the course of a judicious mean between laxity and severity, and both the practical wisdom and the ethical validity of attempting to control human passions by legislation are directly or indirectly questioned. In the *Politics*[12] Aristotle expresses doubt that temperance is likely to be achieved by such legislation, especially where money and sex are involved, and makes the suggestion (echoed by Milton in the *Areopagitica*) that if such laws were enforceable they would still be bad laws, since they would decrease opportunities for the exercise of virtue. It is possible also that the notorious laxity of James's court, in contrast to the decorum (if not purity) of his predecessor's, may not have been wholly absent from Shakespeare's mind when he was writing the play.

However careless he may be about factual details on occasion, Shakespeare is usually both careful and thorough in his exposition, and

---

the blood and baseness of our natures would conduct us to most preposterous conclusions. But we have reason to cool our raging motions, our carnal stings, our unbitted lusts. . . ." (*Othello*, I, iii, 323–31).

[11]Cf. the "Bower of Bliss" episode of Book II of *The Faerie Queene*, of which Temperance is the general theme.

[12]Book II, ch. 9, p. 89.

one of the best ways of searching out the intention of a difficult play
is to give close attention to its first act, and especially its opening
scene. Act I of *Measure for Measure* introduces most of the play's
themes and variations, among which the concept of temperance is
dominant. In the opening scene, however, the motif of temperance is
implied rather than stated, and the emphasis is upon the properties of
government in general and the exercise of authority in particular. No
mention is made here of the problem of licentiousness, and the new
deputy is not directed to correct the consequences of laxity by imposing
the antidote of severity but is told to govern as he sees fit. In other
words the seemingly temperate citizen is given the opportunity to
demonstrate his private virtue in the sphere of public action in which
temperance is transmuted into justice, the virtue which is perfect in
that it is practised towards others than oneself. Angelo's qualities are
to be given the opportunity to "go forth." Office is to prove the man.
No specific limits to Angelo's power are laid down; he is to create his
own image of authority. "What figure of us think you will bear?" the
Duke asks of Escalus, and goes on to define the oppositions inherent
in the exercise of power as "terror" and "love," "mortality" and "mercy."
He entrusts to his deputy the power "So to enforce or qualify the laws /
As to your soul seems good." Angelo's reply shows that his view of his
commission is rather different from the Duke's. He regards himself
not as creating the image of authority but as having that image
stamped upon his "metal" by the office to which he accedes. Even after
he has been told that his power is to be absolute as the Duke's, bounded
only by the limits imposed by his own judgment, Angelo is uncertain
of an authority which has not been specified in law. His "Tis so with
me" echoes Escalus'

> . . . it concerns me
> To look into the bottom of my place.
> A pow'r I have, but of what strength and nature
> I am not yet instructed.
>
> (I, i, 78–81)

Or is he perhaps uncertain of himself, that here, as in II, i, 16–21 and
II, ii, 80, he should be so greatly concerned to divorce the man from
the office.

The Duke has had the foresight officially to make provision against
such a possibility. In addition to the dictates of his own conscience
Angelo is given an experienced guide, the old counsellor Escalus,
whom he is free to consult, though Escalus is limited to acting in an
advisory capacity only. He makes use of this guide, however, only

to ascertain the extent of his own authority and thereafter not only refrains from seeking his appointed counsellor's advice but disregards any which he volunteers. Escalus, however, is not only an advisor but also a model (on the political if not the theological level of the allegory). He is a moderate man who administers justice with mercy. Both theory and practice have taught him that the law is not simple, but complex, depending for its proper functioning on the tempering of many elements. The Duke has listed human nature, place and time as some of them:

> The nature of our people,
> Our city's institutions, and the terms
> For common justice. . . .
>
> (I, i, 10–2)

In these he is as "pregnant" (note that from a number of alternatives Shakespeare chooses a word which suggests that the proper function of the law is a creative rather than a negative or destructive one) "as Art and practice hath enriched any." His advice to Angelo demonstrates his awareness that individual circumstances may sometimes justify the qualifying of law.

In the fewer than ninety lines of Act I, scene i, the problems of political ethics with which the play is to deal are presented. The related problems of individual ethics are introduced in the scene which follows.

As in *Coriolanus* Menenius' re-telling of the Fable of the Belly and the Members draws an analogy between the human body and the body politic, so the Duke's injunction to Angelo to govern "as to your soul seems good" points to the parallels between the government of the state and the government of the soul. In the soul's familiar three-fold division Angelo may be taken as standing for the executive function of the Will, Escalus for the advisory function of the Reason, Lucio and his disreputable acquaintance for the sensual appetites. Scene ii presents the imbalance which the Duke comments upon in scene iii, as well as the setting in motion of the counter-balancing forces which, according to the principles of dialectic, might be expected to correct the imbalance and restore order. In the opening scene the court, as the seat of government, represents the area of moderation which should properly lie between the extremes of laxity and severity, licence and restraint. In the scenes which follow, the extremes on opposite sides of this mean are represented by the brothel and the cloister, though in both areas certain degrees of excess and defect are indicated.

What is significant about the representatives of Vienna's sexual underworld is that however bawdy their conversation, however irresponsible their attitudes, however uninhibited their vices, they are never regarded as unnatural.[13] The appetites which man shares with the animals are as much a part of his proper nature as is the soul which marks his kinship with the angels, and it is on this ground that their spokesman, Pompey, bases his argument for the Defence. Scene ii prepares us for the coming clash of statecraft and sex by means of a thematic modulation from one to the other, which moves rapidly from order to disorder. Lucio and his two companions enter in the midst of a conversation on the current cold-war rumours which soon turns into a cynical commentary on the operation of self-interest in ethical judgments. When the citizens of Vienna pray for peace they are not desiring the peace of the King of Hungary. The pirate excludes "Thou shalt not steal" from his decalogue; the soldier, "Thou shalt not kill." Only grace, which is free from self-interest, is above all controversy, and all three admit that they are far from being in a state of grace. Because of their sexual excesses there is very little of physical or spiritual health in them. "I think I have done myself wrong, have I not?" laughs the First Gentleman, with unconscious ambiguity. Second Gentleman has just replied (with a play on "tainted," and "attainted"), "Yes, that thou hast, whether thou art tainted or free" when Mistress Overdone enters to reveal the disreputable state of Vienna's morals and the new governor's decision to enforce the laws against sexual licence.

With the entrance of Claudio and Juliet under arrest one of the play's patterns of characterization, the Aristotelian pattern of categories and sub-categories, begins to unfold. Lucio and Claudio represent Aristotle's two kinds of sexual intemperance. Lucio's intemperance of excess is ingrained and is reinforced by defects of prudence and responsibility (for he does not behave responsibly either towards others or towards himself). He regards the gratification of sexual appetite as both a pleasure-giving and a natural activity, and therefore as a good, as his reply to Isabella's question concerning the nature of Claudio's offence makes clear:

> . . . that which, if myself might be his judge,
> He should receive his punishment in thanks:
> He hath got his friend with child.
>
> (I, iv, 27–9)

---

[13]Wm. Empson's explication of the "proper bane" passage (I, ii, 122–4) in *Seven Types of Ambiguity* (ch. V) deals with the "naturalness" of original sin in this connection.

His is Aristotle's true intemperance which feels no guilt. Claudio's intemperance is Aristotle's incontinency, the lapse of a passionate man who, lacking fortitude, is incapable of constancy in maintaining his Reason as lord of his will, but who is aware that his error is an error. He accounts for his plight in conventionally dialectical terms:

LUCIO: Why, how now, Claudio, whence comes this restraint?
CLAUD.: From too much liberty, my Lucio, liberty;
         As surfeit is the father of much fast,
         So every scope by the immoderate use
         Turns to restraint.

                    (I, ii, 118–22)

Yet his protest against the publicity attendant upon his arrest shows his awareness that the law's justice and abstract justice are not always identical. Claudio, after all, is only technically guilty, yet,

        Thus can the demigod Authority
        Make us pay down for our offence by weight
        The words of Heaven: on whom it will, it will;
        On whom it will not, so; yet still 'tis just.

                    (I, ii, 114–17)

The lines echo not only Romans 9: 15–18 but Matthew 5: 25–7:

    . . . lest . . . the judge deliver thee to the officer, and thou be cast into prison.
    Verily I say unto thee, Thou shalt by no means come out thence till thou hast paid the uttermost farthing.
    Ye have heard that it was said by them of old time, Thou shalt not commit adultery.

Here as elsewhere in the play, ethical comment is drawn simultaneously from the Christian and from the classical tradition. And appropriately so, for *Measure for Measure*, like Hooker's *Ecclesiastical Polity*, is in its own way a Christian humanist and anti-Puritan document. It supports the cause of tolerance and of the positive morality of unselfish love by precept and by examples both positive and negative.

Scene iii of Act I is devoted to an assessment of the situation presented in the two previous scenes. Shakespeare is being particularly careful, through linking and repetition, to ensure that his audience shall not be confused as to what his play is about, and if more than three centuries of criticism have proved him unsuccessful, it may be because his play is about the complex interrelations of many things. Duke Vincentio, a naturally contemplative man born to a life of action, has "ever loved the life removed," and has chosen a monastery as the retreat which will enable him to view events in Vienna from a position of detachment. Part of his purpose may be self-evaluation, for the Duke is a modest as well as a moderate man, who, according to Escalus, is "a gentleman of all temperance," and "one that, above all other strifes, contended especially to know himself" (III, ii, 222, 219). He does not deny that the responsibility for correcting abuses in the society he governs is properly his own. His predisposition to clemency, his sense of equity and, it would seem, his desire to be loved, have made him incapable of punishing rigorously offences which he had previously seemed to condone.[14] It is usually assumed that the Duke's purpose in appointing Angelo was to expose the hollowness of his reputation, but the text gives no indication that he was certain of the man's corruptness—merely that he had grounds for certain doubts. It is quite possible that he has an open mind about Angelo, that he perhaps hopes to learn something from watching how his deputy discharges his functions. Three courses of action are open to Angelo: he may take the line of least resistance and let things go on much as they have done; he may be moderate in his government, or he may, like the typical new broom, be stiff and severe in his judgments. The character of his life leads the Duke to assume that the last course is the likeliest, and it may be precisely what is needed to restore the balance of order, provided that the rigour intended to counterbalance laxity does not go the extreme of harshness. If that should happen the Duke will be at hand in order to resume power quickly enough to counteract the new imbalance before any irreparable damage is done.

But the Duke seems also to be conducting some sort of psychological experiment. He has chosen to supply his place an outstanding exemplar of the sexual restraint he wishes his subjects to observe, one who should provide the ideal instrument for imposing such restraint upon them by decree as well as encouraging them to emulate his example. But Angelo is perhaps a little too good to be true, or if true, too good to be natural. To what extent, asks the Duke, anticipating Lord Acton, will the test of power show his virtue to be corruptible? All men have their weaknesses. What is his, this man who "scarce confesses that his appetite is more to bread than stone"? tenderness of his reputation? insensibility? hypocrisy? The allusion to Matthew 7:9 ("Or what man is there of you whom if his son ask bread, will give him a stone?") suggests that Angelo will hardly admit to possessing natural affections, let alone fleshly appetites. But equally pertinent are the references to

[14]Cf. *Ethics*, Book II, ch. 9 on applying the principle of the mean.

the love of God for his children which follow in Matthew 7:10 and 11, and especially so the injunction of verse 12: "Therefore, all things whatsoever ye would that men should do to you, do ye even so to them: for this is the law and the prophets."

In the final scene of Act I we move from the monastery to the nunnery in which Isabella is about to commence her novitiate. Her first words mark her as occupying an ethical position at the opposite pole from that of Lucio and his associates:

> ISAB.: And have you nuns no farther privileges?
> FRAN.: Are not these large enough?
> ISAB.: Yes, truly I speak not as desiring more,
> But rather wishing a more strict restraint. . . .
>
> (I, iv, 1–4)

The Sisterhood of Saint Clare was a very strict order, and Isabella's desire for still more restraint is excessive. Its expression also hints at spiritual arrogance in one who has not yet been formally received as a novice.

The two extremes of restraint and licence confront each other when Lucio enters to tell Isabella of Claudio's arrest, and his greeting, "Hail, virgin . . ." is not so much a mocking as an unconsciously ironic parody of the Salutation. Virgin, Isabella is, but she is not as yet full of grace, and her virtue, being negative, gives little promise of spiritual fertility, though her lamp will burn less flickeringly when it is filled with the oil of charity. For Isabella as for Angelo the events of the play will provide an "approbation," and it is Lucio who first points out the parallels between them, however unreliable he may be as a judge. In his eyes, Isabella's renunciation of the flesh makes her "a thing enskied and sainted," her beauty a reflection of that heavenly pattern of the good in which the flesh has no part, and she is therefore not to be jested with and deceived as is his custom with women. If Isabella seems to him more than natural, Lucio agrees with Duke Vincentio in seeing Angelo as perhaps something less than natural, one "not made by man and woman after this downright way of creation" but born of "a sea-maid," or "begot between two stock-fishes." (III, ii, 97–100). He describes him as,

> A man whose blood
> Is very snow-broth, one who never feels
> The wanton stings and motions of the sense,
> But doth rebate and blunt his natural edge
> With profits of the mind, study and fast.
>
> (I, iv, 57–61)

One of the errors for which Lucio will be held to account is his adherence to the double standard. For him the actions which make Isabella a saint label Angelo as less than a man, as the actions which label a woman a whore are in a man "a game of tick-tack" and a badge of virility. As for Isabella, her idea of justice does not, at this point, go beyond the classical concepts of equity and restitution. "Oh, let him marry her" is her immediate reaction to Lucio's news. For her as for most of the citizens of Vienna sexual morality is a private matter, an area in which law properly operates to ensure that wrongs shall be righted, but not as a punitive agent. It is to her credit that she does not appear to find her brother's action shocking, nor does she condemn him for it, however repugnant sexual licence is to her. She may desire to give up the world and the flesh, but she does not insist that others must do likewise, and however rigid she may prove where her own standards are involved she is not a Puritan. When she does turn on her brother, it is because he does not wholly share her views about the sanctity of *her* honour.

Act I has set forth the basic themes of Justice in public action, Temperance in private action. It has established a pattern of characterization which balances one extreme against another and has indicated how the themes of Justice and Temperance are to be interrelated with the plot. As the play proceeds, the complexities and ramifications of these themes are developed. It has already been made plain that the theme of Justice will involve such considerations as the authority and integrity of the judge. In the abstract, Justice may be neatly defined as the mean between Rigour and Laxity and its function in law as the safeguarding of civil and contractual rights. As it affects human lives, however, Justice involves the operation of specific laws, the means of their enforcement, the nature of evidence, the maintenance of equality before the law, procedures for arrest, provision for appeals, prison conditions, and arbitrary or extra-legal proceedings, all of which are touched on in this play. The theme of Temperance also, in its sexual context, is seen as something far more complex, in human terms, than the maintenance of a mathematical equilibrium between lechery and frigidity. It is complicated, in the Christian frame of reference, by a logical conflict between the ideal of virginity and the natural law of self-propagation. As Hooker had pointed out, the law of Nature and the law of God cannot contradict each other, and the law of man which is out of harmony with either is a bad law. Above all, the circumstances of the plot make it impossible to separate considerations of temperance from considerations of law and considerations of love, since the arrest of Claudio has turned the law against lechery to, in the words of the title of the Restoration adaptation, a "law against lovers."

Love, therefore, becomes the theme which binds together the contradictions inherent in these manifold concepts, love in all its aspects sexual and spiritual. Truth and Responsibility, essential elements of love in the courtly, Platonic, and Christian traditions, are concepts which serve to link the world of public justice with the world of individual morality. In Act I, the Duke has already questioned the truth of Angelo's public image; Act II is to prove that his private self-image is equally unreliable, for Angelo is not only a deceiver but is self-deceived. Since the establishing of truth and responsibility is one of the functions of a court of law, it is with a trial scene that Act II opens.

Angelo is recapitulating, to Escalus, what the Duke has already said to Friar Thomas (I, iii) about the retributive and deterrent functions of the law and the consequences of laxity in its enforcement. Escalus exercises his proper function as counsellor by advising moderation, particularly in the case of Claudio, on the ground of the higher law of "measure for measure," that of doing unto others as we would they should do unto us. But Angelo casts himself in the role of the Pharisee in the Temple, certain that he is "not as other men," and thus condemns himself in advance:

> When I, that censure him, do so offend,
> Let mine own judgment pattern out my death,
> And nothing come in partial.
>
> (II, i, 29–31)

He remains adamant, and Claudio is condemned to summary execution. Escalus' aside, "Heaven forgive him, and forgive us all!" not only identifies the audience with the sinners who stand in need of mercy, but foreshadows Isabella's great speech in the ensuing scene and Angelo's fall from grace, since "He that says he is without sin, deceives himself." The effect is strengthened by Angelo's use of the word, "offend," recalling the "miserable offenders" of the General Confession.

But the trial of Claudio has already taken place; it is the complaint of Elbow against Pompey which takes up most of the scene. Angelo's behaviour on the bench hints at his arrogance as well as at the irresponsibility which has led him to break his engagement to Mariana and will lead him to abuse the powers of his office. As a steward, he is not faithful in little things, but grows impatient with the interminable trivialities of Elbow's evidence and goes off, leaving Escalus to deal with such a trifling case, though not without pre-judging it, as indicated by his parting hope that "You'll find good cause to whip them all." What follows is a good deal of standard Elizabethan clowning, but that is not all. Escalus' patient hearing of the case terminates in a warning rather than a whipping for the accused, but it also casts light on yet another aspect of the properties of government. It seems that Lord Angelo is not alone in his disposition to shift irksome responsibilities to others' shoulders, here as elsewhere in the play. The pattern of counterparts is maintained. Elbow is a long-winded and mildly amusing malaprop, but after the audience has had its laugh it is confronted with a serious issue. As a clown, Elbow is ridiculous, but that the ignorant and stupid constable should be a stock figure of fun indicates a situation which is not ridiculous but deplorable.[15] This, of course, is Shaw's trick of getting the audience to laugh and then turning the tables by demonstrating that it is itself responsible for the condition which ridicule has condemned. Elbow is a well-meaning incompetent, utterly incapable of discharging his functions as constable, who retains the office only because he is incapable of doing anything else and because the citizens of his ward have sloughed off their civic responsibility to serve in turn as constables and have hired him as their substitute. Knowing that the man is not to blame for his natural deficiencies, Escalus sympathizes with his difficulty in discharging his duties, but takes steps to see that his fellow citizens, especially the wealthier ones, shall cease to evade theirs. Escalus appears to agree with Aristotle, "Whether he likes it or not, the man fit to hold office should be made to accept it."[16]

The scene ends, as it had begun, with comment on Claudio's condemnation, this time between Escalus and the third of the presiding justices, and with a restatement of the problem of reconciling Justice and Mercy. "There is no remedy," Escalus laments, and "remedy" becomes a key word which is heard again and again throughout the rest of the play, along with "grace" and "justice."

The contrast between the seemingly humble Angelo of Act I, scene i, and the smugly self-sufficient Angelo of Act II, scene i, prepares us for the later revelation of disparity between appearance and reality in his character. We are perhaps less well-prepared for some of the

---

[15]There is a marked contrast of purpose here with *Much Ado about Nothing*, where a precisely similar situation is never allowed to be taken too seriously, and indeed the action of the play turns on the accidental effectiveness of the ignorant honesty of Dogberry and Verges, who are allowed to "get their man."

[16]Aristotle, *Politics*, tr. J. A. Sinclair (Penguin Books, 1962), Book II, ch. 9, p. 89.

surprises other characters have in store for us. For however they may resemble, initially, the personified abstractions of the morality tradition, they soon develop human inconsistencies. Like ourselves, they are vexed with passions of some difference; they posssess an excess of one quality and are defective in another. Even the Duke, whose role of "looker-on" sets him apart from emotional involvement in the action however much he may manipulate the plot, is no exception, though it is his function to provide the touchstone which reveals such inconsistencies, and his purpose to reconcile their conflicts by helping his subjects to supply their deficiencies, curb their excesses, and thus bring them closer to his politic ideal of moderation in all things.

The process of adjustment, however, is set in motion not by the orderly Duke but by his disorderly subject, Lucio, in bringing Angelo and Isabella together in Act II, scene ii. It is one of the play's subtler ironies that the self-confessed "Vice" should lead the woman he professes to regard as "a thing enskied and sainted" into a situation in which the False-Semblant "Angel" shall tell her, in the bluntest possible terms, to "put on the destin'd livery" of a woman. Of Isabella's three great scenes, critical attention has tended to concentrate on the first two, dividing according to the critic's interpretation of her character. Those neo-romantics who see her as the embodiment of the feminine ideal of purity allied with Divine Grace and Mercy rhapsodize over the first and either overlook or condone her language to her brother in the second. R. W. Chambers, for example, justifies her on theological grounds. Those who regard her as a shrew and a prude, and therefore unfit to be a Shakespearean heroine, fulminate against her behaviour to Claudio and dismiss as rhetoric far from "prone and speechless" but highly artificial her passionate eloquence in her first scene with Angelo. Few seem able to reconcile the realities of the human situation in both. Yet when it is examined in terms of the human fallibility which is the centre of reference in the play, Isabella's behaviour is not so difficult to account for. Let us look at Isabella's situation in everyday terms. To consider the implications of her situation when the play opens is not to indulge in Bradleyan speculation. She is certainly young, perhaps seventeen at most, and like most young girls she would appear to be an uncompromising idealist. Though as far as the play gives any indication of her family circumstances she would seem to be an orphan, she has probably led the sheltered life appropriate to young ladies of her station, and she has made the great decision to make her isolation from the world a permanent one by entering a convent as a novice. On this day set aside for the most solemn and sacred occasion of her life, her brother, who seems to be her only relative, finds himself arrested for seducing her best friend and sends for his sister to get him out of trouble. This circumstance, it seems probable from her informing the Mother Superior of her reason for departure, and from her freedom of movement thereafter, makes it necessary for her to defer her entrance into the novitiate. If she had shown herself to be irritated by Claudio's indiscretion as well as distressed for his plight, who could wonder at it? But when she hears the news she gives no sign of concern for herself; her only thought is for her brother's safety.

Yet, when she finally is admitted to an audience with the Deputy she seems tongue-tied, and her pleading is half-hearted. This has puzzled some critics. Yet it is completely in character that she should suffer from shyness and embarrassment as well as distress. Isabella is seemingly overawed by Angelo's high position and his reputation for severity, and is embarrassed by the nature of her brother's offence. It is not merely a matter of a young girl's disinclination to talk about sex with an older man: the divine Desdemona's light chatter with Iago, though repugnant to her, indicates that Elizabethan women seem to have been rather frank in speech on such subjects. But on what grounds can a young woman who has declared her intention of dedicating herself to a life of chastity plead, with sincerity and logical as well as theological consistency, for the pardon of a sexual offender? Does not her decision imply her personal condemnation of the flesh? Hesitantly, she introduces the parallel between human and divine justice by asking Angelo to let the fault, and not her brother, be condemned, in emulation of that supreme Judge "who desireth not the death of a sinner, but rather that he should turn from his wickedness and live." Though Angelo scoffs at her plea, insisting that to grant it would render the judge's function "a very cipher," the argument that the business of the law as well as of Christians was to condemn evils not men, sins not sinners, was a common one enough. We find it stated, for example, in Bacon's essay "Of Judicature":

Specially in case of laws penal, they ought to have a care that that which was meant for terror be not turned into rigour . . . for penal laws pressed are a shower of snares upon the people. Therefore let penal laws, if they have been sleepers of long . . . be confined by wise judges in the execution. . . . In causes of life and death, judges ought (as far as the law permitteth) in justice to remember mercy, and to cast a severe eye upon the example, but a merciful eye upon the person.

Isabella, however, is at first overcome by the logic of Angelo's,

> Condemn the fault and not the actor of it!
> Why, every fault 's condemn'd ere it be done;
>
> (II, ii, 37–8)

and returns to the attack only at Lucio's urging:

> You are too cold: if you should need a pin,
> You could not with more tame a tongue desire it.
>
> (II, ii, 45–6)

Her plaintive, "Must he need die?" receives the stern response, "Maiden, no remedy," and her plea that Angelo show towards Claudio the mercy he would desire in similar circumstances elicits only the harsh dismissal: "Your brother is a forfeit of the law / And you but waste your words." As we have already seen, Angelo resents any suggestion that he may be capable of sin and thus have need of mercy. But when her "prone and speechless dialect" has failed, the words "forfeit" and "remedy" touch off the eloquence which Claudio had praised to Lucio:

> . . . she hath prosperous art
> When she will play with reason and discourse,
> And well she can persuade.
>
> (I, ii, 177–9)

Isabella's embarrassment disappears when the question at issue is no longer that of chastity versus sexual licence but the larger one of justice versus mercy. Here she is on her own theological ground, with Scriptural authority to support her dual theme of "Judge not, that ye be not judged" and mercy as the remedy for all forfeited souls through Christ's redemption.

> O, think on that;
> And mercy then will breathe within your lips
> Like man new made,
>
> (II, ii, 77–9)

she cries, intuitively appealing to Angelo's self-deification in an image which recalls not merely rebirth in grace through the water and spirit of baptism, but the myth of Prometheus, as well as the Prayerbook's "Even as in Adam all died, even so in Christ shall all be made alive." But the reminder that "earthly power doth then show likest God's when mercy seasons justice" has no more effect on Angelo than it had on Shylock.

When this appeal fails, Isabella shows herself to be capable of passion as well as eloquence. In general terms, she launches an angry and scornful attack on the man who enjoys playing God, but this time her context is that of *hubris*, and her allusions are classical rather than Christian. After a brief interlude in which Angelo expounds the deterrent theory of punishment and avails himself of the sophistry of Despair in Book I of *The Faerie Queene* to argue that capital punishment is a blessing, since it prevents the sinner from committing additional sins,[17] Isabella lets off her famous broadside against the abusers of authority. She condemns their lack of discrimination, their subservience to the great and their tyranny over the humble, their irresponsibility, their arrogance, and their folly, and ends with that unforgettable description of the self-image of the self-satisfied man who,

> Most ignorant of what he's most assur'd,
> His glassy essence, like an angry ape,
> Plays such fantastic tricks before high heaven
> As makes the angels weep; who, with our spleens,
> Would all themselves laugh mortal.
>
> (II, ii, 119–23)

"Glassy essence" here suggests both the essential nature of man as the image of God and the mirror before which the ridiculous ape postures. In the end, the fire of her rage has thawed the snow of her embarrassment sufficiently for her to extenuate her brother's fault as a "natural guiltiness" to which even an Angelo might be liable—how liable, we discover in the agonized self-analysis which follows upon his dismissal of Isabella. Up to this point, when he delivers himself of a single, significant aside, Angelo has kept himself rigidly under control, giving no verbal intimation of the turmoil within him. But the audience has nonetheless been conditioned to expect his downfall by an undercurrent of *double-entendre*, not only in Lucio's speeches (where the author probably means us to take them as intentional on the part of the character), but in Isabella's (where he certainly does not). Angelo's subsequently revealed response to her innocence and idealism, as well as her beauty, makes ironical the Provost's "Heaven give thee moving graces!" and Isabella's repeated "Heaven keep your Honour safe!" It invests with ambiguity Lucio's "You are too cold," Isabella's allusion to Angelo's "potency," and possibly even Claudio's tribute to her "prone and speechless dialect." Angelo's "Maiden, no remedy" becomes, in their next encounter, there is no remedy if you remain a maid, and there is no dearth of phallic symbols—the pin, the truncheon, and the

[17]Angelo's argument foreshadows that implied in Isabella's "'Tis best that thou diest quickly" to Claudio (III, i, 152).

sword. Lucio's, "Ay, touch him," and "O, to him, to him . . . / He's coming; I perceive 't" must also be suspect. That there are two levels of connotation, overt and covert, operating is acknowledged when Angelo joins in the word-game with the aside which follows on Isabella's reference to a "natural guiltiness": "She speaks, and 'tis such sense that my sense breeds with it." This signposting makes the sexual ambiguities of Isabella's final plea unmistakable, unconscious and therefore doubly ironic though they are. "Hark how I'll bribe you . . . with such gifts that heaven shall share with you," she begins, and, thanks to Angelo's aside, the audience is aware that the only bribe that can prevail with him is the gift of her body, which, along with her soul, she has resolved to dedicate to Christ. In this context, consider the Elizabethan sexual associations of such words as "fond," "stones," "up," and "fancy," as well as the uncommon spelling of shekels as "sicles" and its association with "tested" in the lines which follow:

> Not with fond sicles of the tested gold,
> Or stones, whose rate are either rich or poor
> As fancy values them; but with true prayers
> That shall be up at heaven and enter there
> Ere sun-rise, prayers from preserved souls,
> From fasting maids, whose minds are dedicate
> To nothing temporal.[18]
>
> (II, ii, 149–55)

Well may Angelo comment that he is going "that way to temptation, / Where prayers cross." Is it fanciful to assume that, in his present mood, Angelo would invest Isabella's words with sexual connotations? I think not. The latent ambiguity points up the opposition between innocence and lust. Thematically, it is related also to the

---

[18]There is an interesting parallel between the language of this passage and that of Jacob Kimedoncius, *Of the Redemption of Man, Three Bookes*, tr. Hugh Ince (London: Felix Kingston, 1598), Sigs. B3, B4. After a reference to I Corinthians: 6, 23, "Ye are bought with a price," he continues (Italics are the translator's): But with what price? S. Peter answereth (Pet. 3, 18) *not with silver and gold, or other transitorie things*, (which nothing at all profit us to the eternall *redemption* of our soules) *but with the precious blood of Christ* . . . this price was not paid to the devill but to God, who had power over us to condemn us, and has made us subject to the power of the devill by his Just Judgement. . . . Therefore Christ satisfied God and reconciled us. . . .

Kimedoncius' treatise begins with a lengthy survey of the arguments in favour of the doctrine that all mankind is to be saved, and concludes with a defence of the doctrine of election. A moderate statement of the controversy, it sheds considerable light on the theological background of *Measure for Measure*. Indeed, on the basis of the arguments which Kimedoncius is attempting to refute, a case could be made for the play as supporting the doctrine of universal salvation.

concept of "natural guiltiness" to which Isabella refers in her excuse for Claudio and to the emphasis on the naturalness of sexual appetite throughout the play. Isabella can abjure this side of her nature and repress it in her conscious actions, but no more than Angelo can she destroy an essential component of her human heritage. There is truth and justice of a kind in Angelo's charge to her, so reminiscent of Macbeth's "I dare do all that can become a man / Who dares do more is none." Forestalling Isabella's protests, he bids her, "Be that you are, / That is, a woman; if you be more, you're none" (II, iv, 134–5). Thus repressed, her natural and innocent sexuality emanates in her physical charm and in the unconscious *doubles-entendres* of her speech, as in Angelo its natural but by no means innocent counterpart explodes in a volcano of guilty lust.

Both have now moved one step from the extreme of insensibility towards the norm. Isabella's anger has proved her capable of passion as well as of restraint, and the flesh she is determined to deny has fulfilled, though she is not yet aware of it, its natural feminine function of attracting a man. Angelo, in experiencing natural desire however reprehensible, has ceased to be a walking iceberg. Lust and guilt are not the only aspects of his nature revealed in Angelo's soliloquy of surrender to a desire which might, had it been transmuted into love, have redeemed him. The obstacle which prevents his ascent of the Platonic staircase is plain. Unlike Spenser,[19] he cannot recognize the

[19]The constructive and destructive responses to physical attraction are clearly differentiated in Spenser's *An Hymne in Honoure of Love*, 176–96:

> For loue is Lord of truth and loialtie,
> Lifting himselfe out of the lowly dust,
> On golden plumes vp to the purest skie,
> Aboue the reach of loathly sinfull lust,
> Whose base affect through cowardly distrust
> Of his weake wings, dare not to heauen fly,
> But like a moldwarpe in the earth doth ly.
> His dunghill thoughts, which do themselues enure
> To dirtie drosse, no higher dare aspyre,
> Ne can his feeble earthly eyes endure
> The flaming light of that celestiall fyre
> Which kindleth loue in generous desyre,
> And makes him mount aboue the natiue might
> Of heauie earth, vp to the heauens hight.
> Such is the powre of that sweet passion,
> That it all sordid basenesse doth expell,
> And the refyned mynd doth newly fashion
> Vnto a fairer forme, which now doth dwell
> In his high thought, that would it selfe excell:
> Which he beholding still with constant sight,
> Admires the mirrour of so heauenly light.

"virtuous mind" of a desirable woman as the reflection of heavenly truth because he sees in it only the reflection of himself. He has fallen in love with the female counterpart of his god-like self-image, and his desire for Isabella is not truly a going forth but is merely a projection of his self-enchantment. Again we are reminded of the Duke's words:

> Thyself and thy belongings
> Are not thine own so proper as to waste
> Thyself upon thy virtues, they on thee.
>
> (I, i, 30–2)

Self-love and selfish love are a denial of love. The Duke's brief interview with Juliet, which follows, serves not only to mark the passing of time but also to contrast his kindly, though theologically precise, attitude to her with Angelo's harshness as indicated by the latter's curt injunction, "See that the fornicatress be removed." Juliet's frank acknowledgment of her error and her equally frank persistence in her love are acceptable evidence of inward grace, and are contrasted with Angelo's attitude as developed in the next scene.

It is remorse without repentance, the anguish of self-disillusionment, that is expressed in Angelo's opening soliloquy. He recognizes that in his private prayers as in his public utterances tongue is far from heart, but, fallen angel as he is, his self-confessed pride will not let him accept his imperfections as the badge of kinship with common humanity, and when he speaks of "the strong and swelling evil of my conception" it is not to original sin that he refers, but to his own black and deep desires. He is still a man of extremes: if he cannot be a saint he will be a devil, taking as his private text, "Evil, be thou my good!" but publicly writing "good angel on the Devil's horn."

In the second meeting between Angelo and Isabella the roles are reversed. Now it is he who is embarrassed, who desperately desires what his position and reputation make it awkward for him to demand openly. The *doubles-entendres* are now out in the open, and when Isabella enters, asking, "I am come to know your pleasure," it is not in an aside that Angelo replies,

> That you might know it would much better please me
> Than to demand what 'tis.
>
> (II, iv, 32–3)

Isabella is as obtuse as she is innocent, and though Angelo, still seeing in her the image of himself, accuses her of seeming so in craft, she is as unaware of his ambiguous communication in this scene as she had been of her own in the previous one. Angelo is forced to state his purpose directly, and in doing so he turns against her her own arguments of the day before: that mercy is above law and that a sexual lapse is a natural and pardonable sin. He urges her to emulate Christ's redemption of man by sacrificing her chastity to save her brother's life. As Angelo's sudden perception of his own depravity has resulted in an outburst of self-disgust, so Isabella's enlightenment results in outrage which goes to extremes. "Lawful mercy / Is nothing kin to foul redemption" is sound doctrine enough. "More than our brother is our chastity," however, and

> Better it were a brother died at once
> Than that a sister, by redeeming him,
> Should die for ever,
>
> (II, iv, 106–8)

mark Isabella as sharing in Angelo's self-righteousness and her virtue, like Angelo's "love," as self-regarding. (The note of arrogance in these statements is the stronger in that they are expressed, respectively, in the plural and in the third person, as general truth rather than personal conviction.)

Angelo's infamous proposal that she, perhaps still wearing the habit of the novice, shall put on the livery of the harlot may be Isabella's first really shocking encounter with the realities of human existence. From this point on, the blows to her cherished and sheltered illusions multiply. Having learned that appearance is not necessarily reality, she is now to learn that truth is not always mighty enough to prevail, that false often outweighs true, and that those we love do not invariably live up to the idealized conceptions we have formed of them:

> To whom should I complain? Did I tell this,
> Who would believe me?
>
> (II, iv, 171–2)

No one but Claudio. Her brother will believe her; to him she will unburden her overcharged soul, and from him she will seek reassurance that honour and righteousness are still to be relied on. Isabella's initiation into the ironies of existence is not yet complete.

It is now, near the mid-point of the play, that the Duke adds the function of moderator to those of observer and touchstone. (He has already tried Juliet and found her current gold.) "Be absolute for death," he urges Claudio, proffering the standard consolations of Stoic philosophy as comfort against tribulation. Why, in terms of his role in the play, does he do so, since he has no intention of letting the condemned man die? Because Claudio's delight in the pleasures of this world is *disproportionate* and his imbalance needs correction through comprehension of their ultimate vanity. Because he needs training in the practice of *fortitude*, because he must learn that only the man who is willing to lose his life shall save it. But the lesson has scarce well begun when Isabella enters, and Claudio's too recently strengthened reason yields to his too easily roused emotion when he learns what bitter medicine of hope is yet available. His weakness, his love of the physical aspects of life, and his terror of the physical aspects of death demonstrate his need of the Duke's instruction.

Isabella's state of extreme emotional tension is indicated by the terseness and bitterness of the language in which she tells her story to Claudio. Everything they say to each other points up the opposed values of brother and sister. She protests, and there is no reason to doubt her sincerity, that if it were but her life which was the price of Claudio's pardon she would throw it down for his deliverance "as frankly as a pin." (Lucio, it should be remembered, had accused her of pleading for Claudio's life as if she desired "a pin.") She who was prepared to renounce the world in life would gladly renounce it in death for an honourable cause. But it is *not* her life which she is asked to sacrifice but her honour, which she values far more than life, and she is incapable of understanding or accepting the possibility that her brother may value his life more than her honour, or that his concept of honour may not be hers. (It is more than coincidence that in this play all the male characters are threatened with death, the female ones with loss of "honour.") She pours out her anger and bitterness at Claudio's betrayal of her standards in language almost as brutal as Lear's when the daughter he loves best disappoints his expectations. If we regard Isabella in this scene merely as the symbol of militant chastity we will find her behaviour intolerable, and the play will make no sense. If we regard her as a young girl in a state of emotional shock, who has not yet learned that it is easier to preach than to practise charity, we may be able to excuse what we cannot admire.

It is important to note, also, that Isabella does not nurse her resentment against Claudio beyond the moment of giving way to her immediate anger. In spite of her

> Might but my bending down
> Reprieve thee from thy fate, it should proceed,
>
> (III, i, 145–6)

the Duke has only to suggest, a moment later, that "a remedy presents itself" by which her brother may yet be saved, for her to reply, "Show me how, good father." Claudio, in his turn, repents of his cowardice as soon as his sister has left him. "Let it come on!" is once more his cry, and he desires only to ask his sister's pardon before he dies.

The "remedy of love" which the Duke proposes is, of course, the much condemned "bed-trick" by which Mariana is to make Angelo guilty of precisely the sin for which he has condemned Claudio, while deceiving him into thinking that he has violated Isabella. By this means, "is your brother saved, your honour untainted, the poor Mariana advantaged, and the corrupt deputy scaled," and "the doubleness of the benefit defends the deceit from reproof," the Duke explains. In other words, the end justifies the means, but most critics feel that the doubleness of the dishonour, not to mention the Duke's double-dealing, requires some further justification than the very problematical benefits the substitution is designed to yield. How can the Duke say, "To bring them thus together is no sin," when he has condemned Juliet for the same action? It would seem probable that in this play Shakespeare is more than usually concerned with the development of his theme and less than usually so with logical motivation of plot and consistency of characterization. For the purposes of the theme it is important to create an exact parallel[20] between Angelo's situation and Claudio's, and to "pay with falsehood false exacting," as well as to present Mariana as an exemplar of the love which bears, believes, hopes, and endures all things. He is willing to let her go cheerfully to bed with her ex-fiancé in order to accomplish these ends, even though to do so makes Isabella tell lies and the Duke contradict himself in insisting that what he had termed sin in Juliet's case is "no sin" in Mariana's, and in spite of the fact that the betrothal contract which might be held to excuse Juliet and Claudio has been abrogated between Mariana and Angelo, civilly if not morally.

Mariana is more completely an allegorical figure than the other characters. She is set apart from the corruption of Vienna by her residence in a country grange, isolated by the moat of Angelo's desertion and slander as well as by the loss of her fortune. The word "grange," originally meaning a barn and later a farmhouse with attached outbuildings, carries the connotation of fertility, and along

---

[20]The parallel extends even to the circumstance that complications of dowry prevent both betrothals from becoming formalized in marriage. But even this similarity is used to point a contrast between the two men. Claudio freely acknowledges that he and Juliet have chosen the lesser good in preferring practical prudence and carnal satisfaction to precise moral rectitude. Angelo, on the other hand, chooses the greater evil in safeguarding his reputation at the expense of Mariana's by refusing to acknowledge the loss of her dowry as the reason for his breaking with her and resorting to slander in order to provide himself with a scripturally authorized excuse (Matthew 5:30) for his breach of contract.

with her name links her with that other maiden, whose espoused husband did *not* desert her in her difficulty and who was likewise lodged in a stable. We first meet Mariana in an atmosphere of harmony, accompanied by a boy who sings her sorrow. It is twice mentioned that she lives at St. Luke's, and it is not like Shakespeare to be so precise about locale without reason. The reason is apparent when we turn from St. Matthew's account of the Sermon on the Mount, so frequently alluded to in this play, to St. Luke's. Both versions include the command, "Love your enemies," but St. Luke's (6: 35–8) is more emphatic about the necessity of forgiveness and demands a more generous outpouring of love:

But love ye your enemies, and do good, and lend, hoping for nothing again; and your reward shall be great, and ye shall be the children of the Highest: for He is kind unto the unthankful and to the evil.

Be ye therefore merciful, as your Father also is merciful.

Judge not, and ye shall not be judged: condemn not, and ye shall not be condemned: forgive, and ye shall be forgiven:

Give, and it shall be given unto you; good measure, pressed down, and shaken together, and running over, shall men give unto your bosom. For with the same measure that ye mete withal it shall be measured to you again.

Such is the measure of Mariana's love—pressed down, shaken together, and running over, or, as the Duke describes it:

. . . his unjust unkindness, that in all reason should have quenched her love, hath, like an impediment in the current, made it more violent and unruly.

(III, i, 233–6)

It is only when Isabella can identify herself with Mariana, when she can kneel with her to sue for Angelo as she had once knelt to him to sue for her brother, that righteousness and mercy are reconciled in her heart.

The remainder of Act III and the first part of Act IV develop minor but significantly related themes. Pompey, as unregenerate nature, having failed to use to good purpose the mercy Escalus has shown him, is brought to justice but remains irrepressible, fulfilling his function as an agent of execution in the same realistic spirit as he had that of an agent of procreation. Indeed, he finds little difference between the world within and the world without the prison walls, now that most of his former fellows and patrons are within. Copulation and death are but different aspects of the process of life, and Pompey, "a poor fellow that would live," is willing to live by either.

Lucio's scurrilous and irresponsible gossip demonstrates his lack of prudence and leads into a discussion of calumny, the obverse of hypocrisy as an obstacle to the reconciliation of Truth and Justice. The subject who slanders the prince is politically as well as ethically culpable, in that his lies not only undermine the people's confidence in authority but also make it more difficult for the citizen with legitimate grievances to find redress. "O place and greatness," laments the Duke,

> Millions of false eyes
> Are stuck upon thee. Volumes of report
> Run with these false, and most contrarious quest
> Upon thy doings.
>
> (IV, i, 58–61)

Slander of the great protects the scoundrel and gives immunity to the hypocrite in office. "Who will believe thee, Isabel?" Justice, as we are made to see in Act V, is unable to recognize the grain of truth where it has been conditioned to expect the chaff of lies.

Truth and justice, appearance and reality, responsibility and seeming, are the favourite themes of the Duke's soliloquies and asides, those sententious pronouncements so clearly set apart by style, line-length, and rhyme from his normal speech. Indeed they are not so much soliloquies in the ordinary Shakespearean sense as the choral comment which these differences proclaim them to be. They are not overheard by the audience, but are directed to it, and in giving the Duke's evaluation of particular situations as formal pronouncements they serve as a reminder that his authority is not abandoned but merely in abeyance. They also serve to prevent the audience from becoming too exclusively concerned with the complications of the plot and thus forgetting what the play is about.

There is much in these middle scenes also about responsibility as related to duty and function. We are allowed to laugh at but at the same time are made to respect Abhorson's pride in his grim but necessary "mystery." We sympathize with the Provost's internal conflict between duty and charity, and are pleased when the Duke resolves his dilemma (at some risk to his own anonymity) by providing him with a higher authority than Angelo's to which he can render obedience without going against his conscience. We are pleased, too, as well as amused, when he mercifully spares Barnardine, the man wholly insensible in spirit, who must be fitted for life in order that he may have time to make himself fit for death. There are many kinds of deficiency of sensibility in this play.

We return to the main stream of the action towards the close of Act IV, scene iii, when the Duke, meeting Isabella, tells her very bluntly that Angelo has welched on his filthy bargain. Again the cry is, "To what end?" What is gained, in terms of the play, by the needless torture of making Isabella believe that Claudio is dead? It is noteworthy that immediately after breaking the news the Duke offers her the chance of vengeance, though his words can bear another interpretation. Lay your grievance before the Duke when he returns, he urges her, and continues:

> If you can, pace your wisdom
> In that good path that I would wish it go,
> And you shall have your bosom on this wretch,
> Grace of the Duke, revenges to your heart,
> And general honour.
>
> (IV, iii, 129–33)

Notice the suggestion of restraint in the word "pace" as well as that of direction, the careful choice of the word "wisdom," the equivocation in the second line, "That good path that I would wish it go," and also between the language of vengeance and the language of love in the third. In intention, this is the counterpart to the Duke's charge to Angelo to administer justice "as to your soul seems good." Isabella will demand such justice as is imaged in her bosom. It is not enough, for the Duke's purposes or Shakespeare's, that she should excuse the insult of an attempted seduction; she must also forgive Angelo for an injury she believes him to have actually committed. Therefore she must be convinced of Claudio's death.

Isabella's cry for justice rings throughout the final act, and it is part of its pervasive irony that she should gain with such difficulty that which she must freely relinquish. For in the beginning, Truth and Justice are still at odds, and reason is mistaken for madness. "O gracious Duke," she pleads,

> Harp not on that; nor do not banish reason
> For inequality; but let your reason serve
> To make the truth appear where it seems hid,
> And hide the false seems true.
>
> (V, i, 64–7)

But she pleads in vain. Angelo's false outweighs her true, and she is carried off guarded. Mariana takes her place as plaintiff, only to be mocked at in her turn and to hear Angelo repeat his former slander of her reputation. Human justice proves itself all too imperfect. Even

Escalus, its best representative, places too much credence in circumstantial evidence and proves to be a respecter of persons. When the Duke, still disguised as the Friar, tells the unvarnished truth about his own administration he is accused of treasonable slander. Truth cries out in the market-place and is not heeded. "Gowns and furr'd robes hide all." Perfect justice requires omniscience, and since only the Duke knows all that it is humanly possible to know, he must resume his authority in order that the earthly justice which is the similitude of the pattern laid up in Heaven *may be seen to be done*. Truth is the daughter of Time, and must await her epiphany until that highly theatrical moment of reversal when Lucio, the Vice, tears off the semblance to reveal the actuality of virtue. *Cuchullus non facit monachem*, but the removal of the cowl makes a duke.

In resuming his authority the Duke accepts the responsibilities of his office in a way he had found it difficult to do at the beginning of the play, and one indication that Shakespeare regarded him as a human protagonist and not merely as a *deus ex machina* or an allegorical figure is that, in common with the other redeemable characters, he grows during the course of the action. He learns to accept the world, with all its imperfections, as his world, for which he, in common with its other citizens, is responsible. He learns Prospero's lesson that "the life removed" is not for the governor, that the end of all knowledge, including self-knowledge, is, in Sidney's words, "virtuous action." The identification of the Duke with his subjects occurs in his soliloquy at the end of Act III:

> Twice treble shame on Angelo,
> To weed my vice and let his grow,
>
> (III, ii, 251-2)

and he admits his responsibility in protesting (as Friar) against the injustice of appointing Angelo to be "judge in his own cause." The faithful Escalus (Justice blindfolded?) having accused him of slander, his justification appears in his public self-accusation:

>   My business in this state
> Made me a looker-on here in Vienna,
> Where I have seen corruption boil and bubble
> Till it o'errun the stew: laws for all faults,
> But faults so countenanc'd that the strong statutes
> Stand like the forfeits in a barber's shop,
> As much in mock as mark.
>
> (V, i, 314-20)

Excess of private licence, especially the sexual licence glanced at in the equivocation on "stew," defect of public restraint, have resulted in chaos, and the Duke's resumption of his authority will not be attended by his former laxity, a laxity based (for all his distaste for "loud applause and Aves vehement") on the desire to retain the approval of public opinion. He has learned that calumny is an inevitable hazard of public office and is ready to accept the uncomfortable consequences of fortitude as applied to firm administration. But the experiment of severity has proved as destructive of justice as laxity has been of order, and in future the Duke will strive to rule in the image of his own temperance. If he is to do so successfully the citizens must learn, as he has learned, the lessons of acceptance and responsibility, and it is in terms of these qualities that he brings about the epiphanies and resolutions of the denouement. Each extreme confronts and reveals its opposite, and through understanding and accepting it is mitigated to the measure of moderation. Those who have the grace to accept their responsibilities are pardoned or rewarded; those who do not, notably Lucio, have responsibility thrust upon them. But the distinction between the justice of restitution and the justice of retribution is clearly drawn. For all his natural resentment of Lucio's slanders of himself the Duke does not hold the babbler to account for them. He exacts no personal vengeance, and his charge to Lucio is the same as that to Claudio: "She . . . that you wronged, look you restore." Since Claudio's "wrong" was an error motivated by love, this is to him no punishment but a boon. To Lucio, who feels nothing but contempt for the whore he has abused and cheated, it is "pressing to death, whipping, and hanging," punishments appropriate, as the Duke only half-jestingly reminds him, to the slanderer of a prince as to a slanderer of love, for love, as the *Symposium* insists, is a mighty prince as well as a god.

Angelo is redeemed by grace, the grace of Providence which has delivered him from actually committing the evil he intended, and the imputed grace of love, which will forgive his trespasses of intention, for Angelo does not change, though Mariana is confident that he will be "much more the better / For being a little bad." He condemns himself as harshly as he had condemned others whose guilt had been brought to the attention of the authorities. His "What's open made to justice, / That justice seizes" (II, i, 21–2) is not far removed in spirit from "When I perceive your Grace, like power divine, / Hath look'd upon my passes," or from Volpone's "To be taken, to be seen, / These have crimes accounted been." He confesses his fault and admits his shame, but, knowing not mercy, "immediate sentence" is "all the grace" he asks. Isabella will soon teach him what mercy is, and Mariana's loving forgiveness may yet make him whole enough to forgive even himself.

Circumstances have involved Isabella in a world from which she desired to exclude herself, and have broadened her comprehension of good and evil. In Angelo she has experienced the depths of baseness; in Mariana the transcendence of love. The authority of religion (in the person of the Friar) has condoned compromise where the choice lay between a lesser and a greater evil. All this has gradually conditioned her to accept the world as what it is instead of rejecting it as being other than she would have it be. But the process of stripping her of her illusions has not diminished but enhanced her goodness by endowing her with charity, without which all her eloquence and faith and self-denial would profit her nothing. The final step, the recognition that mercy is not logical pardon but a free gift of grace, is not an easy one for her, and her heart bestows mercy while her tongue pleads, if no longer for justice, for pardon on logically justifiable grounds. The Duke makes matters more difficult for her by the logic of his rebuttal of her plea, for it is important to him that her grace should "go forth" from her soul, not from her reason alone.

To those on stage unaware of the facts and unfamiliar with the Duke's habit of equivocation, his sentence on the newly married Angelo:

> We do condemn thee to the very block
> Where Claudio stoop'd to death, and with like haste,
> (V, i, 412–13)

is indeed measure for measure, the old law of retribution. When Mariana begs Isabella to join her in pleading for Angelo's pardon, the Duke tells her that such importunity is "against all sense" (i.e., is both unnatural and illogical) and warns Isabella that if she should "kneel down in mercy of this fact" her brother would rise from his grave in horror, since "He dies for Claudio's death." In spite of this powerful appeal not only to her natural feelings but to her self-righteousness, Isabella does kneel, though not, as Mariana had suggested, silently. Still, it is the action rather than the speech which accompanies it that is significant. For Mariana's sake she is ready to forego personal vengeance for Claudio's death, but is reluctant to forego justice. She attempts to justify pardoning Angelo for the offence for which he had himself condemned her brother on the ground that his "act did not o'ertake his bad intent." This may be the way of pragmatic earthly justice, but the text, "He that looketh upon a woman to lust after her

hath committed adultery with her in his heart" makes theological non-
sense of her argument, as she well knows. That she should plead for
her enemy on what to her, though not perhaps to a court of law, must
seem very doubtful grounds is a sign that mercy has conquered rigidity
in her, and forgiveness logic.

Significantly, Isabella begins her speech on behalf of Angelo by
acknowledging that, without either "intent" or "act" on her part, and
therefore without guilt, nevertheless she is in part responsible for his
offence by reason of being what she is, not "a thing enskied and
sainted" but a woman:

> Look, if it please you, on this man condemn'd
> As if my brother liv'd. I partly think
> A due sincerity govern'd his deeds
> Till he did look on me; since it is so,
> Let him not die.
>
> (V, i, 442–5)

Again, her grounds for mercy are not entirely consonant with her
knowledge that "due sincerity" did not govern his actions towards
Mariana, but for that Mariana has forgiven him. For her own part,
however, Isabella thus forgives evil and accepts the flesh as part of
man's nature, and asserts her identity with mankind in both flesh and
spirit. It is true that her growth in grace has made her more than ever
fitted to be the bride of Christ, and

> Thrice-blessed they that master so their blood
> To undergo such maiden pilgrimage;
> But earthlier happy is the rose distill'd
> Than that which withering on the virgin thorn
> Grows, lives, and dies, in single blessedness.
> *Midsummer Night's Dream*, I, i, 74–8)

As a comedy, however, *Measure for Measure* is concerned with earthly
happiness; as an allegory, it is concerned not with the rejection but
with the acceptance of the world, with the reconciliation of things
earthly with things heavenly—of earthly and heavenly love, of flesh
and spirit, of mercy and justice. Therefore we need not be shocked that
this "thing enskied and sainted" should be handed over so casually to
the "fantastical Duke of dark corners," but can regard her marriage as
a natural fulfilment not only of her destiny as a woman but of the
pattern of development of the play. Isabella puts on "the destined
livery" in an honourable union which typifies the Kiss of Peace and
Righteousness prophesied by the Psalmist. We may see Duke Vincentio
not only as the personification of Peace, the instrument of Divine

Providence, but perhaps also as the "courtier not young," who, according to Cardinal Bembo,[21] is most capable of that highest kind of
earthly love which does not exclude the flesh but rises, through an
appreciation of its beauty, to comprehension of the heavenly beauties
of the spirit. In *Measure for Measure* the fifth-act marriages are not
merely devices for tidying up loose ends into a conventionally happy
ending; they are symbols of the various aspects of the reconciliation by
which peace and righteousness, truth and mercy are brought into
agreement in order to establish an ethical polity in Vienna. The result
is not a replica of the heavenly city, perhaps, but it is a model for a
satisfactory earthly commonwealth of tolerably decent citizens. To
Plato, love was the mediator between gods and men;[22] Christian marriage is an image of the spiritual union of Christ and his Church, and
to the Christian humanist it is also a reflection of the Platonic celestial
harmony composed not "of elements which are still in a state of
discord. But . . . of differing notes of higher or lower pitch, which
disagreed once, but are now reconciled."[23]

And how, according to Platonic theory, have these original oppositions and discords been brought to that point of affinity in difference
which is the basis of harmony? By modulation towards the mean. The
process is outlined in Plutarch's Commentary on the *Timaeus*:

Now the better to understand the proportion wherewith he made the soule,
we must take a patterne and example, from the constitution of the bodie of
the worlde: for whereas the two extremes, to wit, pure fire and earth, were
by nature hard to be tempered one with another, or to say more truely,
impossible to be mixed and incorporate together; he placed in the middes
betweene, aire before fire, and water before earth: and so contempered first
these two meane elements, and afterwards by their helpe, the other extremes
also, which he fitted and framed together, both with the said meanes, and
also with themselves . . . . afterwards when these were mixed together he
contempered likewise the extreames, and so warped and wove, as one would
say, the whole forme of the soule, making as far as it was possible, of things
unlike, semblable, and of many, one.[24]

Such is the synthesis of order which has been taking place in *Measure
for Measure*. By the correction of excess and defect through the agency

[21]In Book IV of Castiglione's *The Courtier*.
[22]See Socrates' account of Diotima's definition of Love in *The Symposium*.
[23]Eryximachus' analogy between love and music in *The Symposium*.
[24]In *The Philosophie, commonlie called the Morals written by the learned
Philosopher Plutarch of Chaeronea*, tr. Philemon Holland (London: Arnold Hat-
field, 1603), pp. 1054 ff.
The famous passage on celestial harmony in *The Merchant of Venice* (V, i,
54–65) closely parallels the *Timaeus* on the same theme.

of the Duke as the representative of Temperance, all the major characters have moved at least one step closer to the mean which comprises
the norm of human nature. Those who have denied or retreated from
or been excluded from the normal world have been brought to accept
it or are restored to it. Thus opposites have been modified into
"semblances" by accepting the measure of man's divided heritage,
semblances in which "like doth quit like" and measure balances
measure, not in conflict but in harmony.

Of this humanist allegory of ethical polity Shakespeare, had he been
given to such comment, might have said as Cicero did of his *De Officiis*,
a work which also deals with questions of ethical polity:

Moral goodness, in the truest and fullest sense of the word, . . . could only
be found among those hypothetical people who are endowed with ideal
wisdom. Nobody who falls short of this perfect wisdom can possibly claim
perfect goodness: its semblance is the most he can acquire. And these are
the men, the ordinary men falling short of the ideal, whose moral obligations
form the subject of my present work.[25]

[25]"Of Duties," Cicero, *Selected Works*, tr. Michael Grant (Penguin Books, 1960),
Book III, ch. ii, p. 163.

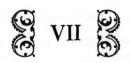

VII

The Poisoned Chalice:
Dualism in *Macbeth*

A land of darkness, as darkness itself; and of the shadow of
death, without any order, and where the light is as darkness.
(Job 10:22)

When thine eye is single, thy whole body also is full of light,
but when thine eye is evil, thy body also is full of darkness.
Take heed, therefore, that the light which is in thee be not
darkness.

(Luke 11:34–5)

SUCH ARE THE DISORDERED inner and outer worlds of *Macbeth*. Yet,
though fair is foul and foul is fair, in none of Shakespeare's tragedies
are the opposed forces of good and evil more clearly defined. Hamlet's
obsessive search for the absolutes of goodness, truth, and beauty and
his inability to accept the evil of this world, lead him to see as rotten
what is merely corrupt—a world of purposes mistook, of mingled good
and evil, a world of dilemmas to which neither passion nor reason can
provide a satisfactory solution. In Macbeth's world, on the other hand,
good and evil are presented as a polarity, in that there is an absolute
idea of good and an absolute idea of evil. But once out of the realm
of the abstract, the poles with which these concepts are traditionally
associated fail to stand firm; like the external macrocosm they reflect
the insurrection in the microcosm of the hero's soul. As he moves from
worldly glory to misery and death, from heroic virtue to deep damnation, his moral revolution is reflected not only in the macrocosms of
external nature and the state but in the behaviour of the individual
inhabitants of his personal world. The normal delimitations of day
and night disappear, as do those of manliness and womanliness, pru-

dence and cowardice. The innocent flee as if guilty; honest men vow allegiance which is nothing more than mouth-honour; responsible men behave irresponsibly, and nothing is but what is not.

But however evil may masquerade as good, and good as evil, no character in the play is more than briefly confused as to which is which, and the audience is never in doubt as it may well have been regarding the character of the hero in the opening scenes of *Othello*, and the character of the villain in the opening scenes of *Hamlet*. The tragic world of *Macbeth* is not merely one in which appearance belies reality, as in *Othello*, nor one in which confusion is triumphant, as in a great part of *King Lear*. It is rather a hell in which the order of nature is turned upside down, in which the image of the good is seen reversed in the dark mirror of evil. A. P. Rossiter, commenting that "Shakespeare wrote in an unstable equilibrium between a 'World' or 'Universe of Thought' of god-ordainedness and another world: the inverted world of belief only in power," notes that the inverted world symbol is familiar in Breughel's pictures as an orb with its cross downwards. One so appears as one of Quarles's *Emblems*.[1] It is such a world, one in which the things of this world are regarded as superior to "the life to come," that Shakespeare shows us in *Macbeth*.

How far this seemingly diabolical, upside-down world is to be taken as the creation of supernatural rather than human agents is a question which he leaves unresolved, perhaps deliberately. The adherents of the opposed doctrines of free-will and predestination are free to interpret the play in whatever sense may please them, and they have not neglected their opportunity.[2] That the weird sisters function as instruments of evil seems clear, their diabolical nature less so, and their

[1]*Angel with Horns and Other Shakespeare Lectures*, edited by Graham Storey (London: Longmans; New York: Theatre Arts Books, 1961), p. 59. The poem and accompanying illustration (*Emblems* I:15) indicate that Quarles is employing the reversed Christian symbol of orb and cross to signify both general and sexual disorder. The orb takes the form of a medallion enclosed by a ring of hearts. It depicts a night scene in which Cupid sits on the ground, his bow thrown aside and an hour-glass in his hand. The vertical member of the cross which serves as a pedestal to the orb is of a shape which suggests sexual symbolism, and the cross-bar is a second hour-glass. It is the generally unsatisfactory state of the world, however, which is chiefly lamented in the poem.

[2]All varieties of opinion as to the nature and degree of Macbeth's deception by the three weird sisters, and the concomitant extent of his moral responsibility for his downfall, may be found in recent as in earlier criticism. For example: Wilson Knight (*The Wheel of Fire*, Oxford University Press, 1930, chs. VI and VII) sees Macbeth's will as suffering a paralysis of fear under the onslaught of absolute evil, which is present both in his internal and in his external worlds, but concludes that "ultimate evil remains a mystery" and "Macbeth is the apocalypse of evil." John F. Danby (*Shakespeare's Doctrine of Nature*, London: Faber and

direct influence upon the events of the play remains in doubt, however much their presence may contribute to the atmosphere of unnaturalness in which these events take place. Shakespeare makes them less the heralds of destiny and more the agents of temptation than he found them in Holinshed, where they are said to resemble "creatures of elder world," held "by common opinion" to be "either the weird sisters, that is (as ye would say) the goddesses of destiny, or else some nymphs or fairies, imbued with the knowledge of prophecy by their necromantical science." There is little in this that is unequivocally indicative of malevolence, the prophecies demonstrating foreknowledge (possibly obtained by evil means) rather than evil intent. In earlier versions of the story[3] they are variously regarded and sometimes omitted. Shakespeare has kept Holinshed's appellation of "weird sisters" as well as calling them "witches," but has endowed them with the attributes of witches, especially of Scottish witches. In Holinshed's account, Macbeth's first thought of murdering his king follows upon the meeting with the sisters, however, whereas in the play it seems clearly to have preceded it.

As witches, the sisters provide a supernatural machinery more appropriate to the theme of inverted order than do Holinshed's Fates, and as such their "soliciting," while it cannot be fatal to Macbeth's

---

Faber, pp. 161–2) regards Macbeth as a man whose moral equilibrium is upset when "his reason is hypnotized by the fortune-telling witches," while Willard Farnham (*Shakespeare's Tragic Frontier*, Berkeley: University of California Press, 1950) considers him one of Shakespeare's "deeply flawed" heroes and suggests that, like Milton's Satan, he possesses a "paradoxical nobility" fused with baseness. Roy Walker (*The Time is Free: A Study of Macbeth*, London: Andrew Dakers, 1949), F. R. Leavis ("Tragedy and the Medium," *The Common Pursuit*, London: Chatto and Windus, 1952; Peregrine Books, 1962) and W. C. Curry (*Shakespeare's Philosophical Patterns*, Baton Rouge: Louisiana State University Press, 1937) agree in seeing Macbeth as possessed by evil, but differ in their emphasis upon external and internal evil. Walker regards the Third Murderer as a projection or personification of Macbeth's guilt (p. 108); Curry insists that the whole drama "is saturated with the malignant presence of fallen angels" who "insnare human souls by means of diabolical persuasion, hallucinations, infernal illusions and possession" (p. 97). He regards Macbeth's moral sense as "rudimentary," since he fears only the immediate, never the ultimate consequences of his acts. Lily B. Campbell (*Shakespeare's Tragic Heroes, Slaves of Passion*, Cambridge University Press, 1930; London, Barnes and Noble, 1960) gives a thorough analysis of Macbeth's character as a "Study of Fear" in the frame of reference of Aristotle's virtue of Fortitude, in which he moves from the excess of rashness to the defect of fear. She regards his personal ambition as a secondary passion, which, according to King James I, was, with lust, one of the two which most predispose men to temptation.

[3]The various versions of the stories of Macbeth and Macdonwald (both of which Shakespeare used for the plot of *Macbeth*) are conveniently summarized in Farnham, *Shakespeare's Tragic Frontier*, pp. 80–93.

spiritual well-being, is not to be taken as either neutral or benevolent. Witches were worshippers of the "dark god," and it was the moral inversion inherent in the denial of Christ and the transfer of spiritual allegiance to his adversary, not the charms and spells of "black magic," which led the medieval Church to condemn witchcraft rites and practices as heresy,[4] in contravention of the earlier *Canon Episcopi* which had declared belief in the supernatural powers of witches and wizards to be itself an error. Accusations of witchcraft levelled against the Cathars, Waldenses, and Albigenses suggest that the Church equated Manichaeism and Dualism generally with Satanism. Understandably so, since the tenet that Satan is coeval with God leads logically enough to the position that the power of Good and the power of Evil are not only co-eternal but co-equal, with Satan presiding over this world and God over the realm of heaven.

The prevalence of the concept in primitive and later religions is commented on by W. C. Curry in his chapter on "The Demonic Metaphysics of *Macbeth*" (see note 2). He notes that the dualist position is clearly reflected in the opening chapters of the Book of Job, that St. Augustine touches on it, and that its elements are present in both Stoic and Neoplatonic philosophy and in Calvin's doctrines of Predestination and Election. In the dualist view, "the two realms of light and darkness, good and evil are eternally opposed, the one to the other, and God and Satan rule over these realms, respectively."

Nowadays, "witchcraft" is usually regarded as synonymous with "sorcery," but a clear distinction between them was maintained by medieval and Renaissance theologians.[5] Though it was assumed that members of witch cults made bargains with the Devil in which they renounced eternal salvation in return for supernatural power in this world, power which they used to advance themselves and harm their

[4]The first such declaration took the form of an edict of the Holy Office of the Inquisition, issued during its campaign of suppression directed against the Waldenses, a thirteenth-century sect which considered the Scriptures to be the final authority in matters of doctrine. The edict charged the Waldenses with practising witchcraft and declared witchcraft a heresy. The edict was subsequently confirmed and extended by the Papal Bulls of Innocent VIII (1484) and Alexander VI (1500).

[5]See Russell Hope Robbins, *Encyclopedia of Witchcraft and Demonology* (New York: Crown Press; London: Peter Neville, 1959), Introduction and entries under "Sorcery" and "Witchcraft." See also K. M. Briggs, *Pale Hecate's Team* (London: Routledge and Kegan Paul, 1962), pp. 3 ff. Miss Briggs cites Michael Dalton, *The Country Justice* (1677), pp. 385–6, as follows: "The witch dealeth rather by a friendly and voluntary Conference or agreement between him (or her) and the Devil or Familiar, to have his or her turn served; and in lieu thereof the Witch giveth (or offereth) his or her Soul, Blood, or other gift unto the Devil." The other gift, especially to a familiar, was usually milk. The confession of

enemies, fortune-telling and spell-casting were regarded as specific acts of sorcery associated with witchcraft, not as the thing itself. In English law (until 1604) such practices were not liable to criminal prosecution until a charge of specific and premeditated injury could be brought against the practitioner. It was Satanism, the transfer of spiritual allegiance from the principle of good to the principle of evil, rather than sorcery, which was damnable in the eyes of the Church, though at the height of the witch-mania the practice of sorcery was accepted as evidence of Satanism. Of course, sorcery practised against the sovereign[6] was capital treason in the eyes of the state, whether successful or not, since disloyalty was obviously its motive.

The fulminators against witchcraft were by no means unaware of the relationship of its rituals (and of certain folk customs) to the rites of pre-Christian fertility cults, nor was this relationship inconsistent with their charge that witches worshipped the Devil. Milton's identification of the fallen angels with ancient deities was common superstition as well as orthodox doctrine, and the Puritans who attacked such survivals as bringing in the May[7] and dancing about Midsummer and Hallowe'en bonfires regarded these practices as relics of paganism, which was, in their view, Satanism. Hence the paradox that a cult recognized as originating in the worship of Nature

---

Margery Sammon, cited in *A True and Just Record of the Information, Examination and Confession of all the Witches taken at St. Oses in the County of Essex* (London, 1582) Sig. f.C. 5, stated that familiars would suck the blood of the witches if they were not fed milk. The references to milk in the play may well be conscious or unconscious allusions to this practice.

The existence of a voluntary bargain with the Devil is also the basis of distinction in Jean Bodin's definition of a witch as "one who knowing God's law tries to bring about some act through an agreement with the Devil" (tr. from *De la démonomanie des sorciers*, Paris, 1580).

[6]As in the trial of Antony Fortescue, formerly comptroller of Cardinal Pole, and others, ordered to be apprehended and brought before the Council on the charge of "contriving mischief against the Queen, by setting up the Scotch Queen's title . . . by dealing with some conjurors to cast their Figures to calculate the Queen's life, the Duration of her Government and the like. . . ." (Strype, *Annals of the Reformation*, London, 1709, as cited in R. Trevor Davies *Four Centuries of Witch Beliefs*, London: Methuen, 1947, p. 20).

[7]Sir James Frazer supports his argument to this effect by citing Stubbes, *Anatomie of Abuses* (1583): "Against May, Whitsunday, or other time, all the young men and maides, olde men and wives, run gadding over night into the woods, groves, hils, and mountains, where they spend al the night in pleasant pastimes; and in the morning they return, bringing with them birch, and branches of trees, to deck their assemblies withall. And no mervaile, for there is a great Lord present amongst them, as superintendent and Lord over their pastimes and sportes, namely Sathan, prince of hel." "Relics of Tree Worship in Modern Europe," (*The Magic Art and the Evolution of Kings*, Vol. II, Part I of *The Golden Bough*, London: Macmillan, 1911, p. 66).

Stubbes goes into further detail on the subject of Maying customs, including

and dedicated to the performance of rites intended to promote natural fertility should so persistently have been associated with unnaturalness and sterility. Since the moral inversion of Satan-worship was regarded as an inversion of human nature, its practices were therefore assumed to be directed towards all manner of subversions of external and physical nature.

Witchcraft was a particularly appropriate frame of reference for the exploration of the theme of moral inversion in a tragedy based on Scottish history. The annals of Scotland are plentifully besprinkled with accounts of sorcery.[8] Not only was James I's *Daemonologie* (1597) one of the most widely read treatises on witchcraft; he and his queen had, as they believed, narrowly escaped death at sea when a group of Scottish witches, suborned by a disgruntled nobleman who was reputed to be a powerful wizard on his own account, had raised a violent storm by diabolical means.[9] James's Parliament had recently

---

those of the setting up of the Maypole and dressing of a youth in spring foliage and bringing him in triumphal procession to the village as the May King. His objection to these revels is not merely the usual Puritan prejudice against "mirth," but specifically that they are pagan rites. For the fertility-sterility paradox, see Briggs, *Pale Hecate's Team*, p. 25, and J. G. Campbell, *Witchcraft and Second Sight in the Highlands and Islands of Scotland*, 1902, p. 13. Macbeth's preoccupation with his lack of "issue" and his willingness to see "nature's germens tumble all together" are related to the witchcraft motifs of the play.

[8]In addition to Holinshed's *Chronicles of Scotland*, see G. F. Black, *A Calendar of Cases of Witchcraft in Scotland* (New York, 1938); George Buchanan, *Rerum Scoticarum Historia*; *Newes from Scotland* (London: Wm. Wright, 1591), and Robert Pitcairn, ed., *Criminal Trials* I, Part ii (Edinburgh, 1833). For example, in 1479 the Earl of Mar was accused of conspiring with twelve witches to shorten the life of James III by melting a waxen image, and in 1537, Janet Douglas, Lady Glamis, was burned on Castle Hill, Edinburgh, for attempting the life of James V by poison and evil charms.

[9]The story is told in the testimony of Agnes Sampson (*alias* Tompson) at the trial of the North Berwickshire Witches, 1590: ". . . at the time when his maiestie was in Denmarke, she being accompanied with the parties before especially named *i.e.* John Fian, Effie McCalyan, and Barbara Napier, tooke a cat and christened it, and afterward bound to each part of that cat, the chiefest parts of a dead man, and severall joynts of his bodie, and that in the night following the said Cat was conveied into the midst of the sea by all these witches sayling in their riddles or Cives . . . and so left the said Cat right before the Towne of Lieth in Scotland. . . . The said Christned Cat was the cause that the Kinges Maiesties Ship at his comming foorth of Denmarke had a contrary wind to the rest of his Ships, then being in his companye, which thing was most strange and true . . . his maiestie had never come safelye from the Sea if his faith had not prevailed above their ententions." (*Newes from Scotland*, pp. 16–17.)

When the storm proved ineffectual the witches resorted to other methods and melted a waxen man at Preston Pans, after pronouncing the words: "This is King James the sext, ordonit to be consumed at the instance of a noble man Francis Erle Bodwell!" (Pitcairn, *Criminal Trials*, I, ii).

(1604) passed a law imposing severe penalties upon those who practised sorcery, which replaced a much milder statute of Elizabeth I. Controversy over the witch question was at its peak, and the presses were pouring forth into the hands of sensation-hungry readers a spate of treatises and pamphlets expressing every shade of opinion from scepticism to the most credulous bigotry.[10] What Shakespeare himself may have believed about these hotly disputed matters has little relevance for the dramatic use he made of commonly received opinions about them. There can be no doubt that he was familiar with these opinions and knew that his audience would be familiar with them also. They could be counted on to respond not only to direct allusions to the concepts and practices of witchcraft, but to subliminal suggestions of their implications conveyed through situation and imagery, such as that of light and darkness, for example, far more sensitively than a modern audience can be expected to do. They were more receptive not merely because they had the habit of allegorizing, nor because, by and large, they were more credulous about such things than we are, but because they were more knowledgeable about them. It is not the fewer than three hundred lines devoted to the speeches of the weird sisters and references to them, which are responsible for the sense of supernatural evil which pervades this play, so much as the iteration of the visual symbolism of duality generally, and specifically of witch-craft motifs, in language, setting, and situation. An examination of the play in terms of the witchcraft frame of reference will not only

[10]Among these, in addition to the pamphlets already mentioned, James I's *Daemonologie, in the Forme of A Dialogue*, 1597, was the most distinguished representative of the semi-rationally credulous, Reginald Scot's *Discoverie of Witchcraft*, 1584, of the lustily sceptical point of view. Among the better known of the pamphlets published in England prior to 1606 are the following: Lambert Daneau, *A Dialogue of Witches*, 1575 (original French, 1564); *The Examination and Confession of Certain Witches at Chelmsford* . . . , 1566 (a second and third series of witch trials took place at Chelmsford in 1582 and 1589, and accounts of these were also published); George Gifford, *A Dialogue Concerning Witches and Witchcraft*, 1587; Sir John Harington, *Nugae Antiquae* (describes his interview with James I in which James questioned him about magic practices with a view to discovering a non-damnable method of knowing the future); Samuel Harsnett, *A Discovery of the Fraudulent Practices of John Darrell* . . . , 1599, *A Declaration of Egregious Popish Practices*, 1603 (this pamphlet is the source of the names of the spirits mentioned by Edgar in *King Lear*); Henry Holland, *A Treatise against Witchcraft*, n.d.; Le Loyer, *IIII Livres des Spectres*, 1586 (tr. into English, 1605); Thomas Nashe, *The Terrors of the Night; or, A Discourse of Apparitions*, 1594; William Perkins, *A Discourse on the Damned Art of Witchcraft*, 1602; *A Rehearsall both straung and true, of Hainous and horrible actes committed by* . . . *Fower notorious Witches* . . ., 1579; *A True and particular observation of a notable piece of witchcraft* . . . , 1589 (later expanded as *The most strange and admirable discovery of the Three Witches of Warboys*, 1593); John Walker, *Dialogical Discourses of Devils and Spirits*, 1601.

demonstrate that such iteration exists, but may also serve to illuminate some of the more puzzling aspects of what Professor G. B. Harrison terms "the least satisfactory of the four great tragedies."[11]

Before proceeding to such an examination, however, it may be helpful to summarize, briefly, the specific practices associated with witchcraft beliefs in the minds of Shakespeare's contemporaries. Pre-eminent among them was the concept of evil masquerading as good. For example, most sources[12] agree that the worship of the principle of evil was conducted in imitation or parody of Christian worship, culminating in a feast of communion with the dark god which paral-leled the ritual of the Mass.[13] The symbolizing of disorder in the inverted Christian emblems of cross and orb also visualizes evil as a parody of good. For witchcraft rites the communion chalice was said sometimes to be filled with blood;[14] sometimes with a dark liquid[15] in which toads, spiders, and other unsavoury objects floated, sometimes with wine spiced with aphrodisiacs,[16] for the Devil was said to com-municate physically as well as spiritually with his elect, this physical union providing the parallel to the symbolic union of Christ and his church in a spiritual marriage. According to the testimony of wit-nesses at trials, the Sabbat ritual was usually conducted by a priestess rather than a priest,[17] a circumstance taken as evidence of a general

[11]Introduction to "The Tragedy of Macbeth," in *Shakespeare: The Complete Works* (New York: Harcourt Brace, 1952), p. 1184.

[12]For example, Pierre De L'Ancre, *Tableau de l'inconstance des mauvaises anges*, 1612, and *L'Incredulité et mescréance du sortilège*, 1622; Paul Guilland, *Des sortilegiés*, II, C iii, n. 6: "Those witches who have solemnly devoted them-selves to the Devil's service, worship him . . . with ceremonial sacrifices, imitating in all respects the worship of Almighty God" (as cited in Harry E. Wedeck, *A Treasury of Witchcraft*, New York: Philosophical Library, 1961). In his *Daemonologie*, James I insists repeatedly that in all things, and especially in the practices of witchcraft, the Devil imitates the role of God in the observances and rituals of religion (see especially p. 37).

[13]The so-called "Black Mass" as practised by modern occultists was a late development. It seems to have originated in its full-fledged form among the more notoriously perverted courtiers of Louis XIV. Something like it, however, is described in the account of the trial of the North Berwickshire witches, 1590.

[14]As at the Sabbats presided over by the Abbé Guibourg, who "was wont to kill young children for his hideous ritual, either by strangulation or more often by piercing their throats with a sharp dagger and letting the hot blood stream into the chalice" (Montague Summers, *The History of Witchcraft and Daemo-nology*, 1926, p. 89) and in the account of the Loudian Witches, published in Scotland in 1678.

[15]Wedeck, *A Treasury of Witchcraft*, p. 145.

[16]*Ibid.*, p. 144.

[17]*Ibid.*, p. 126 and Grillot de Givry, *A Pictorial Anthology of Witchcraft, Magic and Alchemy*, tr. J. Courtenay Locke (Chicago and New York: University Books, 1958), pp. 80 ff. (The priestess was regarded as Satan's favourite and was known as "Queen of the Sabbat" or "The Ancient One," though she was usually young.)

predilection for monstrous and unnatural behaviour on the part of witches, of which another indication was their habit of concluding their rites with a ring-dance in which the celebrants moved counter-clockwise about the circle.[18] The accounts are almost unanimous in insisting that initiates into witchcraft joined of their own free will and not as the result of force or guile,[19] and that they were required to be conscious of the significance of their choice. After formally renouncing their hope of salvation through Christ and enrolling themselves of the Devil's party, they were re-baptized, most commonly in blood, and given a new name. Mothers were required to dedicate their infants to the service of Satan and were said, when called upon, to sacrifice them,[20] especially at the Great Sabbats which were held four times yearly—at Candlemas, May Day, Midsummer Day,[21] and All Hallows. Since the followers of Satan could be vouchsafed no miraculous tran-substantiation of the sacred elements of bread and wine into the body and blood of their god, they were accused of practising cannibalism as well as human sacrifice at these festivals. Cats, toads, and snakes were the forms most commonly taken by the familiar spirits of witches, and the most frequently recurring symbols of the cult were milk, blood, and slaughtered infants. (These last are suggestive of the creative-destructive duality characteristic of most early fertility cults.) The supernatural powers commonly attributed to witches were those of raising storms, of calling down diseases on human beings or animals, of levitation, and of foreknowledge. Most writers insist that these powers were strictly limited. Without the permission of over-ruling Providence, witches were not generally believed to be able to cause death, though they might mislead men into physical danger; and though they might lead a victim into temptation they could not, without his acquiescence, lead him to damnation. (This is in accor-dance with St. Paul, II Thessalonians 1: 2–3, that the power of evil could not prevail "except there come a falling away first.")

[18]Wedeck, *A Treasury of Witchcraft*, p. 141.

[19]Margaret A. Murray, *The Witch-Cult in Western Europe*, sums up the evidence in ch. III ("Admission Ceremonies"), p. 71. Though candidates joined of their own free will, sometimes "the Devil appears to have ordered his followers to perform some action by which to impress the imagination of those who believed in his power though they did not worship him" (p. 113). Cf. *Macbeth*, I, iii, 123–6.

[20]See Scot, *Discoverie*, III, 42.

[21]See Robbins, *Encyclopaedia*, "Sabbat." These are the festivals at which the Druids held their notorious sacrifices. Frazer notes that the traces of human sacri-fice at the Beltane fires in Scotland were "particularly clear and unequivocal" (*The Golden Bough*, abridged ed., New York: Macmillan, 1949, p. 617).

Philosophers and theologians from Plato to Hooker had stressed that love of the good is a distinctive characteristic of man's nature. To desire evil, therefore, and to worship it as good, as devotees of witchcraft were assumed to do, was not only a breach in nature but the ultimate perversion of human nature. It is highly appropriate, therefore, that the opening lines of the tragedy of a good man who deliberately chooses evil should be given to witches, and that their words should evoke the murky hell of Macbeth's world, in which the action moves through darkness, the reek of torches, and the smell of blood until evil and unnaturalness have been exorcised by their own excess and by the forces of the natural and the fruitful. There is truth in the porter's wine, for in giving his body and the jewel of his soul to the common enemy of man, Macbeth makes his heart, his house, and his country a hell of equivocation. If he never admits to repenting of his bargain, once it has been made, on moral grounds (however much remorse he may feel for its consequences) he never seems to be quite sure of his partner. Will the Prince of Evil fulfill his part of the implied contract by giving him power and security for the whole term of his natural life? To be free of retribution here, "on this bank and shoal of time" in the midst of the "multitudinous seas" of eternity, Macbeth is willing to "jump the life to come." It is "judgment here" that he fears, realizing that the example of a bloody act "commends th' ingredience of our poison'd chalice / To our own lips," and that "to every purpose there is time and judgment, therefore the misery of man is great upon him. For he knoweth not that which shall be . . ." (Ecclesiastes 8:6). His pact with Satan is a tacit rather than a formal and specific contract like that of Faustus, and it is for reassurance that he will "live the lease of nature, pay his breath / To time and mortal custom" that he seeks out the witches a second time. Since he regarded his wife as his "partner of greatness" when he made the bargain, it may be this fear of being cheated which underlies his comment on her death, "She should have died hereafter."

Indeed, the "Tomorrow and tomorrow" speech which follows, echoes in its phrasing Old Testament warnings of the judgment which awaits evil-doers in this world. Consider, for example, ". . . there is a time wherein one man ruleth over another to his own hurt," and "Because sentence against an evil work is not executed speedily, therefore the heart of the sons of men is fully set in them to do evil. . . . But it shall not be well with the wicked, neither shall he prolong his days, which are as a shadow, because he feareth not before God" (Ecclesiastes 8:9–13), and "How oft is the candle of the wicked put out! and how oft cometh their destruction upon them." (Job 21:17).

Even if Macbeth does not, as H. N. Paul suggests he does,[22] himself become a necromancer, he makes common cause with the witches by dedicating himself to evil and thus becomes, in spirit, a member of their communion. The dozen lines of their dialogue which so effectively set the mood of the play give the audience a glimpse of the final item of business of a meeting of the inner council or executive committee of a coven,[23] called for the assignment of duties and the setting of a time and place for the next meeting, and it is with reports on the discharge of such tasks that the next scene with the witches begins.

The intervening scene moves, according to epic tradition, from the supernatural to the natural plane, and is correspondingly epic in tone. The multiple ironies of this reporting of Macbeth's heroic exploits on the field of battle merit a fuller analysis than there is room for here. Almost every item of the two accounts is capable of ironic application to later events, almost every detail of Cawdor's treachery is paralleled in the treachery of the Cawdor who succeeds him. But it is not only parallels which are foreshadowed here, but reversals. Almost every item in praise of Macbeth becomes the theme of subsequent condemnation; all too soon, and in other circumstances, Macbeth will again "bathe in reeking wounds," and this time the "multiplying villainies of nature" will be his. The theme of paradox is developed in a passage in which allusions to the sun king's royal favour underlie the surface meaning of the words:

> As whence the sun gins his reflection
> Shipwrecking storms and direful thunders break,
> So from that spring where comfort seem'd to come
> Discomfort swells.
>
> (I, ii, 25–8)

---

[22]H. N. Paul (*The Royal Play of Macbeth*, New York: Macmillan, 1950) regards Macbeth as a necromancer, once he has made his bargain with the forces of evil, and thus the master rather than the deluded victim of the infernal demons and their servants the witches. In this he appears to be possessed of a certitude almost completely lacking in the hero himself, whatever the normal conditions of the contract for the sale of souls as set down in treatises on demonology. It is noteworthy, in this connection, that in *Dr. Faustus* the necromancer's power is limited to commanding the service of subsidiary spirits and evoking diabolical illusions. The Devil's lieutenant, Mephistophelis, is by no means Faustus' slave. He may do him service in so far as it suits his (or Satan's) purpose, but he also commands him.

[23]Murray, *The Witch-Cult*, ch. IV ("Assemblies") Sec. 2 ("The Esbat"), p. 112. The anti-masque of witches in Jonson's *Masque of Queenes* includes a report of activities of witches similar to that of *Macbeth* I, iii.

With Duncan's dismissal,

> No more that Thane of Cawdor shall deceive
> Our bosom interest. Go pronounce his present death,
> And with his former title greet Macbeth.
>
> (I, ii, 65–7)

ringing in their ears, Ross and Angus leave for the Heath, and the King's final words, "What he hath lost, noble Macbeth hath won" echo the witches', "When the battle's lost and won."

The activities of the three weird sisters, as reported or plotted at the beginning of Act I, scene iii, are specifically those of which witches were most commonly accused—the maiming or killing of cattle and the controlling of the winds for evil purposes. They admit that their powers are limited:

> Though his bark cannot be lost,
> Yet it shall be tempest-tost.
>
> (ll. 24–5)

The close connections between the first Witch's plans for the master of the *Tiger*[24] and Macbeth's situation are obvious. "I will drain him dry as hay" is echoed in Macbeth's subsequent lament that his "May[25] of life / Is fall'n into the sear, the yellow leaf," as "He shall live a man forbid" is in the later lines of the same speech (V, iv, 24–8). The references to sleep and to diminished stature similarly condition the audience for the repetition of such references later in the play. The lines,

> Here I have a pilot's thumb,
> Wreck'd as homeward he did come,
>
> (ll. 28–9)

may be taken with equal appropriateness as foreshadowing either the physical destruction of Duncan or the moral shipwreck of Macbeth, his victorious general. The parallels with later events are underlined by the "thumb-come" rhyme-link (repeated with a significant variation in Act IV, i, 44–5) which heralds Macbeth's approach. Winding up their charm with the characteristic circular dance of the witches, the three hags await the conquering hero whose battle with treason, so newly won, is so soon to be lost to the traitor within his own breast.

[24]Remembering that ships are feminine whatever their names, we may find "Tiger" ironically apt. Macbeth can hardly be said to be master of *his* female "tiger."

[25]One of Dr. Johnson's happier emendations, though the Folio's "way" is retained in most modern editions.

The location of the heath on which Macbeth and Banquo appear is an appropriate one, since it was at Forres that Scottish witches were burned, and also at Forres that a celebrated case of witchcraft directed against a king had occurred.[26] The place name is emphasized by Banquo's opening remark, though it is not clear whether "How far is't called to Forres?" is intended as a casual question addressed to Macbeth, as a serious request for information addressed to the weird sisters, or as a humorous comment upon them, as if to say, "Look here! If we can judge by these three specimens we must be getting close to Forres." The theme of inversion of nature, already introduced in the Sergeant's ironic comment that the odds against Macbeth and Banquo had dismayed them "as sparrows eagles, or the hare the lion," is continued in Banquo's remark that the sisters' beards forbid him to regard them as women. Beards were traditionally associated with witches, as in Parson Evans's comment on the disguised Falstaff, "By yea and no, I think the 'oman is a witch indeed. I like not when a 'oman has a great peard." (*Merry Wives of Windsor*, IV, ii, 169–71.)

That women should possess male characteristics, physical or psychological, was not considered merely unnatural and therefore deplorable; along with other "perversions" the reversal of the sexual roles was frequently alleged to be an integral part of the ritual of witchcraft, and such characteristics could be and were taken as legal evidence of criminal conversation with the Evil One. This association of witchcraft with the inversion of sexual roles is important for the understanding of the characterization of Lady Macbeth and, to a lesser extent, of Cleopatra. From the beginning Lady Macbeth is, in her inner nature, what the weird sisters appear outwardly to be—unnatural and therefore "fiend-like." As soon as she reads Macbeth's letter she assumes the initiative, reversing the roles appropriate to husband and wife, to say nothing of violating her natural feminine attributes of tenderness and timidity. The king must die, and it is she who will be high-priestess of the sacrifice, Macbeth merely the executioner, if he is to be allowed

[26]In the year 968, King Duffus, "whilst he was about settling of the Country, and punishing the troublers of the Peace . . . begun to be sore afflicted in his body with a new and unheard of Disease, no Causes of his Sicness appearing in the least." Physicians could do nothing for him and finally news came to court that "night meetings were kept at *Forres*, a town in *Murray*, for taking away the life of the King." The coven was surprised while melting a waxen image of the king and basting it with a poisonous brew. The witches confessed that *their muttered spells during the process were intended to deprive the king of sleep* (final italics mine) (Buchanan, *Rerum Scoticarum Historia*, as quoted in George Sinclair, *Invisible World Discovered*, Edinburgh, 1685, XIII, and cited by Montague Summers in *The Geography of Witchcraft*, p. 203).

even that function. It is under *my*,[27] not *our* (and still less Macbeth's) battlements that the royal victim enters. It is Macbeth who is regarded as having the feminine nature—he is "too full of the milk of human kindness." She uses the image again when she calls on the infernal spirits to unsex her: "Come to my woman's breasts / And take my milk for gall." The bloody Sergeant had reported how Macbeth, "Bellona's bridegroom," "like valour's minion," had carved his passage through the battle to face the merciless Macdonwald, but now the war-goddess herself will pour her merciless spirit, poison-like, into her bridegroom's ear and chastise her minion with the valour of her tongue. The scene ends with Lady Macbeth's announcement to her husband that she is to be the general in this campaign: "You shall put / This night's great business into my despatch," and who can doubt that she intends to be the senior partner in the "solely sovereign sway and masterdom" to come. Though in contrast to her husband's subsequent hesitation she seems whole-souled and firm of purpose, in that she gives no visible sign of any internal conflict, it is in this scene that Lady Macbeth makes her bargain with Evil. Had her nature always been unnaturally evil it would not have been necessary to present her as denying her nature so violently as she does here, and as she must do to make her later disintegration credible. She has, after all, given suck and known what it is to love.

In the next conference between Macbeth and his lady the theme of inversion is further developed in an equivocating discussion of the actions appropriate to a man. Lady Macbeth accuses her husband of being deficient in the masculine virtue of courage, and he replies that he dares "do all that may become a man"; that is, what is proper to the human condition. Who dares do more must deny either his human limitations or his god-like reason, must aspire to be superhuman, or, beast-like, allow his passions to rule his will. It is in the latter sense, in part at least, that Lady Macbeth turns his argument against him, though she chooses for her purposes to assume that aspiration rather than restraint is the distinguishing characteristic of man. She plays upon both the "human" and the "masculine" connotations of the word, however, when she says:

> What beast was't then
> That made you break this enterprise to me?

[27]That until a fairly late date property descended in the female line in Scotland does not alter the fact that Lady Macbeth's words would have sounded strange to Elizabethan ears.

> When you durst do it, then you were a man;
> And to be more than what you were, you would
> Be so much more the man.
>
> 　　　　　　　　　　　　　(I, vii, 47–51)

Again she denies her woman's nature in asserting that she would have dashed out the brains of the child at her breast[28] rather than break her oath had *she* undertaken to murder the king. The rhetoric of the Queen of Night vanquishes her husband's scruples, calling forth from him what is, in the circumstances, an unconsciously ironic tribute:

> Bring forth men-children only;
> For thy undaunted mettle should compose
> Nothing but males.
>
> 　　　　　　　　　　　　　(I, vii, 72–4)

For the remaining lines of the scene the great commander has nothing to say for himself; he merely echoes his wife. He has taken bloody instruction and is ready to drain the poisoned chalice when the mass-bell of the high priestess shall invite him to seal his pact with evil in the blood of his victim.[29]

The inversion of sexual roles is, of course, temporary. As the action of the play proceeds, Macbeth takes on more and more of the characteristics which, in his wife's opinion, "become a man," and, in the eyes of the audience, thereby becomes less and less human. As he takes over the role she had played in the opening scenes, he has less and less need of his wife's undaunted mettle, and Lady Macbeth, her occupation gone, finds her nemesis in the feminine nature she has denied, but can never entirely destroy. For however much they attempt to separate themselves from humanity these two never quite succeed in making themselves complete monsters. Macbeth's self-knowledge keeps him within that great bond which he calls upon darkness to tear and cancel, and Lady Macbeth, though she lacks her husband's awareness, has been unable, after all, to despatch the fatal night's great business, because Duncan resembled her father as he slept.

---

[28]"This must be an infallible rule, that everie . . . month, each witch must kill one child at least . . . ," Scot, III, 42. Summers (*History*, p. 83) quotes similar assertions from less sceptical sources.

[29]John Holloway (*The Story of the Night: Studies of Shakespeare's Major Tragedies*, London: Routledge and Kegan Paul, 1961) comments on the ritual dedication of Macbeth and Lady Macbeth to the Satanic forces but does not specifically associate it with witchcraft. Roy Walker (*The Time is Free*, p. 54) recognizes the "chalice" as the Eucharist cup, but associates it with the reference to blood-drinking in Revelation 16:6: "For they have shed the blood of saints and prophets, and thou hast given them blood to drink, for they are worthy," rather than with witchcraft mass-rituals.

After the murder of Banquo, Macbeth refers to himself as still an "initiate" in evil, and the circumstances of his initiation fulfill, exactly, the procedures laid down for admission into a witchcraft society. When we consider the pains Shakespeare has taken to make it clear that Macbeth has lusted after the crown even before the battle in which he bought golden opinions, the references to the blood bath of "reeking wounds" and the conferring upon him of the title of the traitorous Cawdor whom he had confronted with "self-comparisons" take on a significance in the frame of reference of witchcraft which is additional to the ironic foreshadowing already mentioned. We have not only Lady Macbeth's testimony and Macbeth's guilty start at the witches' greeting as evidence that he has admitted evil into his heart before the meeting on the heath. He himself is well aware of the threat to his integrity and of the nature and cause of the insurrection in his soul:

> . . . why do I yield to that suggestion
> Whose horrid image doth unfix my hair
> And make my seated heart knock at my ribs
> Against the use of nature? Present fears
> Are less than horrible imaginings.
> My thought, whose murder yet is but fantastical,
> Shakes so my single state of man
> That function is smother'd in surmise,
> And nothing is but what is not.
>
> (I, iii, 134–41)

Why "murder"? There is nothing in the witches' prophecy to suggest it. Chance may crown him without his stir. The rebellion in his "state of man" is not a necessary condition of the end he desires, "the sweet fruition of an earthly crown." This is one of those "strange images of death" made by himself, and on this occasion Macbeth *is* afeared of it. Macbeth's chalice of evil, like that commended to Claudius's lips in the last scene of *Hamlet*, is a "poison temper'd by himself."[30] At no time in the play does he lay the blame for his crime either upon the witches or upon Lady Macbeth, though he does eventually damn all those (including himself) who trust in the weird sisters and their companion fiends "that palter with us in a double sense." Like the air-drawn dagger, the weird sisters have merely marshalled him the way that he was going, and if he was seduced into evil he was not beguiled into it.

[30]The concept of the poisoned chalice as the symbol both of Macbeth's dedication to evil and of retribution for it appears to have been developed from a comment of Holinshed's that "the pricke of conscience . . . caused him ever to feare, lest he be served to the same cup as he had ministered to his predecessor."

Like the initiate into a coven, Macbeth, the unforced and undeceived postulant, passes through the ceremonies of acceptance into the communion of evil, resigning his hope of "the life to come," dedicating himself to "the common enemy," being baptized in blood in the Devil's behalf, and feasting (whereas Christians fasted) before the culminating rite—the drinking of blood. It is in these terms that Macbeth sees the murder of Duncan when he has finally decided to partake of the poisoned chalice: "Go bid thy mistress, when my drink is ready, / She strike upon the bell" (II, i, 31–2). And when the bell for this black mass rings, he whispers, "Hear it not, Duncan, for it is a knell / That summons thee to heaven or to hell" (II, i, 63–4).

If the progress of Macbeth's damnation parallels the ritual of admission into the organized worship of evil, the murder of Duncan presents analogies with the ritual sacrifices from which certain of the alleged practices of witchcraft were ultimately derived. The sacrifice of the god-king or sovereign priest is a rite common, in one form or another, to most primitive religions, whether the divine victim is seen as a scapegoat taking upon himself the ills of the community or as a spirit of vegetation bequeathing to it his strength and fertility. The vestiges of such rites have persisted into modern times not only in folk customs the significance of which has long been forgotten, but in the seasonal festivals assimilated into the calendar of the Christian religion, in particular, that of Easter, and the actual practice of ritual sacrifice may not have died out immediately and completely with the official acceptance of Christianity.[31] Some colour is lent to this suggestion by the comparative ease with which usurpers seem to have been able to impose their rule upon the subjects, great and small, of their defeated and deposed or assassinated predecessors, especially if the heir in direct line of succession was not actually present when the transfer of office took place or was not of age to assume office in person. British history presents a number of instances—King John, for one, and these are the circumstances which obtain in *Richard III*, *Hamlet*, and *Macbeth*. Certainly, Macduff, Banquo, Ross, and Lennox make it clear that they have no illusions about the true state of affairs; yet, powerful noblemen though they are, none of them actively opposes Macbeth's investiture. As in *Richard II*, there appears to be a fatalistic acceptance, which only the boldest question, of the principle that the man who proves himself stronger than the king is entitled to his chance to rule in his stead. The confirmation of Henry IV's title by Act of Parliament suggests that the tradition of elective monarchy was not yet entirely forgotten and that trial by combat may have been accepted as definitive

[31]See Frazer, *The Dying God*, and Murray, *God of the Witches, passim.*

in settling questions of kingship as well as criminal causes and legal actions.

The Elizabethans were certainly familiar with the traditional forms of human sacrifice from their reading of the classics and of contemporary accounts[32] of the legendary pre-history of their own island, and such is the persistence of folk-tradition that we cannot assume that the ordinary man of four centuries ago had lost all awareness of the original significance of the burning of harvest effigies and the temporary reigns of festival kings at May Day and Twelfth Night festivals. Indeed, sixteenth-century literature gives abundant indication that he had not,[33] and it should be clear that witchcraft, paganism, and Satanism were closely connected in the minds of Shakespeare's contemporaries with such folk survivals when we recall that it was at precisely these festivals that the sacrificial rites of witchcraft were supposed to take place.

That Shakespeare was familiar with the concepts of the ritual sacrifice of the divine or semi-divine king and the function of blood in fertility rites is beyond question. The state as a garden is a recurrent image in the Histories and is closely associated with the "blood asketh blood" theme, as in Henry IV's lament on hearing of the death of Richard II:

> . . . my soul is full of woe
> That blood should sprinkle me to make me grow.
>
> (*Richard II*, V, vi, 45–6)

In *Julius Caesar*, Calpurnia's barrenness and the fertility rites of Lupercal are associated with Brutus' conviction that the welfare of Rome is dependent on the death of Caesar, who bestrides the narrow world like a Colossus and who is inclined to think and speak of himself as a god. Brutus wishes the assassination to be conducted as a ritual sacrifice, not a cold-blooded political murder,[34] and Decius Brutus' interpretation of Calpurnia's dream[35] and the murderers' bathing of their hands in Caesar's blood are closely connected with fertility ritual.

Nor was the analogy of the Christian doctrine of the Atonement with the fertility-assuring sacrifice of the god-king in primitive societies

[32]For example, Camden's account of the Druids.

[33]For discussion of the relationships between myth and literature there is a plethora of critical reference. Danby touches on king-killing (*Shakespeare's Doctrine of Nature*, II, iv); Holloway does so at greater length (*The Story of the Night*, ch. VIII and App. B.). Barber bases much of his analysis in *Shakespeare's Festive Comedy* on the folk-ritual background of dramatic action. The most rewarding of the general studies in this area is Northrop Frye's *Anatomy of Criticism* (Princeton University Press, 1957), which draws many of its illustrations from Shakespeare.

[34]II, i, 166–74.

[35]II, ii, 83–90.

overlooked by Renaissance writers. Indeed, one of them justifies even the seasonal mass-sacrifices of the Druids as symbolic of the doctrine of Purgatory,[36] and another regards them as a prophetic anticipation of the archetypal death of Christ, the god-king whose sacrifice would redeem the world.[37] In this connection Buchanan's account of the punishment of a Scottish witch is interesting.[38] The Earl of Athole, a ringleader in the murder of James I at Perth, February 20, 1436 (which had been foretold to the king by an Irish witch as he crossed the Water of Leith) was, at his execution, ". . . crowned with a regal diadem of red-hot iron because . . .certain witches . . . had told him that he would be crowned a king in sight of all the people." With an irony not only grim but almost blasphemous, Athole was given his crown of thorns "that it might be fulfilled . . . ," and his executioners must have been conscious of the parallel.

According to orthodox doctrine the human instruments of Divine Providence might be either good or evil; both scourges and ministers played their parts in the working out of the divine plan. Macbeth may be regarded as playing the role of the scourge, Malcolm of performing the function of the minister. Therefore there is nothing inconsistent in seeing both the assassination of Duncan and the retributive execution of Macbeth as ritual sacrifices associated with the theme of national fertility. The murder of Duncan, the Lord's anointed Deputy, by the forces of evil personified in the Macbeths is seen as analogous to the Crucifixion. In order to identify Duncan with the good and fruitful elements of life, Shakespeare has purged him of the weaknesses in character and governance mentioned by Holinshed and endowed him with the Christ-like virtue of humility. He has filled his speeches with references to planting, growth, and tender solicitude for his subjects, whom he regards and who frequently speak of themselves as his children. The sterility of evil, on the other hand, is stressed in Macbeth's obsession with the barrenness of his sceptre and his Herod-like slaughter of Macduff's innocent children. But the identification of the rightful king with the principle of the Good is carried still farther in numerous verbal parallels between the death of Duncan and the Gospel accounts of the last hours of Christ, and by the underlining of these parallels in the verbal allusions to the Mass in presenting the plotting and execution of the murder.

[36]Guillaume Postel, *L'Histoire memorable des expéditions depuys le déluge*, (1552), ff. 47ff., cited in A. L. Owen, *The Mysterious Druids* (Oxford: Clarendon Press, 1962), p. 157.

[37]The author of the poem *La Galliade*, as cited by Owen, *The Mysterious Druids, loc. cit.*

[38]*Rerum Scoticarum Historia*, as cited in Summers, *Geography*, p. 205.

The first of these—an indirect one—comes in that masterpiece of indirection finding direction out, the bloody Sergeant's description of Macbeth's heroism:

> . . . So they doubly redoubled strokes upon the foe.
> Except they meant to bathe in reeking wounds,
> Or memorize another Golgotha,
> I cannot tell. . . .

(I, ii, 38–42)

The divinity which hedges Duncan may not prove an effective impediment to treason, but it is everywhere apparent—in characterization, in incident, in situation, and, above all, in language. His record as a king is without stain; his very murderer can find no fault in him and is fully aware of the moral polarity represented by his victim's meekness and trust and his own treachery and vaulting ambition. Macbeth's analysis of the issues involved (I, vii, 12–28) manifests his realization that the crime he contemplates will be a betrayal of the best in every sense—a violation of honour, hospitality, loyalty, natural affection, and natural justice, as well as of divine law. Like Judas he breaks bread and drinks wine[39] with his victim, and like Judas he leaves before the conclusion of the supper in order to make the final arrangements for his master's destruction.

Biblical allusions[40] and religious imagery permeate the dialogue whenever Duncan is present. Even Lady Macbeth is not immune to the contagion: her speech of welcome compares the duties of the subject to those enjoined in the parable of the good steward:

> your servants ever
> Have theirs, themselves, and what is theirs, in compt,
> To make their audit at your Highness' pleasure,
> Still to return your own.

(I, vi, 25–8)

In the same scene Banquo has referred to the martlet, whose procreant cradles line the castle walls, as "temple-haunting." The epithet is not obviously appropriate to the immediate situation, the irony of which

---

[39]Caesar also drinks with his betrayers just before his assassination (II, ii, 126) and Richard II, at his deposition, compares himself with Christ betrayed (IV, i, 168–71) and brought before Pilate (IV, i, 239–42). See also, John 18:37 and 13:27.

[40]Richmond Noble (*Shakespeare's Biblical Knowledge*) and Walker (*The Time is Free*) list a number of other biblical allusions in *Macbeth*. Holloway (*The Story of the Night*, p. 65) notes that the sound of horses is an echo of the four horsemen of the apocalypse in Revelation 6: 2–8, who bring appropriate retribution for human evil in the form of various disasters—poverty, hunger, sword, death. Those listed here I have found for myself, and the list does not pretend to be either exhaustive or entirely new, though some of the items have not, to my knowledge, been pointed out elsewhere.

lies in the promise of fair weather deduced by Banquo from the birds' nesting habits, whether on the walls of temples or of castles. But temples are more than once associated with Duncan, whose consecrated body is in a special sense the temple of the Holy Spirit, and an earlier reference to the martlet makes it clear that Shakespeare is here drawing a parallel between the natural simplicity of the bird and the innocent, trusting nature of the king. Duncan knows no art to find the mind's construction in the face, and, in the words of the Prince of Aragon, "like the fool multitude," chooses "by show,"

> Not learning more than the fond eye doth teach;
> Which pries not to th' interior, but, like the martlet,
> Builds in the weather on the outward wall,
> Even in the force and road of casualty.
>
> (*Merchant of Venice*, II, ix, 28–31)

Relevant here also is the old superstition that ill-luck will dog the footsteps of those who destroy the nests of martlets, or house-martins, as the birds are more commonly known. Duncan is the martlet, and Macbeth betrays his trust.

After the murder, biblical allusions crowd in one upon another. Like Pilate, Lady Macbeth believes that a little ritual handwashing will clear them of the deed. "Go get some water / And wash this filthy witness from your hand," she bids her husband, recalling Christ's words to Pilate, that his death should "bear witness unto the truth." Macbeth's reply,

> No; this my hand will rather
> The multitudinous seas incarnadine,
> Making the green one red,
>
>   (II, ii, 61–3)

may be an echo of the passage in the Book of Revelation (16:3): "And the second Angel poured out his vial upon the sea; and it became as the blood of a dead man; and every living soul died in the sea." Macduff announces the murder as "the great doom's image," and Macbeth echoes his horror by proclaiming that "Renown and grace is dead, / The wine of life is drawn."[41] Macduff picks up the implied allusion to the body and blood of Christ:

> Confusion now hath made his masterpiece.
> Most sacrilegious murder hath broke ope
> The Lord's anointed temple, and stole thence
> The life o' the building.
>
>   (II, iii, 64–7)

---

[41]There is a triple play on words here, as Macbeth's own renown ("golden opinions") and grace ("the life to come") have also been destroyed by the murder.

This is very close not only to "the stone which the builders rejected," but to "The veil of the temple was rent in twain" (Matthew 27:51). Macduff again echoes St. Matthew's account of the Crucifixion (27: 52–3)—"And the graves were opened; and many bodies of the saints which slept arose, and came out of the graves . . . " when he calls upon Banquo, Malcolm, and Donalbain:

> As from your graves rise up and walk like sprites
> To countenance this horror.
>
> > (II, iii, 77–8)

At Glamis as at Calvary,[42] the earth "was feverous and did shake," and there was darkness by day over all the land:

> . . . the heavens, as troubled with man's act,
> Threatens his bloody stage. By th' clock 'tis day,
> And yet dark night strangles the travelling lamp.
> Is't night's predominance, or the day's shame,
> That darkness does the face of earth entomb,
> When living light should kiss it?
>
> > (II, iv, 5–10)

Many of the motifs associated with the assassination of Duncan are repeated in connection with the murder of Banquo. Compare, for example, the Senecan horrors of the two set murderer's-speeches, with their reference to darkness, unnatural evil, and witchcraft, in the passages cited below. It is strange that Shakespeare should employ, at so late a date, a convention which he had used ironically and mocked openly in *Hamlet* (III, ii, 376–82 and III, ii, 246–8). The second of the two speeches is quieter and more diffuse than the first, yet it is somehow more terrible, perhaps because of its echoes of Lady Macbeth's similar speech in I, v, which demonstrate that Macbeth has taken on her unnaturalness in addition to his own. Her qualities had once been complementary to his; now he is becoming integrated in evil. The reference to "wicked dreams" in the first speech ties in with Banquo's earlier reference to "the cursed thoughts that nature / Gives way to in repose" (II, i, 8–9) and with the emphasis on eyes, sleep, evil, and dreams in the second and succeeding passages.

> Now o'er the one-half world
> Nature seems dead, and wicked dreams abuse
> The curtain'd sleep; now witchcraft celebrates
> Pale Hecate's offerings; and wither'd murder,
> Alarum'd by his sentinel, the wolf,
> Whose howl's his watch, thus with his stealthy pace,
> With Tarquin's ravishing strides, towards his design
> Moves like a ghost.
>
> > (II, i, 48–56)

[42]Matthew 27:45; Mark 15:33; Luke 23:44–5.

The contrast between the wolf-howl and the sound of the watchman's reassuring "Twelve o' the clock, and all's well" adds to the present horror of the time.

> Ere the bat hath flown
> His cloister'd flight; ere to black Hecate's summons
> The shard-borne beetle with his drowsy hums
> Hath rung night's yawning peal, there shall be done
> A deed of dreadful note. . . .
>   Come, seeling night,
> Scarf up the tender eye of pitiful day,
> And with thy bloody and invisible hand
> Cancel and tear to pieces that great bond
> Which keeps me pale. Light thickens, and the crow
> Makes wing to th' rooky wood;
> Good things of day begin to droop and drowse,
> While night's black agents to their preys do rouse.
>   (III, ii, 40–53)

In Shakespeare's later plays a character's use of conventional devices of language is often a sign of his insincerity. It is so in Macbeth's description of Duncan's body, with its "silver skin lac'd with his golden blood." His use of the Senecan clichés of the set murderer's-speech is an indication that he is working himself up to a deed which goes against his nature. Their swift displacement in the speech which precedes Banquo's murder by such everyday things as the drowsy beetle, the tamed falcon, and the gregarious rook show that Macbeth is no longer appalled by the very thought of murder and is resigned to identifying himself with "night's black agents," giving up for lost the "good things of day" which fall blissfully and naturally into the sleep he cannot find.

Banquo is not a king, nor is he invested, like Duncan, with the aura of divinity. His soul is not completely free, in that he accepts the evil Macbeth represents rather than combatting it; he does not yield to temptation, but rather temporizes with it. For all his human weakness he does possess, however, a "royalty of nature" for which Macbeth envies him almost as much as for the weird sisters' promise to him of royal issue. He also fears him, in part because he recognizes in Banquo, with whom he had shared the honours of the battle-field, the man he himself might have been had he not yielded to temptation. Thus, in destroying Banquo Macbeth destroys, for the second time, the better part of himself, and does so because his first act of self-destruction has brought him no real or lasting satisfaction, only the ever-present awareness of guilt, the remorse of conscience without the medicine of repentance. Macbeth has drunk and seen the spider in the "chalice" of his "peace"; those "rancours" he has put there only to make the seed of Banquo kings. He realizes also that his bargain with evil has been a cheat even in terms of material rewards as compared with the loss of true honour and honest friendship. Yet he reconfirms it for two reasons—in hope that the elimination of an exterior threat will rid him of the torments of his conscience and that he can thereby also interfere with the destiny which the weird sisters proclaimed for himself and Banquo. Thus his first crime is committed in mistrust of the prophecy which encouraged him to do the deed, his second as a challenge to the fate which that prophecy represents. He murders his king in order to make double-sure the assurance that he will be Duncan's successor, and procures the murder of his friend to ensure that the witches' foretelling shall prove true only insofar as it applies to himself.

> . . . let the frame of things disjoint, both the worlds suffer,
> Ere we will eat our meal in fear and sleep
> In the affliction of these terrible dreams
> That shake us nightly.
>
> (III, ii, 16–19)

The terror-haunted meal which follows this second sealing of the bargain in blood is again, ostensibly, a feast of fellowship at which the victim is an invited guest. Since he is slain before the feast rather than after it, the parallel may be with the supper at Emmaus (Luke 24:30, 31) at which the risen Christ broke bread with his disciples and then vanished from their sight. If so, the pattern of inversion would suggest that it is the Prince of Evil who, unrecognized, joins the two murderers on the road to Forres, as Jesus joined the two disciples on the road to Emmaus, and who, as a projection of the evil within Macbeth's soul, assumes the shape of Banquo at the feast. Here Macbeth is again overcome with horrible imaginings,[43] and again there is wordplay between husband and wife on the meaning of the word "man":

LADY M.:	Are you a man?
MACB.:	Ay, and a bold one that dare look on that
	Which might appal the Devil.

> (III, iv, 58–60)

[43]Lady Macbeth underlines the parallel:
> This is the very painting of your fear;
> This is the air-drawn dagger which you said
> Led you to Duncan.
>
> (III, iv, 61–3)

and again:

> MACB.: What man dare, I dare.
> Approach thou like the rugged Russian bear,
> The arm'd rhinoceros or th' Hyrcan tiger;
> Take any shape but that, and my firm nerves
> Shall never tremble. Or be alive again,
> And dare me to the desert with thy sword;
> If trembling I inhabit, then protest me
> The baby of a girl. Hence, horrible shadow!
> Unreal mock'ry, hence!
>   Why so, being gone,
> I am a man again.
>
>   (III, iv, 99–108)

And being a man again, his first action is to deny his humanity by confirming his allegiance to evil yet a third time:

> I will to-morrow.
> And betimes I will to the Weird Sisters:
> More shall they speak; for now I am bent to know
> By the worst means the worst. For mine own good
> All causes shall give way.
>
>   (III, iv, 132–6)

Though the infernal powers, once called up, confound earth, air, and sea, church and state, though they make the treasure "of Nature's germens[44] tumble all together / Even till destruction sicken," at whatever cost, he will be answered. Macbeth's is the tragedy of a noble and sensitive soul corrupted and hardened by self-interest; even thus, "the brightest fell." His metal, like that of Brutus though from directly opposite motives, is "wrought from that it is disposed."

From this point on the initiative passes to Malcolm, whose colourlessness makes him one of those meek who shall inherit the earth, as well as preventing him from taking away too much of our sympathy with Macbeth. He is the representative of natural fertility and divinely sanctioned order, and is never seen to shed personally the blood which must be sprinkled to make him grow. In the play's inverted world, however, even the minister of God's Providence must pretend to deny his nature until he is certain that evil is not Macduff's good, as it has become Macbeth's. Malcolm emphasizes the depth of Macbeth's fall:

> This tyrant, whose sole name blisters our tongues,
> Was once thought honest; you have lov'd him well;
> He hath not touch'd you yet.
>
>   (IV, iii, 12–14)

[44]See Curry, *Philosophical Patterns*, pp. 29–49 for the significance of the phrase in medieval and Renaissance philosophy.

Malcolm is no martlet; he has learned from his father's fate the dangers of too much simplicity:

> Angels are bright still, though the brightest fell.
> Though all things foul would wear the brows of grace,
> Yet grace must still look so.

> (IV, iii, 22–4)

Macduff is also an ambiguous figure in this scene. He behaves at first as if the general corruption of Scotland had, in fact, tainted him, giving him something of the emotional insensitivity Macbeth notes as having developed in himself (V, v, 9–14). Until those, his nearest kin, towards whom his affectionate concern should naturally have been directed have been taken from him, he does seem, as his wife complains, to want "the natural touch." He has no answer for Malcolm's sharp question, "Why in that rawness left you wife and child?" and if we attempt to supply one for him we must find it outside the play. He is capable of anger, but appears to be incapable of sympathy, scorning Malcolm's tears for Scotland, and calling upon him to act instead of weeping. Small wonder that the prince fears that this is another emissary who hopes to gain the tyrant's favour by betraying the son of his royal victim. It would be worldly wisdom, in a world in which evil is king,

> To offer up a weak, poor, innocent lamb
> T' appease an angry god

> (IV, iii, 16–17)

and in such a world the sacrificial knife is not, as in the case of Isaac, diverted to an appropriate and convenient ram. Later, when events at Macduff's castle have proved the parallel apter than he knew, Malcolm is able to give the surly thane a taste of his own counsel: "Let's make us med'cines of our great revenge / To cure this deadly grief" (IV, iii, 214–15).

The conference between Malcolm and Macduff is interrupted by the Doctor's account of Edward the Confessor's miraculous power to cure, by his touch, the King's Evil. This account is usually regarded as an intrusive if graceful compliment to James I, who may perhaps have commissioned the play[45] (and possibly even specified that it should deal with Scottish history) for performance on some state occasion. But all is grist that comes to Shakespeare's mill. His theme is the king's evil, which only royalty of nature can cure, and the repetition of the word "touch" helps to integrate the saintly Edward's

[45]See Harrison, "Introduction," p. 1184.

gift[46] not only with the king's "divine right" concept of the sovereign as God's counterpart on earth but with the overall action, in which good is vanquished by evil, which is, in turn, vanquished by good. Macduff lacks the natural "touch" and appears to be suffering from the crippling of emotion which is part of the tyrant's evil, though that evil "hath not touch'd" him yet. When that touch does come it seems a mortal blow, yet it makes Macduff, emotionally, a whole man again. Or is it Edward's grace which Macduff absorbs in England, as in Scotland he had taken on something of Macbeth's hardness? Shakespeare frequently refers to the nature of both good and evil as contagious, and the nature of the sovereign as being communicable to his subjects. This and the ensuing scene contrast sharply the king whose evil infects his land and the king whose piety preserves and restores the health of his people. Both have their doctors who observe and comment on diseases beyond their practice. Macbeth's land is sick, his partner of greatness driven mad by that perilous stuff which weighs upon the heart, and he himself, for all his occasional outbursts of bravado, is as steeped in disillusionment and despair as he is in blood. He speaks almost entirely in images of winter, destruction, disease, and death. The giant's robe upon the dwarfish thief may clothe him like Solomon in all his glory, yet he knows himself to be as "the grass, which today is in the field, and tomorrow is cast into the oven" (Luke 12:27–8).

To Malcolm and his followers is given, on the other hand, the verbal ambience of spring—of flowers and green woods and new life, in which even bloodshed is made to serve the purposes of fertility:

> CAITH.:   Well, march we on
> To give obedience where 'tis truly ow'd.
> Meet we the med'cine of the sickly weal;
> And with him pour we in our country's purge
> Each drop of us.
> LEN.:   Or so much as it needs
> To dew the sovereign flower and drown the weeds.
> (V, ii, 25–30)

Even the camouflage strategy of Birnam Wood becomes part of Malcolm's background of fertility as well as the ironic fulfilment of a prophecy which keeps the word of promise to the ear and breaks it to the hope—of Macbeth, but not of Scotland. The approach of Malcolm's

---

[46]Frazer notes that the belief in England in the efficacy of the royal touch to cure the King's Evil is a relic of the time when the king was considered divine (*Aftermath*, London: Macmillan, 1936, p. 112).

troops to Dunsinane must have presented much the appearance of the May Day procession described by Stubbes,[47] coming to dispossess the old King of Winter and bring in the young King of May whose harvest of peace and public weal "would be planted newly with the time."

Macbeth, the particular man whose dram of evil has corrupted his whole substance, is, if not Everyman, then every man who denies his kinship with humanity by saying, "For mine own good, all causes shall give way," even though he knows in his heart that such good can only be evil. His tragedy results from a double usurpation, for Macbeth is not only a usurper of a throne, but one in whose breast Friar Laurence's "two . . . opposed kings . . . grace and rude will" are encamped, and whose plant of life begins to shrivel into death as soon as the "worser is predominant." Yet, as usually in Shakespearean tragedy, there is a faint and relieving glimmer of hope for the individual as well as for the state even in the dark world of *Macbeth*. Even this man is not seen as totally depraved, though the play presents a treatment of absolute evil, the rejection of God's Providence and reliance upon the powers of Satan, which, according to James I's *Daemonologie*, was the unforgivable sin against the Holy Ghost. But the imagery of darkness in the play is shot with light, and though we have seen the protagonist decline from the praise of "golden opinions" to the epithet of "dead butcher," he is not permitted to lose his human dignity entirely. In his last fight he is shown as retaining something of his original courage, even though the inroads of brutalizing fear have turned fortitude into desperation. His unwillingness to charge his soul with more of Macduff's blood is an indication that he retains also some vestiges of moral sensitivity. Courage and sensitivity are the pillars of his character which frame the story of his downfall. However far astray internal evil and external circumstance have driven him he remains a man, though a man who has dedicated his goodness to the service of evil, who has turned his soul, and his world, upside down. In this, the inverted Morality Play pattern of *Macbeth*, Evil, not Grace, has won the battle for a man's soul, but the harrowing of Scotland's hell is at hand.

Shakespeare's readings of Scottish history and the literature of demonology provided him with an abundance of allusions with which to please the scholarly vanity of his royal patron. The weird sisters belong to the topical aspect of the play; they are such witches as James I would recognize and accept—they had read the same books. But for

[47]See note 7.

the universal aspect of his tragedy, for the conflicts and confusions and inversions of good and evil as they are found in this world, and for the resolution implied by the supreme paradox of a Divine Providence which brings good out of evil, Shakespeare needed a frame of reference broader than the chronicle of a particular king or kings and the witch-mania of a particular period. He found it not in sensational tales of the sorceries of particular witches, but in the archetypal elements of witchcraft: in the symbols of blood, milk and water, the bloody child, the rituals of sacrifice, communion and cleansing, in communal purging and regeneration, in those aspects of witchcraft in which, according to common opinion, the worship of evil masqueraded as the worship of good.

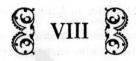

VIII

No Midway: The Structure of
Duality in *Antony and Cleopatra*

> O well-divided disposition! ...
> ... Be'st thou sad or merry,
> The violence of either thee becomes,
> So does it no man else.
>
> (*Antony and Cleopatra*, I, v, 53–61)

IT IS THE VOICE OF LOVE which speaks this evaluation of Antony; the voice of reason, then and now, disagrees, and the sterner moralists among recent critics,[1] when it comes to the relationship between Antony and his "Serpent of old Nile," echo Hamlet. "You cannot," they insist, "call it love." Clifford Leech comments that in late Jacobean and Caroline tragedy the life of the tragic hero is divorced from social action and restricted to sex-life.[2] The Jacobean dramatists, he continues, did not anticipate Freud in considering that the whole of life was governed by sex; they "turned away wilfully from the whole to a part." The point of transition, in his view, is *Antony and Cleopatra* as concerned with "the interrelations of sex and power."

If it is rational to assume that the Jacobean dramatists did not

[1]F. M. Dickey, for example, in *Not Wisely but Too Well* (San Marino, Cal.: Huntington Library, 1957) finds in Antony and Cleopatra, on the basis of his readings of medieval and Renaissance moral philosophers (too many of whom he feels obliged to quote) "patterns of lust, of cruelty, of prodigality, of drunkenness, and, in the end, of despair" (pp. 158–79). He assumes that Shakespeare and the moral philosophers would take the same view of their relationship.

[2]"Love as a Dramatic Theme," in *Shakespeare's Tragedies and Other Studies in Seventeenth Century Drama* (London: Chatto and Windus, 1950, 1961), p. 183.

anticipate Freud, it would seem rational to assume also that Shakespeare did not anticipate the obsession with perverse sexuality which characterizes later Jacobean and Caroline drama, and that the practice of his successors is no safe guide in interpreting Shakespeare's intention in writing this play. I would not quarrel however with Professor Leech's contention that the conflict between sex and power, or, as I should prefer to call it, between passion and public duty, is seen as a problem of integration. The impossibility of maintaining the wholeness of life in the circumstances in which its characters are placed is the play's theme. The opposed forces in *Antony and Cleopatra* profess to seek a reconciliation but fail to find any permanently satisfactory resolution of their conflicts. Politically, the old order of the Republic is dead, the new order of the Empire not yet born. "Things fall apart; the centre cannot hold." The spokesman for this centre is Octavia, whose quiet nature inhabits the middle ground between the passions of Egypt and the policy of Rome. By her own confession her powers of reconciliation are "most weak, most weak," and she finds it impossible to maintain her place in a scheme of things in which there is "no midway twixt these extremes at all."

Yet the play's oppositions, however sharply conflicting, however incapable of reconciliation, are far from being regarded as moral absolutes. Both have their elements of good and of evil, though not the same kinds of good nor the same kinds of evil. Nor are the properties of their composition fixed. Rather, the moral estimate which the audience is invited to form, in both instances, reflects the mutability of the play's universe, of what Cleopatra refers to as "the varying shore of the world."

Indeed this is, in a sense, a tragedy in which there is no hero, no heroine, and no villain. It does not concern itself with the unnatural nor, except on the most superficial level, with the supernatural. It does not deal with crimes against divinely established order, with monstrous ingratitude, or with diabolical evil overcoming saintly purity. It deals with self-destruction and self-aggrandizement, and with other natural human motives. It presents a conflict of opposed views of the good which is predominantly a worldly good, a conflict in which the one suffers a partial defeat in victory and the other a partial victory in defeat. For in defeat one aspect of worldliness is transcendentalized. That this is seldom considered a wholly satisfying tragedy may be due less to its providing too little tragic reconciliation than to its providing too much.

Towards a dramatic conflict of this kind the attitude of the audience is bound to be ambivalent, its allegiance inevitably divided. That the author intended this to be so is indicated by his setting up of oppositions within oppositions and by his presentation of them in a sequence of kaleidoscopic patterns which forces the audience into successive readjustments of its reaction to the dramatic situation. It is not a play towards which any single critical attitude can be maintained. "All for love and the world well lost" and Shaw's description of the play as "a faithful picture of the soldier broken down by debauchery and the typical wanton in whose arms such men perish"[3] are equally unsatisfactory assessments of its theme, yet each possesses a modicum of truth,[4] for the action takes us along on a progress from something like Shaw's view to something close to Dryden's.[5] As we travel, for us as for the participants in the struggle between the values of Egypt and the values of Rome, love and reason keep little company; our minds pull us in one direction, our hearts in another. We identify

[3]Preface to *Caesar and Cleopatra*.

[4]Both schools of thought have their adherents in later criticism, and even those who recognize the play's ambivalence tend, for the most part, to end up as romantics or moralists. Wilson Knight attempts to get around the problem in *The Imperial Theme* (Oxford University Press, 1931; London: Methuen, 1951) by treating the positive and negative aspects in separate chapters and totting up at the end, where the balance is heavily in favour of the transcendental value of love, as indicated by his tribute to Cleopatra as "all womankind, therefore all romantic vision, the origin of love, the origin of life." S. L. Bethell (*Shakespeare and the Popular Dramatic Tradition*, 1944) finds "the basis of the good life rooted deep in the sensual nature." D. A. Traversi (*An Approach to Shakespeare*, London, 1957) walks the tightrope more successfully than most, pointing out that love is treated both as a spiritual value and as a social weakness, and that the presentation of the lovers in Act I, scene i, "calls in the characteristically Shakespearean way for a balance in judgement which will have to be maintained throughout the play" (p. 238). Nevertheless the implications of his analysis make it clear that he believes Shakespeare regarded "social weakness" as the dominating element. To John F. Danby ("*Antony and Cleopatra*: A Shakespearean Adjustment," in *Poets on Fortune's Hill*, London: Faber and Faber, 1952, pp. 128–51) Rome is the World, Egypt the Flesh, in a dramatic world in which there appear to be no other elements. He also notes the play's ambivalence, but after marshalling some excellent evidence on this point fails to come to the conclusions which it warrants. Instead he minimizes Cleopatra's dramatic importance and utterly rejects any suggestion that the world and the flesh are redeemed by love.

[5]Alan Warner, in "A Note on *Antony and Cleopatra*," *English*, XI (Spring, 1957), pp. 139–44, comments that while Shakespeare does not present Cleopatra in so unfavourable a light as Plutarch does in his *Life of Antony*, he uses the imagery of appetite rather than of tenderness in the love scenes, and even the imagery of violence, which pervades the rest of the play. He sees the shifts of attitude to the love theme as related to Antony's feelings about Cleopatra: "Antony's attitude to her continually changes; so does the mode in which Shakespeare presents her to the audience" (p. 142). An interesting suggestion, but one which fails to account for the tone of Act V. Antony does display tenderness to Cleopatra in his death scene and does not urge her to "do what's brave, what's noble" "after the high Roman fashion," but to "seek . . . honour with . . . safety."

ourselves not with one side or the other, but with the fact of their division, for the failure to reconcile them is the tragedy of Man as well as of Antony. Only in Cleopatra's vision does Antony succeed in bestriding the ocean which separates the varying shores of man's middle world, and the melancholy answer to her question, "Think you there was, or might be, such a man? / As this I dreamed of?" is Dolabella's "Gentle madam, no."

The catastrophe which results from this insoluble conflict involves not only the major but also many of the minor figures in despicable or lamentable victory, however glorious, or in noble or magnanimous defeat, however ignominious—Pompey, Octavia, Enobarbus, Eros, Iras, and Charmian among them. Caesar "gets money where he loses hearts" as he moves towards the mastery of the Mediterranean world which will usher in the *Pax Romana*. Antony suffers what he regards as the ultimate dishonour, despair, and eventual death, but enhances his characteristic magnanimity as he achieves self-knowledge in defeat. Cleopatra passes from quean to queen, uniting in her death the passion of Egypt and the dignity of Rome.

In *Antony and Cleopatra* we have, reflecting the pervasive ambivalence of the play, not one dramatic movement but two, each of which is parallel to the other but contrary in its motion. For Caesar and for Antony the internal and external actions move in opposite directions along the diagonals of a square, the one rising as the other falls. The pairs of parallel lines meet at that midway point of the play where there is "no midway twixt these extremes at all," where Octavia's prayers cross, and prayer "destroys the prayer" (III, iv, 19). Duality is omnipresent—in structure, setting, characterization, incident, and imagery; in irony and paradox, in parallel and contrast of all these, and in every sort of wordplay, as in theme. It is especially evident in the emphasis which the plot places upon choice. Over and over, characters find themselves in situations in which they must choose between opposed goods or opposed evils, and which is the lesser and which the greater good or evil is seldom discernible by reason alone.

Often such a choice is illuminated by and itself serves to illuminate an opposite choice. Thus, Pompey must choose between personal integrity (or, if we are less charitable, reputation) and personal ambition, Caesar between the pursuit of the power he believes necessary for the peace of the Roman world and loyalty to his pledged word. That the less important character makes what seems the nobler if less expedient choice leads the audience to judge Caesar in part by Pompey. Menas and Enobarbus must choose between fidelity and what they regard as commonsense, and the different ways in which they come to similar conclusions give us more sympathy for Enobarbus than we might otherwise have had. Ventidius must choose between honour for Rome's sake and prudence for his own, and his choice tells us something about Rome and about Antony. Dolabella must choose between loyalty and truth, Eros between obedience and devotion, and from their choices we learn as much about Caesar, Cleopatra, and Antony as about Dolabella and Eros. These are all inescapable choices, without possibility of compromise. Circumstances preclude the middle way, and, for all the tricks she plays later in order to call "great Caesar, ass unpolicied," even that pastmistress of vacillation, Cleopatra, comes in the end to realize that this is the heart of the matter:

> ANT.: Of Caesar seek your honour, with your safety. O!
> CLEO.: They do not go together.
>
> (IV, xv, 46–7)

"The stars irreconciliable" so divide not only men but values that they cannot "stall together in the whole world."

In the parallel patterns of development of the three main tragic figures, each does not pass through precisely the same stage at the same time, but the three climaxes do occur in successive scenes (III, v, vi, and vii). The *agon* of each is a paradox, exemplifying an aspect of the disintegration of one order in moving towards the establishment of another. Like Lear, Antony must be stripped of all command, all respect, external and internal, declining from the heroic governor divinely descended from Hercules to unaccommodated man before he can know, accept, and command himself. Caesar follows the opposite course, and is least admirable when he is most successful, though he moves, in his own estimation and public acclaim, from boy to god. Cleopatra is most royal when her realm has shrunk to the proportions of her own monument. For all three the pattern of conflict is the epic one, commencing *in medias res* and setting aside exposition for later narration—in Caesar's conversation with Lepidus, in Enobarbus' description of the meeting of Antony and Cleopatra, and in Antony's reminiscences of Philippi. At the beginning of the play the positive forces in Caesar and the negative ones in Antony are already in operation, and for a full understanding of the extent of the latter's decline we must take into consideration the pre-Alexandrian Antony as others describe him.

In this earlier, more youthful Antony the "elements," if not so well mixed as he believed them to be in Brutus, were those of a whole man. Antony fought hard and lived hard; he was luxury-loving, even licentious, but strong both in his passions and in his ability to endure the hardships of the field. He had the vices and virtues of youth, and the contrasting elements of his nature functioned in the circumstances appropriate to them. He might justifiably, at that period, be said to possess a "well-divided disposition," with what would in Shakespeare's times have been classed as a sanguine predominance. Later, he had proved himself a shrewd politician and a great general, both as a strategist and as a leader of men. But his "little moment" of perfection is past. Circumstances have combined with the fading of youthful energy, the corrupting effects of power, and the charms of Cleopatra, to put Antony off-balance. He has gone soft. He has delegated his wars to subordinates, and in absenting himself (physically, spiritually, and politically) from Rome he has neglected not only his public duty but his private interest. He has been what is worse than merely self-indulgent; he has been self-indulgent at the wrong time, as Caesar is quick to point out (I, iv, 16–33). Pleasure is for him no longer merely a pastime; it has become his business, as his "no messenger but thine" to Cleopatra, when he dismisses the embassy from Rome, and Enobarbus' punning on the "business" which demands his presence in Egypt make abundantly clear. He has lost his balanced composition, his internal "order." That this is the view not only of Antony's rivals but of his supporters is evidenced by the comments of Philo, that spokesman of rational devotion who makes his brief appearance in the opening scene:

> Nay, but this dotage of our general's
> O'erflows the measure. . . .
> His captain's heart,
> Which in the scuffles of great fights hath burst
> The buckles on his breast, reneges all temper.
>
> (I, i, 1–7)

Antony has lost sight of the Roman ideal of the golden mean, and the excesses excusable in youth and appropriate in war have no place in maturity and peace. There is no midway, no moderation in Antony's middle age. The heyday in his blood is not tame; it does not wait upon the judgment. (It is interesting, if not necessarily relevant, that in 1607 Shakespeare was very probably Antony's age.) Philo continues his account to Demetrius:

> Sir, sometimes when he is not Antony,
> He comes too short of that great property
> Which still should go with Antony.
>
> (I, i, 57–9)

By nature, Antony is endowed with the qualities of greatness, but he is no longer a whole, a balanced man. Sometimes he is one part of himself, sometimes another, erring both in excess and in defect. As Octavian says of the "common body" of Rome, he "goes to and back, lackying the varying tide." He has lost the ability to keep the parts of his divided disposition in balance and so give them purposeful integration. He recognizes the fact of this division in himself, but he does not accept it as an aspect of his nature for the management of which he alone must ultimately be responsible. He makes his will lord of his reason, laying his difficulties at the doors of others. Until the news of his wife's death reaches him he is inclined to blame Fulvia and his brother, not his own neglect of duty, for his difficulties with Caesar. Thereafter, it is his "enchanting queen" whose "strong Egyptian fetters" he must break or "lose himself." Cleopatra has conquered a part of his soul, but it is Antony, as Enobarbus later points out, who allows that part to enslave the rest. In Act I, however, Antony's will is as yet "but conquer'd merely," not yielded utterly; his sense of duty not dead, but asleep. When a Roman thought awakens him "Antony will be himself." Though the foundations of his prestige in Rome have been weakened by the scandalous rumours from Egypt, they have not crumbled, and Antony has not declined *noticeably* from the peak of his political power and military reputation when the play opens. His internal decline, however, is already far advanced. Though he still casts the shadow of a hero in the Roman world, to the audience he seems to lack some of the substance of a man. He has been brought drunken forth, Cleopatra has been presented in the posture of a whore, and the audience has seen the seeds of Antony's destruction—negligence, sensuality, over-estimation of himself, and under-estimation of Octavius —planted in the mud of Nilus.

The opening scenes give us a taste of Cleopatra's infinite variety, but its emphasis is predominantly negative. Airs and graces she displays in abundance, but little "grace" and less majesty until the moment of Antony's departure, when the alternating inarticulateness and quiet dignity of her farewell reveal the sincerity and tenderness buried beneath the quick and often shrewish wit of her earlier speeches. It is her passion rather than her cleverness, on the other hand, which is stressed in the Egyptian scenes of Act II. She is still an extremist, whether she is expressing the love-melancholy of sexual frustration or the termagant fury of a woman scorned, but her very violence precludes any doubt of the depth of her feelings or the keenness of her sense of loss. For Cleopatra, Egypt without her Roman is sterile; for Antony, Rome without his "royal Egypt" is futile. Without duty *and* pleasure, reason *and* passion, honour *and* love—without the fullness of life—there can be no fruitfulness.

In the four years since Philippi the scarce-bearded Caesar has emerged from his pupillage and is thinking of his former mentor as his "great competitor," whose failings deserve to be "chid as we rate boys." He is flexing his political muscles but does not yet feel entirely sure of himself, as his *apologia* to Lepidus indicates. He will not long care what Lepidus approves or disapproves, though he never quite loses the habit of self-justification. Octavius has to excess the qualities in which Antony is defective, and he has added to his native prudence and far-sightedness the shrewd opportunism for which Antony has provided the example in earlier days. If his blood is not very snow-broth, it certainly lacks warmth. Caesar's passions will never lead him into folly, but will be managed with the detachment of one who knows instinctively when it is politic to weep, to be generous to a defeated rival, to display righteous indignation. He is not likely to fight elsewhere than on his own ground for either a woman's whim or a rival's challenge, and if pleasure has become Antony's business, business would seem to be Caesar's pleasure. The word is often in his mouth.

In the *De Officiis*, a work familiar to every Elizabethan schoolboy, Cicero sketches two "characters" of men unfit for public office. The one neglects his duty for his pleasure; the other punctiliously fulfills the demands of office not for the good of the state but for personal aggrandizement. There is little doubt that he modelled his portraits on the two triumvirs who had already tried to bring about his downfall and were soon to hound him to his death. In seeing the vices and virtues of these two men as complementary Shakespeare follows his lead. Where Antony is reckless, Caesar is calculating; where Antony is magnanimous, Caesar is just but ungenerous; where Antony is erratic, Caesar is steadily purposeful; where Antony is a libertine, Caesar is a prude. Indeed, like Malvolio, he is "sometimes a kind of Puritan."

Yet, as everywhere in this play, we must beware of over-simplification. Just as we judge Antony by what he has been as well as what he is when the play opens, so we tend to judge Caesar not merely by what he is in Act I but also by what we know him to have become after the play ends. Considered in isolation, however, the Caesar of Act I is an honourable man and a just one, understandably irritated by the irresponsible behaviour of his partner. He gives credit where it is due. Indeed, it is from his lips that we are reminded of Antony's past greatness, and his regret that Antony is so careless of his reputation appears to be genuine, if not untinged with personal pique.

At this stage the secondary characters function in various ways as links between these mighty opposites, for as yet the issues between them have not become so sharply defined as to turn the middle way into a no-man's-land where none can live between two fires. Yet it is already dangerous ground, a quicksand which will disappear after swallowing those who inhabit it. Pompey, whose threatened wars have brought a patched-up quarrel between Antony and Caesar to a patched-up peace, is the first to go. In Pompey "the ancient Roman honour more appears" than in any that draws breath in this play. He is proud, honest, honourable, gracious, and reasonable, and the trium-virs do well to take seriously his popularity with the Roman masses, for he has his father's charm, if not his father's greatness. Although his scathing comments on Cleopatra's waning graces and their effect upon her "amorous surfeiter" prove ironically inaccurate, they express the general contemporary opinion in Rome, if we can judge by the propa-ganda of Horace and others. On the other hand, Pompey takes a lively interest in things Egyptian, and is concerned that the hospitality aboard his ship should approach if it cannot hope to equal the sumptuousness of an "Alexandrian feast." His view of life encompasses both sides; he is a balanced man who is capable of compromise, an exemplar of the mean, and therefore he is doomed. The effect of this feast of fellowship upon the various characters is revealing. As host, Pompey enters fully into the spirit of the occasion, yet stays relatively sober. Lepidus has a weak head and falls by the wayside early. Antony leads the Bacchanalian dance, and Enobarbus, "weaker than the wine" though still on his feet, decides to stay on board with Menas[6] instead of attempting to go with Antony. Caesar does what is required of him, under protest. He dislikes conviviality, and "frowns at this levity" as inappropriate to the serious "business" in hand. He is more interested in negotiating an advantageous peace than in celebrating it.

The trimmer Lepidus is the second representative of the mean to disappear. Like Octavia, who soon follows him into oblivion as far as the play is concerned, he is a "swan's down feather / That stands upon the swell at full of tide / And neither way inclines." Finally Enobarbus, the restorer of balances, who is hard-headedly Roman in Egypt and

[6]In view of Menas' earlier comment regarding Pompey's refusal to indulge in a little politic assassination, "For this / I'll never follow thy pall'd fortunes more," the pairing of these two here cannot be taken as accidental.

sensuously poetic (on the subject of Egypt) when in Rome, withdraws.
His comment on the fate of Lepidus foreshadows his own:

> Then, world, thou hast a pair of chaps—no more;
> And throw between them all the food thou hast,
> They'll grind the one the other.
>
> (III, v, 13–15)

Similar methods of exposition have been used for the three main characters. First, a dominant characteristic has been presented in strong outline, then has been mitigated by demonstrating that its opposite is also part of the truth. The idle sensualist, however soft the beds i' the east, is persuaded that he must give up his pleasure for his peace, which is also his profit. Caesar has been admirable if unlovable until the moment when he gives his sister, who deserves "no worse a husband than the best of men" to one whom he has already condemned as "the abstract of all faults." The glamorous royal harlot has shown herself, long before Act V, to be commanded "by such poor passions as the maid that milks." It is of course nothing new for Shakespeare to begin a play by presenting conflicting views of his hero. Iago's scurrilous slanders are our introduction to the noble Moor of Venice, and a whole scene is devoted to glowing accounts of Macbeth's brave and devoted service to his king. But *Antony and Cleopatra* is unusual in that *all* the major characters are given this double presentation, in which comment and action alternate and are frequently inconsistent in themselves as well as in conflict with each other.

This insistent emphasis on the dialectic pattern, which goes far beyond the normal requirements of dramatic conflict, may have been dictated in part by the restrictions imposed on the author by historic fact as well as legend. For the events covered by the time-span of the play are not so much the clashes of equal and mighty opposites as the successive stages in the decline of Antony's fortunes and the rise of Caesar's, and though the action and its consequences are politically significant, this is not, as *Coriolanus* is, primarily a political tragedy. To treat the conflict between Antony and the young Caesar as simply a political one and the play as a chronicle, would be to fly in the face of historical and literary tradition, which had firmly established Antony's infatuation with Cleopatra as the cause of his downfall. But a struggle for power between an ambitious young man and an older man who has lost his ambition does not provide material for an effective dramatic conflict. In such a contest the dice are so heavily loaded that the catastrophe is more likely to evoke pathos than tragic awe.

The dying lion must be accepted as a part of the pattern of natural order. Shakespeare therefore compensated for the lack of dramatic issues in his external conflict by emphasizing all the other oppositions in theme, character, and situation, and, wherever possible, by universalizing them. Cosmic imagery recalls to us the epic significance of Antony's internal division. The insurrection in Antony's soul is seen as the reflection of a world in flux, Rome and Egypt as the conflicting elements of reason and passion in man's soul. The dissensions and reconciliations of the lovers take on overtones of the age-old battle of the sexes with its love-hate ambivalence, and indeed, almost every action in the play is seen in terms of dilemma or paradox.

The first part of *Antony and Cleopatra* deviates from Shakespeare's usual tragic structure in devoting almost equal attention to each of the main characters rather than concentrating on one, and in developing a number of minor characters in considerable depth. The latter part also deviates in various ways from the norm, as, for example, in the management of climax. Where there are so many significant choices, the climactic ones which motivate the reversal do not stand out as sharply as any one of them might do on a less crowded canvas. It might even be possible to argue that there is no real reversal in this play, as Octavius has had the direction of the action in his hands from the beginning, and Antony responds to circumstances rather than creating them. The turn of fortune is, however, clearly marked by a choice which makes reconciliation between them impossible instead of improbable, or rather by two choices, one on Antony's part and one on Caesar's. Caesar initiates the new movement, and, having made his choice between profit and honour by breaking peace with Pompey (who had protested that his profit did not lead his honour), and dismissing Lepidus without consulting the third member of the triumvirate, he forges steadily ahead to his goal of temporal greatness. At every step he demonstrates his confidence that the end can always be made to justify the means, as well as the sense of situation and firmness of purpose which mark him as a man of destiny. But every step also gives evidence of his progressive spiritual deterioration, and he touches bottom as a man in that moment of triumph when he gloats over the defeat of his old friend, replying to Antony's gallant if unrealistic challenge to personal combat with,

> Let the old ruffian know
> I have many other ways to die, meantime
> Laugh at his challenge.

> (IV, i, 4–6)

If this, in the eyes of the audience, is Caesar's nadir, it must be that it is so regarded because bad manners are often more distressing than dishonesty. For by Act V, Caesar is no longer taking the trouble to keep up even a pretence of truthfulness—at least where Cleopatra is concerned:

> Come hither, Proculeius. Go and say
> We purpose her no shame. Give her what comforts
> The quality of her passion shall require,
> Lest, in her greatness, by some mortal stroke
> She do defeat us; for her life in Rome
> Would be eternal in our triumph.
>
> 					(V, i, 61–6)

In *Hamlet* and *Macbeth* Shakespeare follows the usual tragic pattern in removing the hero from the stage for some time after the climax, and focussing attention upon his antagonist. It is perhaps some support for the contention that this play lacks a hero that he does not do the same with Antony. Instead, he continues to alternate his scenes between Antony's camp and Caesar's and, if anything, increases rather than diminishes the emphasis on Antony. Normally the dramatic focus returns from the antagonist to the hero in Act V, and this particular variation may be dictated by the fact that Antony's tragedy must be accomplished by the end of Act IV, the fifth act being reserved for Cleopatra, but its effect is to define more sharply the action–reaction pattern of the play's structure and to weight the scales of dramatic interest more evenly between the victor and the vanquished. Such a counterweight is needed, for not only the acclaim of Virgil and Horace, hailing him as the bringer of peace and the restorer of order, but all the historical and legendary grandeur of the golden age of Imperial Rome, so familiar to Shakespeare's contemporaries, load the scales on Caesar's side. The audience must never lose sight of the *internal* view of Antony if he is to retain the essential core of sympathy without which the catastrophe would have no tragic impact, for, viewed externally, his actions during most of Act III and a great part of Act IV have in them more of folly than of magnanimity or magnificence, the heroic virtues commonly associated with the great age of Rome.

Having made his last politic gesture by marrying his "occasion," as Enobarbus puts it, at the end of Act II, Antony thereafter proves incapable of either reconciling the extremes of his divided disposition or choosing between them. He makes and unmakes choices, consciously goes against the dictates of his reason and afterwards bewails the consequences of his folly. No sooner has he allowed Octavia to go to

Rome to mediate between himself and Caesar than he is off to "his
Egyptian dish again," an action which makes all mediation futile and
drives the mediator into the enemy's camp. Whether Cleopatra's subsequent actions are those of an infinitely various or of an incorrigibly
fickle woman, they reinforce Antony's divisions in nature, if not—to
indulge in a Shakespearean quibble—in the field. As she veers with
every breeze, from courage to cowardice, sincerity to coquetry, loyalty
to trickery, Antony's attitude to his "grave charm" alternates between
doting and detestation. She is the armourer of his heart, whose single
tear is "worth all that's won and lost"; she is also "the foul Egyptian"
and a "triple-turned whore." At times it is true that Antony "is not
more manlike / Than Cleopatra, nor the Queen of Ptolemy / More
womanly than he." When she demands recognition as the head of a
state which bears a charge "i' the war" and insists that she "will appear
there for a man," she is more concerned to demonstrate her superiority
over Antony by making him fight at sea than to win the battle against
Caesar by land. Having made her point, she pleads feminine timidity
as the excuse for her navy's craven desertion in the midst of the fight.
She is accusing and penitent, imperious and humble, straightforward
and devious. Yet she is allowed one significant and redeeming action,
one which is often too lightly regarded if not overlooked. She is given
her chance to pack cards with Caesar, and while she temporizes with
his messenger she does not take advantage of the opportunity Caesar
offers her to buy her own safety at Antony's expense. We are given,
also, a few brief glimpses of another Antony than the dotard and the
railer. In Act IV yet another shift of emphasis presents the man who
was once and still might be a magnanimous leader, a courageous and
successful general, and, finally, a man who, in both senses, knows his
own mind.

Yet it is small wonder that in the midst of such violent and contrary
storms of passion and folly the rational, balanced man should begin to
doubt his function. Is loyalty to folly in itself folly? asks Enobarbus.
Having seen the depths of degradation into which the man who makes
his will lord of his reason can fall, he decides to follow his head rather
than his heart, only to discover that wisdom can be infamous and folly
noble. Yet among the heaped-up paradoxes of Act IV the supreme and
significant irony of making the man who is not passion's slave die of
a broken heart is often missed.

Antony, after Cleopatra's second desertion in battle, rejects utterly
the "right gypsy" who has beguiled him "to the very heart of loss," and
condemns her to die. Yet, when news of her supposed death reaches

him, he knows that this, not military defeat and disgrace, is the true heart of loss which makes all length torture. The god Eros may have brought him to his downfall, but his human namesake cannot, for very love of him, kill Antony when commanded to do so. If he is to preserve such honour as is left to him, Antony, the man who had evaded the responsibilities of duty, must assume full responsibility for his own death. Yet even this last attempt to play "the firm Roman" is only partly successful. It is not only historical fact but also effective drama that the man who could not live apart from Cleopatra should not die apart from her. And when the fatal results of her last, desperate deception of Antony are brought home to her, Cleopatra takes on the elements of the "firm Roman" in Antony, becoming most fully "royal Egypt" in her determination to do "what's brave, what's noble" after the high, Roman fashion. Yet she remains herself, addressing death in the language of love, assured of her power to conquer this last of her conquerors and make him "proud to take" her.

Caesar has the glory of his victory, Antony his dram of consolation in knowing that however sharply nobility and baseness may have contended for mastery in his life he does "not now basely die." But in Act V, if the power is Caesar's the glory is Cleopatra's. "Bravest at the last," she is again for Cydnus in all the majesty of queenliness and love. Yet here as throughout the play even the strongest emphasis is not long maintained without its counter-balance. In the midst of her exaltation and grief, Cleopatra can rail as bitterly at Seleucis as she had railed at the messenger who brought her the news of Antony's marriage, can still jest about being jealous of a ghost who will give his first disembodied kiss to the handmaid who dies before her, still pretend to entertain the idea of coming to terms with Caesar, as in Act III, scene xiii. The oppositions extend to her eloquence, in which golden rhetoric and lyric simplicity fuse in a heavenly mingle. Even the cold heart of Caesar is sufficiently warmed by the rising sun of destiny to enable him to be touched by Cleopatra's beauty and majesty in death, if not in life, and to weep the "declining day" of his old comrade, who, now he is safely dead, is no longer "the abstract of all faults" but one in whom "taints and honours wag'd equal."

The danger of handling a tragic theme by the methods Shakespeare has chosen for *Antony and Cleopatra* is that the play will become not merely complex but diffuse. In the theatre, much of the diffuseness is eliminated by returning to the flexible, open stage of Shakespeare's day. But even there, and much more in reading, the multiplicity of persons, scenes, and episodes, as well as the multiplicity of dualities, can work against unity of impression. To counteract this tendency, to find a solution to the familiar Renaissance problem of creating unity in diversity, Shakespeare makes use of every poetic and dramatic device. One is to accept and indeed to exploit the limitations—or rather lack of limitation—of his subject. By giving generous development to a number of characters rather than a few he is able to set up illuminating parallels and contrasts. Instead of exalting the fashionable ideal of *gloire* as the highest if not the only worthy goal of noble endeavour, he makes ambivalence central to his treatment of the conflict of love and honour and builds a symmetrical structure on the patterns of equation and opposition. Another of his methods of integration is to make the fullest possible use of parallels of situation. A third is to use every sort of verbal echo—recurrent motifs, symbols and images, direct repetition and ironic contrast—to bind together into a dramatic whole the discordant elements of political and spiritual disintegration and re-integration.

Our earlier discussion of the importance of choice has indicated some of the uses of parallels of situation. Other instances abound, but some of the episodes are minor ones and the echoes they set ringing are subtle, much less insistent than the recurrence of handwashing in *Macbeth*, or Laertes' willingness to cut the throat of his father's murderer "i' the church." Some of these parallels, such as Caesar's list of charges against Antony in Act I, scene iv and Act III, scene vi, and Antony's against Caesar in Act III, scene iv are part of the formal symmetry of the play, but others, such as the hand-kissing incidents and those involving the reception of bad news serve additional purposes. Antony's rage at finding Thyreus, Caesar's envoy, kissing Cleopatra's hand is, like most of Antony's attitudes in Act III, excessive. It demonstrates three things, however: that he places the highest value on Cleopatra's favours, that he is not certain of her fidelity, and that he is capable of being a lion and an ass at the same time. Antony has some justification for his doubts. As he reminds her, Cleopatra has three times previously given her passionate heart along with her politic hand, and she herself reminds Thyreus that "your Caesar's father" had often "rain'd kisses" on that hand. Earlier in the play she had tendered the hand "that kings have lipp'd, and trembled kissing" to another messenger from Rome, only to turn on him with a rage equal to Antony's against Thyreus when the terrified courier informed her of her lover's bondage to Octavia for "the best turn i' the bed." Both incidents are associated with infidelity, actual or suspected; each is verbally linked with Cleopatra's imperial amours, and each ends in violence to a messenger. Antony's slashing "Take hence this Jack and whip him!" has been anticipated by Cleopatra's threat to the hapless slave she has been haling up and down by the hair:

> Thou shalt be whipp'd with wire and stew'd in brine,
> Smarting in ling'ring pickle.
>
> (II, v, 65–6)

To these associations the hand-kissing incident of Act IV, scene viii, provides a contrast. It is the magnanimous, not the irrational Antony who insists that his "day o' the world" shall allow the faithful Scarus to kiss her hand as a reward for his service in the victory which intervenes between Antony's two disastrous defeats. Here, there is no reference to kings previously so honoured, and all violence has been honourably expended on the battlefield. This third hand-kissing episode demonstrates that Antony's previous rage had not (like Cleopatra's) been motivated solely by sexual jealousy, and also distinguishes between various kinds of service—that of the lover and the soldier, which merit favour, and that of the time-serving intriguer, the go-between, which does not. All three are woven into and intensify an emotional context of love and war, passion and policy, devotion and disloyalty.

Having returned to his Roman mood in Act I, scene ii, Antony receives the messengers from Rome with the firmness and stoical calm which are the complement to his hedonism, even though their budget of news is uniformly bad. "The nature of bad news infects the teller," protests the hesitant envoy. "When it concerns the fool or coward," is Antony's sententious reply.

> Who tells me true, though in his tale lie death,
> I hear him as he flatter'd.
>
> (I, ii, 92–3)

It is only after she has given way to irrational anger that Cleopatra, on the other hand, admits the folly of her behaviour towards the bringer of bad news, and, characteristically, her remorse is self-regarding:

> These hands do lack nobility, that they strike
> A meaner than myself. . . .
>
> (II, v, 82–3)

Her subsequent remarks to the messenger are worldly wise rather than logically sound:

> Though it be honest, it is never good
> To bring bad news. Give to a gracious message
> An host of tongues; but let ill tidings tell
> Themselves when they be felt.
>
> (II, v, 85–8)

The third component of the bad-news triad harks back to Antony's boast, "though in his tale lie death, / I hear him as he flatter'd." The word of Fulvia's death he may be able to bear with equanimity, but events prove how unfounded was Cleopatra's taunt, "Now I see, I see, / In Fulvia's death how mine receiv'd shall be" (I, iii, 64-5). Hard on Antony's "She hath betray'd me, and shall die the death" (IV, xiv, 26) comes Mardian's,

> Death of one person can be paid but once,
> And that she has discharg'd.

Antony does not receive Mardian's piteous tale "as he flatter'd," but, now that he has lost "the armourer" of his heart, calls on Eros to disarm his body also, dismissing the messenger with "That thou depart'st hence safe / Does pay thy labour richly." In this tale lies not only Cleopatra's death, but his own, and totally disarmed, he is beyond both rage and reason.

Reference has already been made to Octavius' unwillingness to remain *in statu pupillari* with regard to Antony. Around this relationship is woven a complex of associations which accentuate the "the younger rises when the old doth fall" aspect of the conflict between them. Caesar suggests that Antony's follies are more appropriate to adolescence than to middle age, and should be rebuked,

> As we rate boys who, being mature in knowledge,
> Pawn their experience to their present pleasure,
> And so rebel to judgment.
>
> (I, iv, 31-3)

It is one of the many paradoxes of the play that Antony, for all his twenty additional years, does indeed seem younger in heart and mind than Caesar. The issue of precedence raises its head again at their first meeting in Rome, when each graciously urges the other to "sit," and yet again when Caesar derives a special satisfaction from the fact that Antony is reduced to sending "so poor a pinion of his wing" as his schoolmaster to treat for terms of peace. Antony cannot comprehend how the stripling who "at Philippi kept / His sword e'en like a dancer" and "no practice had / In the brave squares of war" (III, xi, 35-9) can have defeated him, and challenges him to single combat in words calculated to rouse Caesar's ire:

> Tell him he wears the rose
> of youth upon him; from which the world should note
> Something particular. His coin, ships, legions,
> May be a coward's, whose ministers would prevail
> Under the service of a child as soon
> As i' th' command of Caesar.
>
> (III, xiii, 20-5)

Caesar's resentment is clearly indicated in his reply to this challenge of age to youth:

> He calls me boy, and chides as he had power
> To beat me out of Egypt. My messenger[7]
> He hath whipt with rods; dares me to personal combat,
> Caesar to Antony. Let the old ruffian know
> I have many other ways to die. . . .
>
> (IV, i, 1–5)

All this, in addition to binding the various episodes together, suggests that the conflict between Antony and Caesar is part of the age-old battle of the generations. Along with Caesar's reference to Antony's "declining day" they associate it with the necessary and incontestable mutability of the natural order,[8] and the impression of inevitability thus imputed to the events of the play serves to make Antony's downfall less his own fault. With the same effect, Antony counsels Cleopatra to remember not his "crooked eclipses" but his "main of light."

> The miserable change now at my end
> Lament nor sorrow at; but please your thoughts
> In feeding them with those my former fortunes
> Wherein I liv'd the greatest prince o' th' world,
> The noblest. . . .
>
> (IV, xv, 51–5)

The general dramatic irony established by the circumstance that the audience knows in advance the outcome of the action is extended and supported by many other kinds of irony. Even so small a detail as the naming of characters contributes to this pervasive irony of tone. For example, Shakespeare found in Plutarch only the name of Domitius Enobarbus; the character is his own creation, and he is the personification of irony. Not only is his function that of the ironic commentator; his fate, by its own irony, demonstrates that man cannot live by reason alone, that ironic detachment, consistently maintained, is unnatural. But there is more. "Enobarbus" means, literally, "bronze-bearded," and

---

[7]That the accredited messenger was considered a proxy for the person of his master as well as the bearer of his message, and that an injury to the messenger was regarded as tantamount to an injury to the sender, is made clear in Lear's reaction to the stocking of Kent (II, ii and iii). Caesar's references in this speech to "boy" and "whip" make it obvious that he resents the whipping of Thyreus (as Antony no doubt meant him to do) as a personal affront, as if he had himself been chastised like a schoolboy.

[8]For an illuminating discussion of the death of the tragic hero as associated with "the solemn sympathy of Nature," see Northrop Frye, *An Anatomy of Criticism* (Princeton University Press, 1957), pp. 36 ff.

according to medieval physiognomy red hair was a sign of excessive passion. It was also associated with treachery, and Judas was usually depicted as red-haired. Upon this hint Shakespeare builds a complex of contradictions. The spokesman of reason and commonsense, who jests at passion, sees love as the "business" of lust, and finds the only natural causes of tears in an onion and a head-cold, is Antony's best friend as well as his severest critic only as long as he sees reason. But the logic which justifies his desertion cannot suspend the operations of human nature. In the end, the emotions he had derided in others and suppressed in himself rise up and destroy him.

Other names provide material for various kinds of wordplay. As the play opens, Philo is describing Antony's excesses to Demetrius. "Philo," of course, is judicious devotion as opposed to "Eros," passion. The name Demetrius is derived from "Demeter," the goddess of natural fertility and harvest bounty, and her name suggests "beyond measure." Shakespeare begins to play with these concepts in Philo's opening words: "Nay, but this dotage of our General's / O'erflows the measure." Antony's eyes now turn "the office and devotion of their view" not upon the front of war and public service but upon "a tawny front." The word "office" is used here equivocally, meaning "function," in the Aristotelian sense, and civic "duty," as in Cicero's *De Officiis*. His heart, which appropriately had burst the buckles of his harness in battle, now inappropriately "reneges all temper." Here, "temper" has the force of "balance," as well as the hardening of steel for armour, through which latter connotation it is associated with the blacksmith's forge and thus with the "bellows" to come. "The bellows and the fan," usually thought of as opposed in function—the one serving to produce heat, the other to mitigate it—may both be used to blow up a fire, and in Antony's heart they serve to nourish the fire of unquenchable lust that grows by what it feeds on.

Though Philo introduces the first movement of the play, his opposite appears with the beginning of the second, meeting (significantly) Enobarbus head-on in Act III, scene v. Philo talks too much like Caesar to be needed after the latter has stated his case in Act I, scene iv. Neither does Demetrius appear again, but the train of thought set in motion by his name continues through repeated references to Antony's bounty. To Enobarbus he is "a mine of bounty," and to Cleopatra that mine was inexhaustible:

> For his bounty,
> There was no winter in't, an autumn 'twas
> That grew the more by reaping.
>
> (V, ii, 86–8)

It is a measure of Cleopatra's progress that this is not the language of
insatiable lust, but of love, recalling Juliet's:

> My bounty is as boundless as the sea,
> My love as deep: the more I give to thee,
> The more I have, for both are infinite.
>
> (*Romeo and Juliet*, II, ii, 133–5)

Wordplay on Dolabella's name serves to contrast Antony's bounty
with Caesar's. For all that his name means "fine trick," Dolabella does
not "laugh when boys or women tell their dreams," though Cleopatra
asks him if that is not his *trick*. He is sympathetic, straightforward, and
honest with her, scorning to deceive her by false pretences as to
Caesar's bounty. It is Proculeius, the one man about Caesar Antony
has told her to trust, who protests that his master is "so full of grace
that it flows over / On all that need" and immediately thereafter takes
her prisoner by trickery.

Classical allusions are also used for many purposes, of which
rhetorical ornament is only one. Antony is frequently likened to Mars,
Cleopatra to Venus. Mars and Venus, as Danby reminds us,[9] was a
favourite subject in Baroque canvases. Even the poor eunuch Mardian,
who centres his imaginings on "what Venus did with Mars," probably
had in mind a less celestial couple closer to hand. Nowhere is the
metaphor worked out specifically, but the repeated allusions suggest
that Shakespeare had in mind the story of Mars and Venus caught in
the net of Vulcan, the lame artificer of the gods. Octavius is represented
as emotionally crippled, and as a political craftsman. He has a trades-
man's soul. Support for this suggestion may be found in Cleopatra's
welcome to Antony after his victory in Act IV, scene viii:

> O infinite virtue [i.e. valour] com'st thou smiling from
> The world's great snare uncaught?
>
> (ll. 17–18)

Antony is frequently likened to his legendary ancestor, Hercules.[10]
The comparison is in some respects appropriate, in others ironically
inappropriate. Hercules, given the choice of luxury, personified by a
beautiful young girl, and fame, personified by a hard-featured crone,
had chosen the laborious road of fame. Yet he was ultimately destroyed
by a woman's trickery, a circumstance to which Antony alludes in the
following lines:

[9]*Poets on Fortune's Hill*, p. 150.
[10]See Eugene M. Waith, *The Herculean Hero in Marlowe, Chapman, Shakespeare and Dryden* (London: Chatto and Windus, 1962), pp. 113–20.

> Eros, ho!
> The shirt of Nessus is upon me; teach me,
> Alcides, thou mine ancestor, thy rage;
> Let me lodge Lichas on the horns o' th' moon,
> And with those hands that grasp'd the heaviest club
> Subdue my worthiest self. The witch shall die.
> To the young Roman boy she hath sold me, and I fall
> Under this plot. She dies for't. Eros, ho!
>
> (IV, xii, 42–9)

The *Hercules Furens* was one of the most familiar of Seneca's tragedies to Renaissance readers. Its purple patches were studied as models of style and widely quoted and paraphrased. An Elizabethan audience would be prepared to appreciate the interplay of ideas in this bit of bombast, which not only alludes to the madness of Hercules but mimics his ravings. The summonses to Eros are an appropriate frame, not only because Antony's lust has brought him to destruction but because Hercules, in his madness, had destroyed all those whom he loved, including his page boy, Lichas. It is unlikely that Antony had any intention of tossing the actual Eros up to the cold, fruitless moon, but his outburst is a rejection of physical passion as well as of its object, and their association here contrasts with their similar association in Act IV, scene xiv.

> Eros!—I come, my queen.—Eros!—Stay for me;
> Where souls do couch on flowers, we'll hand in hand,
> And with our sprightly port make the ghosts gaze.
> Dido and her Aeneas shall want troops,
> And all the haunt be ours.—Come, Eros, Eros!
>
> (ll. 49–54)

And again:

> Thou teachest me, O valiant Eros, what
> I should, and thou couldst not. My queen and Eros
> Have, by their brave instruction, got upon me
> A nobleness in record. But I will be
> A bridegroom in my death, and run into't
> As to a lover's bed. Come, then; and, Eros,
> Thy master dies thy scholar. To do thus
> I learn'd of thee.
>
> (ll. 96–103)

There is more here than the usual sexual pun on "die" and the commonplace about meeting death like a bridegroom. Eros has taught Antony how to die for love as in the act of love, for honour and with honour, and his image of the wedding-bed of death is echoed in

Cleopatra's "Husband, I come!" and her "the stroke [More equivocation!] of death is like a lover's pinch / Which hurts, and is desir'd."

Sometimes the connotations of particular words, such as "royal," "charm," "business," repeated in various contexts, serve not only to evoke a desired response but to bind episodes together. References to particular kinds of action, such as gambling or fishing, perform similar functions, as does the cosmic imagery[11] found throughout the play. Sometimes concepts which reflect the duality of theme and action are alluded to, either frequently or, as a framing device, at key points early and late in the action. Examples of these last two uses of repetition may be found in the serpent and the fig, and they are especially interesting because they occur in conjunction.

The connotative ambivalence of "serpent" is obvious, possibly even archetypal. Long before Freud it was a symbol of sexual fertility; it is associated with Aesculapius, the god of health, and with Hermes, the trickster. The transformation of Aaron's rod into a serpent is his warrant of priesthood. Yet the serpent is traditionally the enemy of man, and in Christian mythology is the symbol of absolute Evil. Caesar alludes to a popular superstition in seeing the threat of Pompey as potential rather than actual, as having "like the courser's hair, but life / And not a serpent's poison." Shakespeare makes much of the "strange serpents" believed to be spontaneously generated by the mud left behind by the Nile's receding floodwaters, and for Antony the spell of his "Serpent of Old Nile" was so strong that he could protest,

> Let Rome in Tiber melt, and the wide arch
> Of the rang'd empire fall! Here is my space.
>
> (I, i, 33–4)

His vehemence is equalled in Cleopatra's outburst against Antony's subsequent defection to Rome:

> Melt Egypt into Nile! And kindly creatures
> Turn all to serpents! (II, v, 77–8)

Antony's behaviour seems to her as unnatural as the birth of Nile's serpents. If he can be disloyal, all Nature must be disordered.

---

[11]See Wilson Knight, *The Imperial Theme*, for a rewarding discussion of the cosmic imagery of the play, in particular the imagery of the four elements. The poetic orchestration of the final scenes is fully analyzed in John Middleton Murry's *Shakespeare* (London, Jonathan Cape, 1936, pp. 352–79). A judicious study of both the verbal and the theatrical imagery of the play (along the lines suggested by R. A. Foakes in "Suggestions for a New Approach to Shakespeare's Imagery," *Shakespeare Survey* 5, pp. 85–6) is given by Maurice Charney in *Shakespeare's Roman Plays; The Function of Imagery in the Drama* (Cambridge, Mass., Harvard University Press, 1961).

The fig is similarly, though not so obviously, ambiguous in connotation.[12] The scriptures associate the fig with the vine as symbols of natural fertility blessed of the Lord. In the expression, "a fig for it" the word, at best, signifies something so commonplace as to be of no value, if not an object of scorn. In Jacobean writing it frequently serves as a euphemism for the verb of similar sound denoting sexual intercourse. Shakespeare so uses it in *II Henry IV*, V, iii, 17: "When Pistol lies, do this; and fig me. . . ."

The serpent and the fig, with their various and contradictory connotations, reflect the play's attitude to Egypt and what it stands for. Serpents are not mentioned directly when the first reference to figs occurs in Act I, scene ii, but the fertility of "the overflowing Nilus" is (and in a sexual context), and in this play the two concepts are inseparable. This brief encounter with the soothsayer serves a number of purposes, one of which is to evoke the heavily sensual atmosphere of Egypt without associating it exclusively and irrevocably with Egypt's queen. The saltier bawdries are restricted to conversation on the secondary social level. A more obvious intention is that of ironic foreshadowing, not only in the actual fortune-telling but in seemingly inconsequential talk which later events will make significant.

"Keep decorum, dear Isis, and fortune him accordingly," prays Iras, joking with Alexas. In other words, let him get the fortune he deserves. Enobarbus, who is present during this teasing, later reports the fulfilment of Iras' wish:

> Alexas did revolt, and went to Jewry on
> Affairs of Antony; there did dissuade
> Great Herod to incline himself to Caesar
> And leave his master Antony. For this pains
> Caesar hath hang'd him.
>
> (IV, vi, 11–16)

Alexas is a person of no importance, and this report of him shows how careful was Shakespeare's attention to detail. Not even the most trivial possibility of a linking irony is overlooked. Far more telling is the use made of Charmian's request, ". . . companion me with my mistress." The soothsayer replies, seemingly denying but actually confirming her wish, "You shall outlive the lady whom you serve." Here

---

[12]Certain ideas of mine already in gestation regarding the functions of Eros and the significance of figs in the play were matured and defined in a discussion with Professor Nevill Coghill in November, 1962, during the course of which he was kind enough to read to me an unpublished paper which touched on some of the points I have treated here.

the ironic impact does not depend upon subsequent information. Plutarch's account was so familiar that only the most ignorant members of the audience would be unaware that Charmian outlived her mistress by approximately one minute. But if they do not need to be informed they may need to be reminded, and the author takes no risk of missing his effect. Charmian's rejoinder is, "O, excellent! I love long life better than figs," and she is at her mistress's side when the guard enters to announce the "rural fellow" who "brings you figs." "He brings me liberty," is Cleopatra's reply, welcoming the gift which conceals "the pretty worm of Nilus . . . / That kills and pains not," whose "stroke of death is like a lover's pinch / That hurts, and is desir'd." Death and life, destruction and fertility, innocence and lust, are reconciled in the serpent hidden in the fruit—the symbol of the fortunate fall which led to the redemption of Man. This is the image which underlies the metamorphosis by which the asp, taken from its nest in the tawny globes of fruit, becomes the baby at Cleopatra's breast, "that rocks the nurse asleep."

In his Preface to *Three Plays for Puritans*, Shaw accuses Shakespeare of straining all the resources of his poetry to persuade the audience of *Antony and Cleopatra* that "the world was well lost by the twain." Like so much of Shaw's criticism this aims directly at the centre of the target and ends up just wide of the mark. Certainly Shakespeare makes no attempt to persuade us that it was not a good thing for the *world*, for the twain to lose it. The worldly and rational side has all the best of it in a worldly and rational sense. Antony's defeat is the basis of the *pax Romana*; it ensures that "the three-nook'd world, may bear the olive freely." The new order is founded upon his defeat and Caesar's victory. Nor does Shakespeare gloss over, as Shaw admits, the fact that the union between Antony and Cleopatra is lustful, adulterous, and destructive. What he is concerned to do is demonstrate that all love is potentially good and to communicate through his poetry the emergence of good out of evil. He accomplishes this purpose, this "justification," if you will, by careful modulation of poetic tone—expository, rhetorical, epic, and lyric. In the early scenes of the play the lyric touches are rare, present only frequently enough to allow of later development. They are confined almost entirely to the dialogue of the lovers, in such phrases as "bliss in our brows' bent," and such exchanges as:

CLEO.: I'll set a bourne how far to be belov'd.
ANT.:   Then must thou needs find out new heaven, new earth.

For the rest, the language is grave, witty, cynical, bawdy, or forthright, at need. If at his best Antony's speech rises to epic grandeur, at its worst it is inflated (deliberately) into bombast. Cleopatra's is incisive, shallow, or sensuous, according to her mood. Enobarbus' account of Cleopatra's barge transmutes North's rich prose into the pictorial vividness of Ovidian descriptive poetry, but the passage is not characteristic of the speaker nor of the prevailing tone of this part of the play; its soarings are an isolated promise of things to come. Antony's abrupt breaking of the tone in moving from Herculean railing to the lyric simplicity of "ten low words" in his, "Unarm, Eros, the long day's task is done, and we must sleep" signals the counter-movement from decline towards redemption. From this point on, in the language as in the persons, the elements of "baser life" are gradually purged, leaving the poetry of "air and fire" in possession. Variety remains, but discord vanishes, conquered by celestial harmony as Cleopatra's death scene is presented in verse "propertied," like Antony's remembered voice, "to all the tuned spheres." "It is well done"; indeed so well that Shakespeare does not hesitate to risk breaking the illusion of his newly established atmosphere by reminding us of its opposite as his boy actor delivers the lines:

> Saucy lictors
> Will catch at us like strumpets, and scald rhymers
> Ballad us out o' tune; the quick comedians
> Extemporally will stage us, and present
> Our Alexandrian revels; Antony
> Shall be brought drunken forth, and I shall see
> Some squeaking Cleopatra boy my greatness
> I' th' posture of a whore.
>
> (V, ii, 213–20)

Royal Egypt a bawd at the cart's tail? Our imaginations refuse admittance to any such picture.

There is none of the insincerity imputed to it by Shaw in the poetry of the final scenes, for to Shakespeare inconsistencies were not incongruities but reflections of the substance of life. The qualities which in one light might appear as vanity, fickleness, and extravagance, in another might be revealed as dignity, prudent compromise, and regal splendour, especially if they were possessed by a queen who reigned in perilous times. The man had "seen some majesty, and should know." It is not beyond the possibility of conjecture that in *Antony and Cleopatra* the poet who appears to have contributed no formal eulogy to Elizabeth's obsequies may have given expression in his portrait of the royal harlot to his mixed feelings about the virgin queen whose "variety" was as notorious as it was "infinite," and who successfully kept up the pretence that age could not wither her. A tribute "fitting for a Princess descended of so many royal Kings!"—the irony would have pleased him.

This is not wholly fanciful speculation. At least one passage in Plutarch's *Life of Antony*[13] might have suggested the parallel:

And besides her beauty, the good grace she had to talk and to discourse . . . was a spur that pricked to the quick. Furthermore, besides all these, her voice and words were marvellous pleasant for her tongue was an instrument of music to diverse sports and pastimes, the which she turned to any language that pleased her. She spake unto few barbarous people by interpreter, but made answer herself, or at least the most part of them . . . whose language she had learned.

Elizabeth's linguistic ability is well attested, not only by her tutor, Ascham, but by visitors to the English court who speak of precisely this facility in replying to ambassadors either in Latin or in their own tongues.

[13]See Tucker Brooke, ed., *Shakespeare's Plutarch* (1909), II, 40.

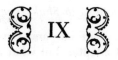

IX

Mockery and Cherished Purpose: Duality of Intention in *The Tempest*

> Yet sit and see,
> Minding true things by what their mock'ries be.
> (*Henry V*, IV, Prol.)

AS THEY ARE "GUARDING" their sleeping companions in Act II, scene i of *The Tempest*, Antonio points out to Sebastian that he is letting slip one of those critical tides in the affairs of men which should be taken at the flood. Sebastian, who suffers from "hereditary sloth" and is more inclined to "ebb" than to "flow," does not at first see the relevance of the metaphor. His Machiavellian friend thereupon proceeds to further instruction, with the following preamble:

> If you but knew how you the purpose cherish,
> Whiles thus you mock it! how, in stripping it,
> You more invest it!

(ll. 214–17)

The remark might as appropriately be applied to the playwright as to the heavy-witted Sebastian, for *The Tempest* "strips the ragged follies" of romance while at the same time investing them with serious, indeed almost religious purpose. Shakespeare's treatment of the theme of honour in the "Henriad," of the epic heroes and heroic values in *Troilus and Cressida*, and of pastoral conventions in *As You Like It*, provides ample precedent for such duality of approach. But the satiric undercurrent has been largely overlooked in the preoccupation of criticism with tracing the path of allegory through the cloudy symbols of this high romance.

In his use of dramatic materials and devices, Shakespeare is not only an experimenter and adapter, but what a psychologist would call a "limit-tester." He likes to push a theme or convention as far as it will go and see what happens. Sometimes, intentionally or otherwise, he reduces it to absurdity. Sometimes, "ranging freely within the zodiac of his own wit," he extends its scope to "find out new heaven, new earth." Sometimes, as in *The Tempest*, he does both. Having already tested romance conventions in three plays, he is here pointing out their limitations as well as demonstrating a method of overcoming them, in part, by going beyond their normal limits and directing his positive and negative approaches to the romance forms towards the two sides of a single theme. Underlying the play's reconciliation of the discordant elements of human existence, a vein of mock-romance satirizes contemporary romantic drama for its failure to hold up the mirror to the *whole* of that existence, for its abandonment of serious purpose, for its flight from the realities of the human spirit.

With a certain amount of equivocation (seldom out of place in talking about Shakespeare) the satirical elements in *The Tempest* may be said to complement the treatment of the theme of Nature and Grace in the play. *The Winter's Tale* had asserted the superiority of the grace of Nature to the grace of Art. In this play, however, the supernatural perfection of Divine Grace is seen as superior to human imperfection however natural; but even so, human nature however imperfect is superior to the illusions of the romance world which, however graceful, are unnatural. In the context of the fantasy world of romance, art and enchantment are equated. It is against this *unnaturalness* rather than the *supernatural* elements of romantic drama, against its artifice as revealed in the unreality of its themes, setting, incidents, and characters, that Shakespeare directs the familiar weapons of mockery—burlesque, irony, exaggeration, diminution, incongruity, and failure to fulfill conventional expectations.

Both serious and satiric purposes are served by the blurring of the dividing line between illusion and reality in *The Tempest*, a rejection of "divided and distinguished worlds" which goes beyond pointing out that "all the world's a stage" and that "we are such stuff as dreams are made on." This mingling and confusing of illusion and reality works in two directions and on two levels. It not only points out that what we consider reality is, *sub specie aeternitatis*, an illusion, but also argues that the theatre, which in the temporal frame of reference is recognized as the world of illusion, should concern itself with the realities of human experience, temporal as well as spiritual, with the emphasis on human nature with all its imperfections and contradictions. It is a corruption of nature, in life or in art, to treat men as puppets.

The Tempest is therefore a criticism of literature as well as of life, and in the literary frame of reference Prospero is the central figure in an allegory of the theatre, an allegory which is sometimes romantic, sometimes satirical. His function is in part that of the romantic playwright as summed up in Una Ellis-Fermor's description[1] of the attitudes of Beaumont and Fletcher towards their characters:

> . . . the characters . . . do not necessarily act like those of everyday life, and the rare and strange events which befall them beget emotions and motives that are a little strange, a little unaccountable. They do not do what ordinary people, illuminated by the light of common day, would do, but, more happily for the author, . . . what he would have them do, in order that such and such further situations might arise. . . . he foresees situations which he will enjoy exploring, plans for them emotions and experiences in which he will enjoy watching them, and then sets them therein.

But Prospero is more than the artist-magician, the clever manipulator of men and events. He is the trickster who exposes his own trickery, the Pirandello-like author-actor-manager who repeatedly and deliberately shatters his own dramatic illusion in order to take the audience into his confidence and explain to them the strange and subtle nature of his art.

Since *The Tempest*, like *Love's Labour's Lost*, is both a court play and a satire on courtly conventions and courtly drama, Prospero's serious role in the romance elements of the plot also serves a double purpose. The romantic dramatist and the Duke of Milan alike have withdrawn from the totality of human experience. In either world, the literary or the political, withdrawal from life is denial of life, a failure in stewardship, as Prospero half admits in accounting to Miranda for his past:

> I thus neglecting worldly ends, all dedicated
> To closeness and the bettering of my mind
> With that which, but by being so retir'd,
> O'er-priz'd all popular rate . . . my false brother,
>   . . . did believe
> He was indeed the Duke. . . .
> . . . Me, poor man—my library
> Was dukedom large enough—

>   (I, ii, 89–110)

[1] *The Jacobean Drama* (London: Methuen, 1936, 1958), p. 206.

How shall the world—and the Globe—be served when its Prosperos withdraw into the enchanted world of romance, however white its magic? By Antonios "on the make," who are not above prizing "popular rate," and who will turn the Globe, whose stage is for all the world, as all the world is a stage, into a theatre for citizens and apprentices who cannot get into the Blackfriars.

Prospero's failure to fulfill his worldly function is appropriately punished by the addition of physical to intellectual isolation. He is rebuked for his one-sidedness by being given a surfeit of his heart's desire. Enchantment then becomes the only reality and charms become the only instrument of power for the ruler who has neglected the world of men for the world of magic. The uncharted and enchanted island which provides a unified setting for *The Tempest*, in contrast to the multiple setting usual in the romances, can be seen as a satirical exaggeration of the romance world. It is not merely out of this world but uncounted leagues beyond even Tunis, which is said to be "ten leagues beyond man's life." It not only exaggerates and oversimplifies the elements of the real world as the romances do; it exaggerates the exaggeration. The ruler of this strange microcosm is no mere king by divine right but an almost superhuman figure, a magician whose symbolic function has been variously interpreted as that of the creative imagination, the human reason, Divine Grace, the monarchical principle, and God the Father. An allegorical figure he certainly seems to be, but as with the characters of *The Faerie Queene* his allegorical significance is multiple and not always consistent. Though Miranda, both wonderful and full of wonder, is, as romance convention demanded, at once sexually naïve and extremely vocal about her chastity, Shakespeare, tongue in cheek, has taken no chances; he makes Miranda virtuous both by nature and by force of circumstance. While using Caliban's dastardly intention to fulfill the satyr-shepherdess attempted-rape convention of romance fiction, he ensures that Miranda shall not, since infancy, have beheld a male other than her father who is "honour'd with human shape." Ariel and Caliban, the king's sole subjects, represent the bournes just beyond the opposite extremes of human nature. The one is too spiritual to be human, though he possesses the virtue of "humanity." The other is a sub-human savage, almost wholly bestial though, like Spenser's satyrs in Book I of *The Faerie Queene*, he can recognize and desire if not comprehend the good and the beautiful. Flesh and spirit, reason and imagination, innocence and experience, are the implicit poles of characterization. The action and reaction of the impact of reality on this unreal world of the enchanted island, and of its unreality upon the representatives of the real world, form the basis of a plot in which reality and unreality become so confused as to be almost indistinguishable—by the characters, if not by the audience.

The plot of *The Tempest* follows the tragi-comic pattern, although the elements of the standard tragedy of blood are here transcendentalized to achieve a logically and aesthetically satisfying reconciliation rather than the facile and superficially satisfying happy ending of romantic tragi-comedy. But Shakespeare's attitude towards his plots and plotters past and present, serious and comic, is a somewhat ambivalent one. The evil-doers are subjected to moral condemnation and are forgiven when repentant, and all this is presented with the highest seriousness. Yet the conspirators are presented as foolish as well as wicked; they are laughed at as well as thwarted and condemned, ridiculed as well as redeemed. Even the theme of redemption itself becomes a matter for burlesque in the comic sub-plot, which, as we shall see, is also concerned, if in a rather different sense from the main plot, with salvation by water and the spirit.

It is a commonplace of criticism that as it came to be increasingly dependent upon court patronage the Jacobean drama went out of its way to flatter its courtly audiences. According to convention, then, the opening scene of *The Tempest* should afford the noble personages on board the storm-tossed vessel an opportunity to display their heroism, their stoical calmness in the face of death, and their selfless concern for the welfare of their sovereign, possibly in contrast to the cowardice of the base-born mariners. What happens, of course, is the exact reverse. The behaviour of the crew and passengers of the stricken vessel is presented with as much ironic realism as is the illusory storm itself.

While the mariners do their best to fulfill their function, the representatives of the nobility fail to measure up to theirs. Even that good old lord, Gonzalo, grumbles, while Antonio and Sebastian make royal nuisances of themselves according to their own particular brands of unpleasantness. Not only do they "assist the storm"; they are neither nobly courageous nor stoically calm. Sebastian even commits the sacrilege of suggesting that they leave the king to sink or swim. The Boatswain's retort when these "gentlemen" attempt to "pull rank" on him even in the face of Death the Leveller, is in sharp and perhaps not accidental contrast to Amintor's attitude in Beaumont and Fletcher's

The Maid's Tragedy. There, the duped bridegroom's bloody intentions are dissipated by Evadne's taunt that it is the King who is her lover. "The King?" repeats Amintor,

> . . . thou hast nam'd a word that wipes away
> All thoughts revengeful! In that sacred name
> "The King," there lies a terror. What frail man
> Dares lift his hand against it?
>
> (II, i, 308 ff.)

But the forces of nature are immune to "the glories of our blood and state." "What cares these roarers for the name of king?" cries the Boatswain.

The unheroic behaviour of the courtiers, including the play's romantic hero, is expanded upon in Ariel's report to Prospero. Indeed, Prospero underlines the point by questioning him specifically on the matter:

> Who was so firm, so constant, that this coil
> Would not infect his reason?
>
> (I, ii, 207–8)

Thoroughly enjoying the joke, Ariel replies:

> not a soul
> . . . . All but mariners
> Plung'd in the foaming brine, and quit the vessel,
> . . . the King's son, Ferdinand . . .
> Was the first man that leapt. . . .
>
> (I, ii, 208–14)

The account follows hard upon Miranda's plea to her father to "allay" "the wild waters" and save the

> brave vessel,
> Who had no doubt some noble creature in her.
>
> (I, ii, 6)

With Prospero's reply to Miranda begins the curious and repeated insistence on the unreality of the events presented which runs throughout the play. These illusions, Prospero implies in this first explanation, are designed to arouse the tragic emotions of pity and awe while stopping short of the fatal consequences attendant upon natural, as opposed to magical, phenomena of the same sort. Their life-like pageantry is the illusion created by his art, and the seas are only imaginatively perilous.

>   . . . tell your piteous heart
> There's no harm done. . . .
>   No harm. . . .
> Wipe thou thine eyes; have comfort.
> The direful spectacle of the wreck, which touch'd
> The very virtue of compassion in thee,
> I have with such provision in mine art
> So safely ordered that there is no soul—
> No, not so much perdition as an hair
> Betid to any creature in the vessel
> Which thou heard'st cry, which thou saw'st sink.

(I, ii, 14–32)

This is not the standard danger without death of tragi-comedy, but the illusion of the danger of death. A similar serio-satiric ambivalence of intention may be seen in the frequent testimonials to the "miraculous salt-water cleaning process" which has left the garments of the ship-wrecked passengers, "not stained, but fresher than before." As so often in Shakespeare, the apparel proclaims the man, and the sea-bath is the redemption of baptism, yet the scoffing of Antonio and Sebastian indicates how ridiculous such a statement seems to the literal-minded man.

All this playing with the concepts of reality and illusion, is very much like what goes on in the Athens Trades and Labour Dramatic Society, though on a higher social level. One cannot have lions among ladies. We do not hesitate to laugh when Snout suggests that "Another prologue must tell them that he is not a lion," or when Bottom insists that half the player's face must be seen through the lion's neck and he must entreat them "not to fear, not to tremble," and that he must "tell them plainly that he is Snug, the Joiner." Storm? Shipwreck?—"Tell your piteous heart there's no harm done."

Prospero's assurances to Miranda are followed by the play's formal exposition, upon the merits of which criticism is so sharply divided. It is said to be both highly effective and hopelessly inept. From Shakespeare's double point of view it might well have been both. Una Ellis-Fermor assures us[2] that it illustrates "the full measure of the structural freedom of exposition of the Jacobean tragic writers" and that it is "a remarkable instance of the non-realistic opening which serves its purpose directly and economically, often through abandoning verisimilitude altogether." She does not mention that Prospero commences it with the ritual gesture of casting aside his cloak of invisibility and with the injunction "Lie there, my art!" *Ars est celare artem.* In this

[2]*The Jacobean Drama*, p. 33.

exposition he will reveal himself as fully and (in both senses) as artlessly as he can.

As an adventure story Prospero's is, indeed, as Miranda insisted when caught nodding, "a tale that would cure deafness," though needlessly long in the telling. What makes it so long is that it is not merely an exposition; it is also Prospero's attempt at self-justification, his confession of human weakness, of his inability to keep illusion in its proper place. Now that the secret studies which had been his indulgence have become his prison, even his sole remaining human relationship, that with his daughter, is distorted by illusions of his own creation. After all, the artist must have his audience. Only when he has given her to the protection of the greater magic of love, and himself to the self-denial of forgiveness, that "rarer action" which is virtue, can he abandon trickery as well as vengeance.[3] But that self-denial is still in the future; and to that end, his art must be expended "most preciously" during the next four hours. Now, after scolding Miranda for failing to give to his story the rapt attention he demands, he admits to the audience that he has been putting her to sleep all along " . . . 'tis a good dullness, / And give it way. I know thou canst not choose."

The second part of the exposition, following Ariel's entrance, is even more long-winded than the first, though its ostensible purpose is to exhort Ariel to greater liveliness, not to put him to sleep. From the point of view of literary criticism the most interesting thing about it, aside from Prospero's inadequately motivated irritability, is the insistent signposting of time. The structure of *The Winter's Tale* had followed, almost exactly, Sidney's famous account of contemporary abuses of the dramatic unities of time and place. *The Tempest*, Prospero informs Ariel, will go to the opposite extreme, observing the unity of time more realistically than even the strictest Italian critics demanded. The action will be completed, not in a calendar day, not in a solar day, but in no more than twice the time actually occupied in the two-hours' traffic of the stage. Prospero even takes care to pin-point the exact moment at which he is actually speaking, assuming that the play began at the customary hour of 2 P.M.:

[3]In suggesting that, in the earlier acts of the play, Prospero is motivated largely by self-interest, I should not go so far as does George Garrett, who argues in his essay, "That Four-Flusher Prospero" (*Shakespeare Survey Pamphlet*, ed. by William Empson and George Garrett, London: Brendin, 1937, pp. 37–62), that the expatriate Duke abuses his power throughout and manipulates events (including the love between Ferdinand and Miranda) for the *sole* purpose of recovering his duchy.

PRO.: What is the time o' th' day?
ARI.: Past the mid-season.
PRO.: At least two glasses. The time 'twixt six and now
Must by us both be spent most preciously.

(I, ii, 239–41)

It is the double demand for speed-up and overtime which sets off the quarrel between Prospero and Ariel, a quarrel in which justice seems to be on Ariel's side. He has been promised a year off from his indentures for good behaviour, and the time appointed for his emancipation is at hand. Clearly, the demand for extra work is outside the terms of the agreement between the artist and his imagination, and Prospero's threatened penalty of twelve years' imprisonment in an oak tree for Ariel's mild protest against a breach of contract would be considered unreasonable if not tyrannical according to any Renaissance theory of government. Prospero is here playing the role of the wicked magician of romance in such a way as to lend some credibility to Caliban's claim that all his attendant spirits "do hate him / As rootedly as I."

A hundred lines or so before the end of this omnibus scene, a marked change in point of view occurs. At the entrance of love in the person of Ferdinand, Prospero and Miranda cease to be merely spectators, and step into the framework of dramatic illusion to become actors in what might be called a "micro-romance." Had the scale been the larger one of narrative romance, the tale might have begun thus:

> Hard by a cave in that enchanted wood
> A gentle prince went wandering to the west,
> Whom songs of sirens tempting toward the flood,
> Nor demon voices rousing him from rest,
> Could long deter from his appointed quest;
> Though beauty's canker stain'd his rosy cheek
> And pious grief lay heavy on his breast,
> Though with his long wayfaring wan and weak,
> His father's shipwreck'd corse he sought and still did seek.

The perils which beset Ferdinand are the standard sirens, monsters, and personifications of despair, but as illusions they are so "translated" as to be robbed of their terror, and are either invested with a mysterious and melancholy beauty, or made to seem familiar, everyday things. Thus the sirens become dancing sea-nymphs, the roars of monsters the homely barking of dogs and crowing of cocks; the Dirge describes the horrors of dissolution as a "sea change into something rich and strange." As in the mock heroic, the tone is diminished by the triviality of the machinery. The traditional three trials withstood, the denouement is inevitable: the knight is captured by an enchanter with whose beautiful daughter he falls in love, and he wins her hand and release from the spell by fulfilling a seemingly impossible task imposed by the tyrant. In our micro-romance none of the standard elements is omitted; all are mocked by diminution, reversal, and incongruity, and by blurring the division between illusion and reality. When Ferdinand first comes on stage, Prospero's "The fringed curtains of thine eyes advance" is not merely an overstrained conceit; it is his invitation to Miranda to view yet another theatrical illusion presented for her entertainment, though, within the framework of the larger illusion of the island, this one happens to be a reality. In presenting reality as illusion the incident parallels the subsequent drawing of the curtains of the inner stage to "discover" Ferdinand and Miranda playing at chess, a scene which Alonzo is in doubt whether to receive as truth or as a "vision of the island."

No sooner has Prospero assured Miranda that Prince Charming is real than he plunges her into confusion by a completely unmotivated change of character—from fond to tyrannous father, from magnanimous to sinister ruler—which provokes in her the entirely logical question, "Why speaks my father so ungently?" Her bewilderment is understandable. As she comments a little later, "My father's of a better nature / Than he appears by speech. This is unwonted / Which now comes from him." She has never "known him so distemper'd." But Prospero's behaviour is only slightly more perverse than that of other romance fathers. In *Philaster*, for example, the Sicilian tyrant's changes of attitude towards his daughter Arethusa are almost as inadequately motivated. Lest the audience be as bewildered as the lovers, however, Prospero's asides remind them that he is merely putting Ferdinand through the motions of the conventional romance love-trial and that they are not to take anything he says too seriously. And what form does the impossible task take? Merely giving Caliban a hand with the woodpile, and the impossibility is social rather than physical. Nevertheless, the ritual is strictly observed. The courtly lover insists that his heart as well as his service is in willing bondage to his lady, the paragon of all perfections, and that no task is impossible if she is near. "And she, poor fool, doth fond as much on him." If Miranda does not, as does Bellario-Euphrasia, avouch her eagerness to die to give pleasure to her beloved, she does offer to carry his logs for him. Fortunately the diminutive scale of this mock romance makes Ferdinand's probation as "patient logman" a brief one.

Act II, scene i, takes us to "another part of the island," where Gonzalo's plagiarized[4] description of the delights of primitive society recalls our earlier introduction to that noble savage, Caliban. Antonio and Sebastian play the ironic commentator. "Yet he would be king on't," mutters Sebastian, when Gonzalo lists the absence of sovereignty as one of the blessings of his golden world. But the cynical realist has a beam in his own eye. Though he taunts Gonzalo with acting as if he could take the island home in his pocket and give it his son for an apple, his vision of his own golden future is similarly irrational. His conspiracy with Antonio is based on the illusion that the island is Naples and that, Ferdinand being drowned, the assassination of the king will clear the way for him, since the other heir, Claribel, dwells at Tunis, "ten leagues beyond man's life." Yet the plotters themselves are marooned without hope of rescue on an undiscovered island far beyond Tunis! Realists also may be the victims of illusions—self-created and self-flattering ones.

Mock romance combines with echoes of the mumming plays to suggest that the literary satire of the comic sub-plot may be directed against the citizen romances, rather than the courtly variety. Readers of prose romances from *Euphues* down as well as frequenters of romantic plays would certainly find familiar Stephano's discovery of the body of his shipwrecked friend. Not only is Doctor Stephano's restoration of St. George–Trinculo and Dwarf–Caliban by means of a miraculous draught from his "bottle of salvation" clearly in the romance-mumming tradition; mock allegory is indicated by his repeated commands to "kiss the book" as he administers additional restorative and swears his subjects to his allegiance. In view of the play's date, and the use of the bottle in pledging the oath, Stephano's promise to "fill it with new contents by and by" suggests that even the Authorized Version met with the suspiciously resentful reception which has greeted all subsequent translations of the Bible, a suggestion which is supported by the elaborate self-justification of the Translators' Preface of 1611.

Though in the latter part of the play Shakespeare increasingly shifts his emphasis from mockery to cherished purpose, he does not let slip any opportunity to play tricks with dramatic convention. His handling of the betrothal masque may serve as an example. Here Prospero finds himself in the awkward position of having to "double" in two major roles in the one scene. The romantic mood is at its peak

[4]From Montaigne's essay, "Of Cannibals."

in the entertainment which he has arranged as the seal of his approval
of the union of Ferdinand and Miranda. But, as every theatre-goer
knew, a dramatic performance in a revenge play is either the murderer's
opportunity or the avenger's mousetrap. Either way, convention
demanded that the masque be interrupted, and the only possible
role for Prospero is either that of the royal murder-victim or that of
the producer-avenger who uses the entertainment to unmask and
punish his enemies. The first will not do at all, and it would defeat
Prospero's purposes to play the second one straight at this moment.
To allow the low-comedy conspirators to come in on cue would shatter
the poetic mood so carefully built up in the masque. But Prospero is
too old a hand at the producer's game to be caught more than momentarily in such a dilemma. He interrupts the masque himself with an
aside to the audience to the effect that he has been so absorbed in
his own dramatic illusion as to have forgotten "that foul conspiracy /
Of Caliban and his associates." Since logical motivation has no place
in romance, any excuse will do for Ferdinand and Miranda, to whom
he pleads a touch of migraine.

Thereafter, mockery all but disappears as Prospero turns to making
his fifth act a mirror of judgment, in which he uses his charms for the
last time not to call up ministers of vengeance but to call down the
"heavenly music" of reconciliation. Once again he plays multiple
roles. He is both the particular man more sinned against than sinning
and the exemplar and symbol of the order of divine justice. He must
attain to a state of grace in the first rôle before he can function as the
bestower of grace in the second.

It is at the prompting of the "spirit," Ariel, that Prospero at last
realizes that his cherished purpose has been not to punish his enemies
but to bring them to confession and repentance, that he does not desire
the death of these sinners but that "they shall turn from their wickedness and live."

> ARI.:   . . . If you now beheld them your affections
>   Would become tender.
> PRO.:   Dost thou think so, spirit?
> ARI.:   Mine would, sir, were I human.
> PRO.:   And mine shall.
>   Hast thou, which art but air, a touch, a feeling
>   Of their afflictions, and shall not myself,
>   One of their kind, that relish all as sharply,
>   Passion as they, be kindlier mov'd than thou art?
>   Though with their high wrongs I am struck to th' quick,

> Yet with my nobler reason 'gainst my fury
> Do I take part; the rarer action is
> In virtue than in vengeance; they being penitent,
> The sole drift of my purpose doth extend
> Not a frown further. Go release them, Ariel.
>
> (V, i, 18–30)

The release from bondage is general: Ariel will be missed, but he is freed from the service of art to sport in the innocent world of nature; even the unrepentant Sebastian and the incorrigible Caliban are included in the general pardon as losses are restored and sorrows end in love.

His cherished purpose fulfilled in repentance and forgiveness, Prospero, in his third role as playwright-producer, concludes his allegory of the theatre by bidding a long farewell to the rough magic of his fairy-tale world—to its supernatural characters, romantic illusions, and unnatural events. As his charms dissolve, the characters become "themselves"—and at the same time new selves—as the tide of life returns to fill the reasonable shore. Even Caliban ceases to follow after false gods and vows to "seek for grace," so that it is possible to conceive that he and Ariel may share the island in harmony. But it is the audience, as the epilogue makes clear, which must decide whether the magician, who in breaking his wand and identifying himself with both Caliban and Ariel has reasserted his divided humanity, is to remain a prisoner of enchantment or return, with their approbation, to the world of "beauteous mankind." Only the breath of their applause can fill the sails which will carry him back to Naples and Milan, to the temporal reality of illusion in that brave old world of a drama which has *people* in it.

It is *The Tempest* which gives fullest expression to the theme which persists, in one guise or another, throughout the work of Shakespeare's maturity—that of the acceptance of oppositions as the basis of the natural, and therefore divinely appointed, pattern of being. The questionings and inversions of his middle period are sufficient indication of the persistent search and acute struggle which led, sometimes winning near, sometimes losing sight of the goal, to that acceptance. Even in the early plays and more particularly in the poems, Shakespeare's sensitivity to the problems posed by the dualities of existence is often at odds with his seeming acceptance of received notions of order. But sensitivity, struggle, and acceptance are alike exploited in the service of his art, so that Shakespeare's richness of difference is at least in part the harvest of his probing for an underlying unity in the diversity of human experience. The deeper the probing, the more fully are the elements of duality reflected in theme and tone, in irony of circumstance, ambivalence of character, and ambiguity of language. In the final plays especially, symbolism supports all these in expressing the double vision, as the search for an immediate and personally satisfying resolution of the human dilemma gives way to acceptance of mutability and contradiction as active forces working towards an ultimate resolution in a larger frame of reference.

As both dramatist and humanist, Shakespeare naturally tends to see and to present the conflict of good and evil not only as between particular men but in terms of a particular man—of the one defect in the substance of an otherwise noble nature, or the one saving grace in a nature otherwise corrupt, of the evidences of human dignity and depravity, the relish and the passion in the human soul which make the whole world kin. More often than not he gives universal significance to individual instances by setting them against a background of cosmic or national disturbance in which a parallel pattern of conflict is writ large. Inversely, the higher resolution of oppositions in ultimate harmony as presented in the final plays is manifested in terms of individual human experience, in the restoration of a lost good and in forgiveness of error, more often than not set against the background of the natural cycle, which mirrors, in its winter and spring, its storms and sunshine, the dialectic of human life.

In the eternal pattern, conflict is the basis of harmony, a celestial music whose echo can be heard by those individuals who accept the temporal world with all its imperfections, ethical dilemmas, and warring values rather than attempting to reconstitute the composition of life or rejecting it in whole or in part. Hamlet seeks complete justice and brings about a general massacre; Macbeth cannot wait to allow destiny to shape itself for his good, and ends as the bondslave of evil; Othello sets certitude above faith and robs life of all meaning. Only those who can accept as ultimately good the nunnery and the brothel, the olive and the sword, can weather the storm of life and come, under the conduct of the "high miracle" of love, into that haven of reconciliation where contraries meet in one, and where they can say, with Ferdinand,

> Though the seas threaten they are merciful;
> I have curs'd them without cause.

INDEX

Index

LIST OF ABBREVIATIONS

AC: *Antony and Cleopatra*
AYL: *As You Like It*
CE: *The Comedy of Errors*
Cor: *Coriolanus*
FQ: *The Faerie Queene*
Ham: *Hamlet*
1H4: *Henry the Fourth, Part I*
1(2,3)H6: *Henry the Sixth, Part I (II, III)*
JC: *Julius Caesar*
Lear: *King Lear*
LLL: *Love's Labour's Lost*
Macb: *Macbeth*
MM: *Measure for Measure*

MV: *The Merchant of Venice*
MN: *A Midsummer Night's Dream*
Oth: *Othello*
Per: *Pericles*
R3: *Richard III*
RJ: *Romeo and Juliet*
Son: *Sonnets*
TShrew: *The Taming of the Shrew*
Temp: *The Tempest*
Timon: *Timon of Athens*
TrC: *Troilus and Cressida*
TN: *Twelfth Night*
VA: *Venus and Adonis*
WT: *The Winter's Tale*